The Herne's Egg

Manuscript Materials

THE CORNELL YEATS

PLAYS

The Death of Cuchulain, edited by Phillip L. Marcus
Purgatory, edited by Sandra F. Siegel
The Herne's Egg, edited by Alison Armstrong

POEMS

The Early Poetry, Volume I: "Mosada" and "The Island of Statues," edited by George Bornstein
The Wind Among the Reeds, edited by Carolyn Holdsworth
The Early Poetry, Volume II: "The Wanderings of Oisin" and Other Early Poems to 1895, edited by George Bornstein

The Herne's Egg
Manuscript Materials

BY W. B. YEATS

EDITED BY
ALISON ARMSTRONG

Cornell University Press

ITHACA AND LONDON

This edition has been supported by a grant from the National Endowment for the Humanities, an independent federal agency.

First published 1993 by Cornell University Press.

Library of Congress Cataloging-in-Publication Data

Yeats, W. B. (William Butler), 1865–1939.
The herne's egg : manuscript materials / by W. B. Yeats ; edited by Alison Armstrong.
p. cm. -- (The Cornell Yeats)
Includes bibliographical references and index.
ISBN 0-8014-2818-1
1. Yeats, W. B. (William Butler), 1865–1939. Herne's egg—Criticism, Textual. 2. Yeats, W. B. (William Butler), 1865–1939—Manuscripts. 3. Manuscripts, English. I. Armstrong, Alison, 1943– . II. Title. III. Series: Yeats, W. B. (William Butler), 1865–1939. Works. 1982.
PR5904.H4 1993
821'.8--dc20 92-54709

Printed in the United States of America

♾ The paper in this book meets the minimum requirements of the American National Standard for Information Sciences—Permanence of Paper for Printed Library Materials, ANSI Z39.48-1984.

THE CORNELL YEATS

The volumes in this series will present the manuscripts of W. B. Yeats's poems (all extant versions), plays (complete insofar as possible), and other materials (including selected occult writings) from the rich archives preserved in the collections of Senator Michael B. Yeats, the National Library of Ireland, and elsewhere. The primary goal of the editors is to achieve the greatest possible fidelity in transcription. Photographic facsimiles will be used extensively to supplement the texts.

The series will include some important unpublished works of high literary quality, and individually and as a whole the volumes will help to illuminate Yeats's creative process. They will be essential reference works for scholars who wish to establish definitive texts of the published works. The emphasis throughout, however, will be on the documents themselves, and critical analysis will be limited to discussion of their significance in relation to the published texts; the editors assume that the publication of the documents will stimulate critical studies as a matter of course.

THE YEATS EDITORIAL BOARD

Contents

Acknowledgments

My work on this manuscript is greatly indebted to the pioneering labor on Yeats's manuscripts by Curtis Bradford, David R. Clark, Phillip L. Marcus, George P. Mayhew, Michael Sidnell, and Jon Stallworthy, as well as to the labors of Stephen Gill and others in the Cornell Wordsworth Series edited by Stephen M. Parrish.

Grateful acknowledgments are due to Miss Anne Yeats and Senator Michael Yeats for permission to examine and to publish the manuscript of *The Herne's Egg*, and to A. P. Watt Ltd. to quote material copyrighted by and in some cases belonging to them, and to Senator Yeats also for his efforts to find further material relating to the writing of the play.

Special thanks are due to David R. Clark of the University of Massachussetts at Amherst for initially suggesting that I transcribe and edit NLI MS. 8770 and for his advice during the early stages of the edition. My thanks also go to Patrick Henchy, director of the National Library of Ireland, to his successors Ailfrid MacLochlainn and Michael Hewson, and to the staff of the library's manuscript room, for their courteous assistance. I also thank the staff of the Royal Irish Academy for their courtesy and help, and the staff of the British Library manuscripts room for assistance with attempts to locate the typescripts and galley proofs of *The Herne's Egg* among the Macmillan papers. My grateful thanks also go to Professor Richard Finneran, who located the typescript in the Scribner's Archive at the Harry Ransom Humanities Research Center, Austin, Texas; to Cathy Henderson of the center for assistance with material from the archive in 1984–1985; to Peter van de Kamp of University College, Dublin, for transcribing material in the possession of Anne Butler Yeats; and to James Pethica, for assisting in the preparation of this volume for publication. I am also indebted to the staffs of the Bodleian Library, Oxford; the University of Notre Dame Library in Indiana; the Ohio State University Library; the Berg Collection of the New York Public Library; the Stony Brook Melville Memorial Library Special Collections; and the Kenyon College Library, Gambier, Ohio.

I owe gratitude to the late Richard Ellmann, for his supervision and advice, and to John Kelly, who kindly allowed me access to unpublished letters of Yeats and for his assistance in deciphering some difficult passages in the manuscript. I am deeply grateful to Sean Golden for his encouragement and help during my work in Dublin and for making excellent color slides of the more complicated manuscript pages. I also owe thanks to the late John Jordan and Liam Miller for information about the first performances of the play in Dublin in 1950.

My parents, Mr. and Mrs. John Trimble Armstrong, contributed more than can be expressed here, as has my son, Edward Armstrong Nice, who grew to manhood while the volume was in preparation.

St. Hugh's College, Oxford, and the Meyerstein Fund and the English Faculty Board of Oxford University gave financial aid in 1977 and 1979. Very special thanks are due to the

Academic Board of Bedford College, University of London, for an Una Ellis-Fermor Memorial Research Grant, awarded in 1978, which helped to support the preparation of the transcription. I am also indebted to Professors Phillip Marcus, Stephen Parrish and Jon Stallworthy of the Cornell Yeats Editorial Board, and to Professor Warwick Gould, editor of the *Yeats Annual*, for their assistance.

A. A.

Census of Manuscripts

ABY A copy of the 1938 printing of *The Herne's Egg* in the possession of Anne Butler Yeats, with revisions entered by WBY toward a later edition.

Harvard Proof sheets, dated 1937, of *The Herne's Egg* (London, 1938). Stamped "Second Proof" with corrections and revisions. Inscribed on cover: "for Frank O'Connor." EC9. Y 3455.938, in the Houghton Library, Harvard University.

Macmillan A copy of the 1938 (London) printing of *The Herne's Egg* in the Macmillan archive, Basingstoke, with revisions in pen and pencil entered by George Yeats and Thomas Mark and perhaps others, apparently toward the 1952 printing in *Collected Plays*. Most revisions involve spacing, punctuation, the removal of parentheses around stage directions, and the like, and there is no reason to attribute them to WBY. Twelve pages bear verbal revisions; nine of these duplicate revisions written into ABY, but three are unique and are given in the apparatus, below, pages 165, 175 and 197. Inscribed on flyleaf: "George Yeats./Corrected Copy."

NLI 8770 (1) Twenty-three leaves of holograph on 3-hole notebook paper ruled with blue lines at intervals of 0.6 cm (double red rules at top), measuring 22.8 cm by 18 cm, watermarked WALKER'S / LOOSE / LEAF. Twenty-two leaves are numbered in top right corner 1–22; between 11 and 12 is inserted an unnumbered leaf containing revisions to drafts on 10^v and 11^v. The text runs from the beginning of the play through scene 2. Fully transcribed in this volume.

NLI 8770 (2) Thirty leaves of holograph. The first leaf, evidently belonging to NLI 8770 (1), is numbered 23 and is the same paper as NLI 8770 (1). The remaining leaves are 3-hole notebook paper, 22.9 cm by 18.25 cm, watermarked WALKER'S / L$^{\text{OOSE}}_{\text{EAF}}$ / MADE IN GT BRITAIN. The first ten leaves (of the twenty-nine with this watermark) are numbered 1–10 in pencil, and are followed by one unnumbered leaf, six leaves lettered *a–f*, and twelve further unnumbered leaves. The text begins with scene 3 and runs through the end of the play. Fully transcribed in this volume.

NLI 13,593 (37) One leaf, holograph, of 3-hole notebook paper with same watermark as NLI 8770(2), ruled with blue lines 0.9 cm apart, measuring 22.8 cm by 18 cm, containing (at top) 5 lines of draft for *The Herne's Egg* and (at bottom) a stanza of draft toward "A Bronze Head," published in *Last Poems* (1939). In apparatus criticus to page 27 of The Texas Typescript in this volume.

NLI 30,119 Seven pages of typescript, 10 inches by 8 inches, watermarked Swiftbrook / Bond, two of which contain "Corrections and additions to 'The Herne's Egg'" for the Scribner edition (never published), keyed by page to the first edition of *The Herne's Egg* (1938). These two pages duplicate Texas (1), below, without any editorial annotations. The last three pages, containing "Corrections to Yeats' Poems," are dated March 1938 and "April," in pencil.

NLI 30,485 Contains six leaves of holograph revisions, keyed by page and line to a typescript or set of proofs of *The Herne's Egg*, not located. Same paper as NLI 8770(1). The revisions are incorporated in The Texas Typescript and in the Harvard proofs.

Texas Forty-one-page carbon typescript prepared for the Scribner edition. The paper is 26.6 cm by 20.3 cm, watermarked with an emblem over DEVON VALLEY / PARCHMENT. Six pages carry additions or revisions in the hand of an editor, probably "BS"—see Texas (1)—one in WBY's hand. All appear to be copied from entries on Texas (1), below.

Texas (1) Two pages watermarked Swiftbrook Bond, headed SCRIBNER EDITION, containing typed "Corrections and Additions to 'The Herne's Egg' made by W. B. Yeats / Macmillan & Co's edition," evidently taken from ABY. Duplicate of NLI 30,119, but with annotations. At top of first page is inscribed "Yeats Vol V" and "10/25/40 Corrections transferred by BS." Annotations are in the hand of BS save for one correction of a typographical error in the hand of George Yeats. Corrections and additions are keyed, in type, to pages of the first edition of *The Herne's Egg* (1938) and, in pencil, to pages of The Texas Typescript—called "MS copy"—where they are entered in ink.

Introduction

I

> "The Herne's Egg" was written in the happier moments of a long illness that had so separated me from life that I felt irresponsible; the plot echoes that of Samuel Ferguson's "Congal" and in one form or another had been in my head since my early twenties.[1]

The Herne's Egg is perhaps Yeats's least understood and least appreciated dramatic work, yet it exemplifies those symbols, themes, and beliefs which constitute the essence of all his later poetic dramatic writing. When he was twenty-one, Yeats wrote about that moment in Celtic myth/history, the "sunset of Irish heathendom,"[2] which opened the way to Christianity. And for nearly five decades he kept in his head the story that ultimately found expression in what he called the "tragi-comedy"[3] of the confrontation between the civilized Congal and the pre- or anti-Christian Great Herne through the medium of Attracta, a virgin-seductress, or type of Cathleen ni Houlihan.

The Herne's Egg was not written until 1935–1936—long after Yeats had the initial inspiration for its story. Once he had completed the manuscript (even before he had corrected the galley proofs), he attempted to have the play performed at the Mercury Theatre, without success. But after the play had been published in 1938 and had met with hostility or indifference, he began to be relieved that it was not being performed (the first public performance did not occur until 1950). Perhaps it is fitting that *The Herne's Egg* has encountered conflict; to those who do not delve the play's subtle and very Yeatsian message, the superficial aspects of this philosophic farce seem quite strange, even shocking. We must look to what might be called the ritual substructure of art for an understanding of the relation among the various states of composition of Yeats's work; whether this analysis of the drafts of a single late play affords a new or broader view of Yeats is for the scholarly reader to judge. By the time Yeats wrote *The Herne's Egg*, he had pretty much succeeded in reshaping the Irish mythological cycle in and for his own art. Ailing, yet imaginatively a "wild old wicked man," and in the interim between two other tasks (aside from ongoing Cuala Press work and public and theater life)—finishing his editorial work on *The Oxford Book of Modern Verse* and commencing to translate, with Shri

---

[1]Preface to *The Herne's Egg and Other Plays* (New York: Macmillan, 1938), p. v.

[2]In *The Irish Fireside* of October 9, 1886.

[3]He used this phrase in a letter to Dorothy Wellesley, November 28, 1935, cited, as are all such letters quoted below, from *Letters on Poetry from W. B. Yeats to Dorothy Wellesley* (New York: Oxford University Press, 1940).

Purohit Swami, the *Ten Principal Upanishads*—Yeats found in Majorca a sense of irresponsibility and distance from the world which was perhaps what he most needed to consolidate his thought in the play's strangely evocative way.

The plot of *The Herne's Egg* concerns the breakdown of ancient social patterns when the heroic will defies divine will. It is the classical and medieval concern of Choice versus Chance reworked in an Irish tribal context. This dramatic theme is exemplified in the hero Congal's career, from its heights of glory and confidence to an ignominious physical downfall which nevertheless leaves open the question of his spiritual status. In asserting his will against divine forces, the hero brings about his own fate: physical metamorphosis punishes spiritual pride. In Yeats's plot we can follow the poet's manipulation—through Attracta and her servant Corney—of this hero's development toward consciousness and death.

Yeats uses themes and images from Celtic and Indian sources to create an ancient and mysterious context for his story. The basis for the structure of the play, these themes result from Yeats's enduring fascination with antinomies—the balance between East and West, the interaction between the moral and the divine—and can be enumerated as follows.

1. *The Herne's Egg* incorporates what Yeats recognized as the two major aspects of Irish myth. One is a world view that assumes perpetual tribal war as a condition of life; the other is a set of ancient symbols—the Four Talismans of the Tuatha de Danaan.

2. The fateful substitution of an egg that, together with its classical allusion to Leda and suggestion of the Blakean egg of Los and Plato's cosmic egg, had its origin for Yeats in Irish mythology as a goose's "egg of discord," which caused the battle of Magh Rath.

3. The two animal images of herne (as antithetical) and stuffed donkey on wheels (as primary), Yeats borrowed from Celtic myth and from Indian plays. In a story in *The Secret Rose* (1897),[4] and in his play *Calvary* (1920), the heron or herne represents timeless, extra-worldly, pre-Christian attitudes. The stuffed donkey is probably based, as Richard Taylor suggests, on toys used in classical Indian theater.[5]

4) Reincarnation as a donkey probably came from a story in Alexandra David-Neel's book *Mystiques et magiciens du Thibet* (translated into English in 1932), about a priest who attempts to give human form to the wandering soul of his deceased lama by having intercourse on the road with a young girl—but before he can act two donkeys copulate in a nearby field, thus causing the lama to be reborn as a donkey.

5. The hero's death at the hands of a fool is taken from *The Battle of Magh Rath*, developed by Samuel Ferguson in his epic poem *Congal* and used by Yeats in this play as well as in *The Death of Cuchulain* (1939).

6. The hero's contact with the supernatural through the intermediary of a woman is an archetypal theme. The juxtaposition of sexual and religious themes and the intermingling of physical and spiritual aspirations and knowledge are traditional in most literatures. As Yeats wrote to Olivia Shakespear on May 25, 1926: "the mystic way and sexual love use the same means."

Although the plays of Yeats's late period are violent and extreme in content and highly stylized in form, *The Herne's Egg* is based on traditional materials. Behind Ferguson's *Congal* (1872) lies Gilla-Bridghe MacConmidhe's epic poems *The Banquet of Dun na n-Gedh* and *The*

---

[4] "The Old Men of the Twilight."

[5] *The Drama of W. B. Yeats: Irish Myth and the Japanese No* (New Haven: Yale University Press, 1976), p. 180.

Battle of Magh Rath, both in their Gaelic original and in the 1842 translation by John O'Donovan.[6] That Yeats was interested in these sources is confirmed by a youthful article titled "Bardic Ireland," which he published in *The Scots Observer* in 1890:

> The bards, kept by the rules of their order apart from war and common affairs of men, rode hither and thither gathering up the dim feelings of the time, and making them conscious. In the history one sees Ireland ever struggling vainly to attain some kind of unity. In the bardic tales it is ever one, warring within itself, indeed, but always obedient, unless under some great provocation, to its high king. The *Tain Bo*, the greatest of all these epics, is full of this devotion. Later, when things were less plastic, men rose against their *ard-reigh* for any and everything : one because at dinner he was given a hen's egg instead of a duck's.[7]

Yeats refers here to the account found both in Ferguson's *Congal* and in *The Banquet of Dun na n-Gedh* (which means "the Fort of the Geese").[8] At this banquet, offence is taken over a substitution:

> then a goose egg was brought on a silver dish before every king in the house; and when the dish and the egg were placed before Congal Claen, the silver dish was transformed into a wooden one, and the goose egg into the egg of a red-feathered hen.[9]

Congal Claen, a satellite king of the *ard-reigh* (or more correctly, *ard-righ*), that is to say, the High King, Domnall (who is also his foster father), is then urged by one of his own followers—against all custom and manners—to rise in indignation against Domnall. However, Domnall was responsible for the magical transformation (and hence devaluation) of the egg only in that his men had stolen the goose eggs from Saint Erc for their banquet, which they had prepared in the hope of uniting Domnall with all his people.

> [King Domnall] saw the eggs, and asked who ate a part of the broken egg (pointing to that which Congal had broken [before the banquet had begun] for he knew that the first person who should partake of the banquet which had been cursed [by Saint Erc] would be the man who would destroy Erin and disobey himself.[10]

This saint does avenge himself with the curse, or *geis*, which transformed the goose egg into

---

[6]Although written in the fifteenth century, both tales record putative seventh-century events. In his article on the poetry of Samuel Ferguson in *The Irish Fireside* Yeats wrote: "Congal was a heathen; his enemy the arch-King Ardrigh, was a Christian. This war was the sunset of Irish heathendom." See *Uncollected Prose by W. B. Yeats,* ed. John Frayne, vol. 1 (New York: Columbia University Press, 1970), p. 84; hereafter cited as UP 1. The battle of Magh Rath occurred in 637 A.D.

[7]UP 1, p. 163. Yeats here confuses a duck's egg with the goose's egg of the Irish tale.

[8]Or Darts, depending on one's reading of the fifteenth century Irish. See *The Miscellany of the Celtic Society*, edited by John O'Donovan (Dublin: 1851), p. 16: "In . . no. 60 of Ms. collection of Messrs. Hodges and Smith, is written Dun na n-Gaedh, i.e., the fort of the darts or wounds . . . [the name] does not appear to be derived from the goose eggs which are made the principal cause of the battle of Magh Rath."

[9]Ibid., p. 29.

[10]Ibid., p. 26.

the common hen's egg, thus indicating and condemning the man who would become the unwitting Judas of Erin. Although Congal Claen is clearly a model for Yeats's Congal, close reading in the Irish source makes it plain that Saint Erc and his curse are parallels to the Great Herne and his curse. Saint Erc and the Herne share the habit of standing in water all day—behavior associated with spiritual powers.

Yeats's interest in Ferguson's plot for *Congal* and its Irish sources can be traced to a date even earlier than his 1890 review. In October and November 1886, Yeats praised Ferguson, who had died in August, in two essays titled "The Poetry of Sir Samuel Ferguson."[11] In these he discusses and quotes lengthy passages from *Congal* after relating its story to other Irish tales. Ferguson's long poem is in five books and cleverly condenses the sagas of the banquet and the battle from the two original Irish texts. Yeats was most taken, he says, with a "wonderful incident full of Celtic irony." This is the confrontation, in book 5, between the provincial king Congal Claen and "an idiot boy with a bill-hook for sword and the head of a cauldron for a shield. Congal turns away half in scorn and half in pity, but as he turns the idiot wounds him mortally with the bill-hook."[12] In gratitude, the *ard-righ* promises the idiot great gifts, much as Yeats would have his fools in *The Herne's Egg* and *The Death of Cuchulain* persuaded to kill the hero to "get all the pennies." This episode, which is also in the Irish source, incorporates the substitution of kitchen implements for heroic weapons (in parody of the mystical qualities of the Four Talismans of the Tuatha de Danaan), the wounding of the hero by a fool, and the fool's reward for the deed—elements Yeats would incorporate into his own work fifty years later. In the same essay Yeats discusses Ferguson's "Deirdre" along with Congal, and quotes a long passage from the lament of Deirdre in which herons are mentioned. Even at that early date Yeats was beginning to connect the story of Congal with the symbol of heron or herne. In "The Old Men of the Twilight" Yeats recounts that druids who would not be converted to Christianity were changed into herons by Saint Patrick.[13]

Yeats seems to have been most strongly influenced by books 2 and 5 of Ferguson's *Congal*. In his adaptation of the story for *The Herne's Egg*, he incorporates the two crucial turns in the plot which Ferguson adapted from the Irish sources: the unintentional slight at the royal banquet (book 2), and the final overthrow by the Fool (book 5). Yeats also based his male characters, in a modified and simplified form, on those in Ferguson. Domnall, High King of all Ireland, becomes Aedh,[14] King of Tara; Congal Claen, provincial King of Ulster, becomes Congal, King of Connaught. In Yeats's play, however, the two kings have parity in prowess, East (Tara) versus West (Connaught), until the balance is destroyed by the effect of the Herne's egg on Congal's drunken pride.

The motivation for the stealing of the eggs, the insulting substitution (due to supernatural influence) of the hen's egg at the royal banquet, the resulting battle that brings about a change in historical relations, and the confrontation between hero and fool are less elaborated in Yeats's play than in either Ferguson's epic or its Irish sources. Yeats deliberately kept the story simple:

---

[11]See UP 1, pp. 81–104. The essays were first published in the *Irish Fireside*, October 9, 1886, and the *Dublin University Review*, November 1886.

[12]Yeats thus paraphrases Ferguson, UP 1, p. 99.

[13]In *The Secret Rose* (1897).

[14]This is a name found in Ferguson and in the Irish sources as belonging to various characters. In the Irish epics, this is the name of Domnall's father as well as a component in the names of the fathers of two other chieftains. "Aedh" is speaker of some of the poems in *The Wind Among the Reeds* (1899).

the many complexities of character and plot in the sources are streamlined to enhance the irony and philosophic depth in Yeats's modern version. To the structure of the epic story, Yeats added two elements: the rape of the priestess and the attempt by Congal to thwart the divine curse by suicide.

The major changes Yeats made were in the nature of the female character and in that of the supernatural being. Ferguson had added the character Lafinda and reduced the importance of other female characters of the original sources except for the prophetic Washer at the Ford, whom Yeats converted into Attracta, the Herne's bride. Lafinda, betrothed to Congal Claen, serves as an ideal type of feminine purity. By book 5 she has become a nun who emerges from the convent of Saint Brigid long enough to comfort the heathen Congal as he dies. Yeats turns her into Attracta, a kind of vestal virgin/divine harlot, dedicated to the service of the Herne-god. He provides her with three innocent girls as attendants. Preternatural elements that, in the sources, take various forms are concentrated by Yeats into the "only reality" of the Great Herne, who seems to have been monotheistically based on both the "evil" and the "good" prophetic figures of the Washer at the Ford and Saint Erc.

Various explanations for the source of the character Attracta have been put forward. F. A. C. Wilson stresses Balzac's *Seraphita*;[15] Georgio Melchiori suggests the pagan Salome.[16] In spite of many echoes, however, neither of these is closely akin to Yeats's Attracta, any more than is the Christian Lafinda in Ferguson's poem. Attracta's name was probably inspired by the fifth-century Saint Attracta, said to be the Abbess of Boyle (in Connaught), who, according to local tradition, was given the veil by Saint Patrick.[17] She is said to have built the causeway that runs part way across Lough Gara by carrying stones in her apron. When a passing fisherman commented on her pretty legs she dropped her skirt in modesty and abandoned the project. She then began another causeway across Lough Kee only to have the same interruption.

Yeats's Attracta, a pagan priestess of the invented "mystery of the Great Herne," shares with Leda and the Virgin Mary the experience of intercourse with godhead in the form of a bird—a link more important than her affinity with either Seraphita or Salome. That is to say, her role as feminine agent of a god's will (thus uniting the sexual and the religious) outweighs her importance as man's muse or temptress. The ambiguity of Attracta's nature reflects that of Mary, the nominal wife of Joseph and the actual bride of God—at once married and virginal, impregnated not by man but by the Holy Ghost, represented in art by a dove. Yeats explored the idea of dual sexual allegiance not only in Attracta but also in the two characters Decima and

---

[15]F. A. C. Wilson, *W. B. Yeats and Tradition* (London: Gollancz, 1958), pp. 104–105.

[16]Giorgio Melchiori, *The Whole Mystery of Art* (London: Routledge and Kegan Paul, 1960), p. 196.

[17]See *The Life and Writings of St. Patrick*, by The Most Reverend Dr. [John] Healy, Archbishop of Tuam (Dublin: Gill, Sealy, Bryers and Walker, 1905), pp. 214–215: "the local details are strikingly like truth; yet there are difficulties about the chronology. According to the statement here given by the Tripartite, which is in all points confirmed by Tirechan, an older authority, this Saint Attracta . . . must have been at least sixteen years of age when she received the veil from St. Patrick, most probably about the year 437 or 438. It is not likely, therefore, that she lived much beyond the fifth century; yet her Life, as given by Colgan, represents the saint as contemporary with . . . personages who flourished in the sixth and early part of the seventh century." After giving the veil to Attracta, "Patrick . . . went further on towards Boyle to preach to the sons of Erc 'at the place where the nuns now live'. . . . But the godless crew stole the Saint's horses, at the Ford of the Sons of Erc, whereupon he [Saint Patrick] cursed them." So we see that the names Attracta and Erc are closely associated with curses and fords; the nunnery, built after Patrick's time, is near this ford on the River Boyle and Attracta's Abbess of Boyle may have been a later namesake of that Attracta who took the veil from Patrick, who lived for 373 to 493 A.D., or 120 years! All this Yeats could have learned on his visit to Douglas Hyde at his home at Frenchpark, near Lough Gara and Lough Kee, in 1895.

the Queen, in *The Player Queen*, and in the Lady and her Chambermaid in his late poem "The Three Bushes," which he began drafting on the back of the last page of the manuscript of *The Herne's Egg*.

Yeats's tendency was always to blend Christian and pagan elements through his iconography. The "woman out of nature" or the virgin entranced by divine influence, experiencing the horror and ecstasy of superhuman knowledge, is a powerful decoy and threat to mortal man. In *The Resurrection* (1931) the choric songs portray a sinister trance comparable to Attracta's.

I saw a staring virgin stand
Where holy Dionysus died,
And tear the heart out of his side,
And lay the heart upon her hand
And bear that beating heart away;

Attracta's trance (scene 2 of *The Herne's Egg*), in which she makes the fateful substitution of the herne's egg for the hen's egg, is dramatized by the accounts given by her girls, who only partly understand the mystery. These girls are Yeats's closest approximation to a "chorus" in this play.

AGNES
Her god is calling her.
KATE
Look, look, she takes
An egg out of the basket.
. . . .
MARY
Her eyes grow glassy, she moves
According to the notes of the flute.
AGNES
Her limbs grow rigid, she seems
A doll upon a wire.

II

Yeats had begun planning the composition of *The Herne's Egg* by November 1935. In letters of that month he repeatedly writes of a play he has "in my head." On November 28 he informed his sister Lilly: "I am going away [to Majorca] partly to escape the chance of another illness and partly to write without interruption. I have a three act play in my head." And to his sister Lolly: "I go to warmth and the chance of concentrating upon a big piece of work I have in my head."[18] On the same day he also wrote to Dorothy Wellesley: "My work on the anthology [*The Oxford*

[18]Unpublished letters, to Susan Mary Yeats and Elizabeth Corbet Yeats, both written at Riversdale, Rathfarnham, Dublin. These and all subsequent unpublished letters quoted were shown to me in Oxford by John S. Kelly, general editor of Yeats's correspondence.

Book of Modern Verse] is finished—the rest, the business arrangements, are my wife's task. I have a three-act tragi-comedy in my head to write in Majorca, not in blank verse but in short line like 'Fire' but a larger number of four stress lines—as wild a play as 'Player Queen', as amusing but more tragedy and philosophic depth."[19]

The letters he sent from Palma, Majorca, and from Riversdale, near Dublin—to his wife, to Margot Ruddock, to Dorothy Wellesley, and to his sisters—refer to the development of *The Herne's Egg* between November 1935 and August 1936, and their information is often repeated to the various recipients. In them we can trace the development, to some extent, of the attitude Yeats had to his writing of the play. On Christmas Day, 1935, he wrote to Margot Ruddock:

> I wish I could have seen more of your acting, it would have helped me to write the strange play I am now writing. My heroine, a holy woman, is raped by seven men, and the next day calls upon the heavens to testify that she has never lain in any arms but those of her god. Heaven thunders three times, and the men who have raped her fall upon their knees. This is but one episode in a wild fantastic humorous, half-earnest play, my first full-length play. . . .
>
> Swami and I are translating the Upanishads together—we are both to put our names on the title page. Here is a sentence I like: "Mere preachers and soldiers are his food, death its condiment; how then can a common man understand Him."[20]

On December 7, on his arrival at the Hotel Terramar in Palma, Majorca, Yeats wrote to his wife: "Yesterday I finished the scenario & today began writing the play in verse—short lines, rhymed here and there. I think I shall write it quickly, have it [illegible] blocked in, in a month . . . 3 acts, Act 2 with 3 scenes. All I think amusing & strange. There is a donkey, like a childs toy, on wheels but life size, an important character. My days are not long enough for all I have to do."[21] And later: "Dear Dobbs, I have got great confidence in myself. Yesterday morning the last crumple of my play smoothed itself out & now all is complete in my head, at last my work is all in all with me."[22] What that "last crumple" was and whether its smoothing out was the result of Shri Purohit Swami's companionship and their discussion of the *Ten Principal Upanishads* remain a mystery. To judge from some of the massive deletions in the manuscript, though, Yeats did not have the form of the play quite so firmly in his mind as he seemed to think. On December 16, he wrote again to Dorothy Wellesley: "I work in my bed till noon at a verse play, though as yet it is but prose scenario—very wild but I think very well constructed. I think of writing for the first time in sprung verse (four stresses) with a certain amount of rhyme, part may be in the verse of your 'Fire'. Shri Purohit Swami is with me, and the play is his philosophy in a fable, or mine confirmed by him." He then began to turn the scenario into what he called sprung verse but soon developed a more fluent metre. The original prose scenario has not survived, nor have his initial efforts at "sprung verse."

---

[19]Cited from *Letters on Poetry from W. B. Yeats to Dorothy Wellesley* (New York: Oxford University Press, 1940).

[20]*Ah, Sweet Dancer: W. B. Yeats, Margot Ruddock, A Correspondence,* ed. Roger McHugh (London: Macmillan, Gill and Macmillan, 1970), p. 65.

[21]Unpublished letter.

[22]Unpublished letter to his wife George, whom he called "Dobbs," sent (probably in mid-December) "c/o Thomas Cook," from Majorca (n.d.).

Hotel Terramar,
Dec. 21 [1935]

Dear Lady Dorothy,
. . . Yesterday I finished the scenario of my new play and to-day began the verse. It has begun well, but much of it will I am certain be artificial till I re-write and re-write. I am writing in short lines but think that I shall not use "sprung verse"—now that I am close to it I dislike the constant uncertainty as to where the accent falls; it seems to make the verse vague and weak. I like a strong driving force. If there should be a subtle hesitating rhythm I can make it. I do not want it as part of the metrical scheme. I shall write "sprung verse" only if I find it comes spontaneously— if a foot of four syllables seems natural I shall know I am in for it. My play will I think be a full evening's entertainment if it is ever played—my first full length play. One of the characters is a donkey, represented by a toy donkey with wheels but life size. I am trusting to this play to give me a new mass of thought and feeling overflowing into lyrics (these are now in play).

Scene 1 of the published versions of the play, like act I of the manuscript, is almost entirely in short three-stress lines. On "Dec. 22 (I think)," Yeats wrote to Dorothy Wellesley: "When I wrote yesterday that you had a more natural style than the rest of us, I was thinking mainly of 'Fire' which I am trying to emulate in my play. I do not know whether it is the change from your three stress lines to four stress, or sheer incapacity to handle a natural speech, but I have hitherto failed to do so. I rewrote a longish scene to-day, keeping 'Fire' in my mind."

The three-stress lines in the beginning of the play gradually give way to lines with mostly four stresses and a greater number of unstressed syllables between stresses. A few lines from "Fire" may be compared.

Modern Man! the mystical
Core of life, and the carnal
Are one with that you have slain,
One with the fire, Cain![23]

Yeats's shift from three to four-stress lines is illustrated by the following passages from scenes 1 and 2 of *The Herne's Egg*:

CONGAL
How many men have you lost?
AEDH
Some five-and-twenty men.
CONGAL
No need to ask my losses.

[23]"Fire," in *The Oxford Book of Modern Verse*, ed. W. B. Yeats (Oxford: Clarendon Press, 1936), p. 309. Note that the "message" of the first lines of Wellesley's stanza quoted above—that the "mystical Core of life, and the carnal" are at odds—is also a significant aspect of the meaning of *The Herne's Egg* and of "The Three Bushes."

AEDH
Your losses equal mine.

And,

ATTRACTA
For a thousand or ten thousand years,
For who can count so many years,
Some woman has lived among these rocks,
The Great Herne's bride, or promised bride,
And when a visitor has played the flute
Has come or not. What would you ask?

Compare this published version of Attracta's speech with the revision in his working manuscript, now in the National Library of Ireland, MS. 8770 (1), 8^{r}, ll. 8–12, which Yeats then deleted and replaced with 7^{v}, ll. 10–15, given below. (Note that the lines are four-stress, yet their content and order are not identical with those of the first version above.)

For a thousand or ten thousand years
For who can count so many years
A visitor has played upon the flute
A Woman sang among the rock
Hernes ~~Hawk~~ s, ~~or~~ Bride, or promised to the ~~hawk herne~~ Herne
Your question is permitted—speak

A third development of this speech, on 8^{v}, is nearer to the published text:

For a thousand or ten thousand years
For who can count so many yea[rs]
Some woman has lived among these [rocks]
The great Hernes bride or promised bride
And when a visitor has played this flu[te]
Has answered with the song that I have sung
What would you ask.

The manuscript indicates that Yeats originally associated the function of the table leg (with which the drunken Congal slays Aedh in scene 4) with that of the egg. The table leg is a substitute, and an inferior one, for the sword; the hen's egg is a substitute for the herne's egg, which, in turn, is substituted for by Attracta, who is raped as a substitute for unsuccessful attempts at stoning the Great Herne. On MS. 8770 (2), 5^{v} and 6^{r}, a deleted song of Attracta's indicates that it is *because* Congal played the fool with both table leg and herne's egg (using one as a weapon to kill his friend, the other as a target for his men to throw hats at when determining the order of rape) that his fate is to die at the hands of a fool. The song was meant to follow Mathias's speech that begins, "Look, look" (the rest is mostly deleted); see 6^{r}, ll. 10–14. Attracta's "Song" was then moved to 5^{v}, ll. 13–19, to follow new material to be interpolated before Congal's speech at 6^{r}, l. 15. In the published versions of the play, the curse results from stealing the herne's eggs. In MS. 8770 (1), 15^r, ll. 1–5, motivation for the curse shifts to Attracta's statement that Congal only asks her permission in mockery. She then gives him a choice of putting the eggs back or keeping them and so being condemned to "carry the curse upon his back" (just as the creels of stolen eggs are borne upon the donkey's back—indeed, are *painted* upon its back—evidence of *that* rapscallion's curse and an implication that a previous soldier-king had trespassed into the sacred hernery).

It is generally accepted that Yeats gave this particular fate to Congal as a result of having read the anecdote in Alexandra David-Neel's *Magic and Mystery in Tibet*, in which a saintly lama suddenly tries to have sexual intercourse with a young girl and justifies his behavior thus to her:

> the Grand Lama of the neighbouring monastery has died in ignorance, having neglected all occasions of instruction. I saw his 'spirit' . . . drawn towards a bad rebirth, and, out of compassion, I wished to procure him a human body. But the power of his evil deeds has not permitted this. You escaped, and while you were at the village, the asses in that field near by coupled. The Grand Lama will soon be reborn as a donkey.[24]

Note the reversal of emphasis in Corney's speech in comparison with the lama's: while the lama says that soon his master must be reborn as a donkey, Corney says

> I have heard that a donkey carries its young
> Longer than any other beast,
> Thirteen months it must carry it.
> All that trouble and nothing to show for it .

This final speech acknowledges the compulsive regenerative forces in brute nature. After the heroic personal achievement in which Congal takes responsibility for his own, only partially forseeable, fate in his attempt to direct his own destiny, he is dragged back into the mire and blood of bestial nature.[25] Attracta's invitation to Corney to mate with her,

> there's a work
> That should be done, and that work needs
> The imperfection of a man,

is answered by "The sound of a donkey braying." The imperfection of the beast ensures that the cycle of spiritual evolution and physical reincarnation must, for Congal, begin again from a degraded level, echoing the degraded symbols of table leg for sword and hen's egg for herne's. The braying of the lusty donkey—no longer a mere painted toy on wheels—can be heard as a rude song of celebration and affirmation of the flesh, a relief from the spiritual and ethical concerns that precede it.

---

[24]Alexandra David-Neel, *Magic and Mystery in Tibet* (New York: Dover , 1971), p. 24.

[25]In an unpublished letter to "Dobbs" of September 1935, Yeats says that he saw and was impressed by T. S. Eliot's play *Murder in the Cathedral*, in which Becket foresees his own martyrdom and struggles to "perfect his will": this may have provided a partial model for the character Congal's development, although Eliot's notion of *will* as an obstacle to grace is, on the surface, antithetical to Yeats's notion of *Will* as essential to achieving one's (heroic or artistic) destiny.

Yeats's retrospective statement (in his Introduction to *The Herne's Egg and Other Plays*) that refers to "happier moments of a long illness that had so separated me from life that I felt irresponsible," seems somewhat apologetic in light of remarks about his state of mind which he made during the composition of the play. For example, he told his wife: "I do not think my head has ever been so full of imaginative inspiration. I think of a saying in the Upanishads, 'I am full of longing. They have put a gold stopper in the neck of truth; pull it out Lord, let our reality'."[26] The courage to combine frank sexual content with bizarre imagery taken from such divergent sources may, as he said, have come from an "irresponsible" feeling—a lifting of his concern for the carefully cultivated public mask and the reputation of dramatist and poet that he had, until his final decade, consciously maintained. Yet this attempt to give some ultimate turbulent view of the pairing of Chance and Choice demonstrates his lifelong concern with the responsibility of the poet's task.

III

Yeats began composing his play, in the pages now gathered as MS. 8770 in the National Library of Ireland, soon after he had composed a prose scenario, not extant. In one letter to his wife, sent probably in early January 1936, he remarks in a postscript: "I have finished and am copying out my first act."[27] On January 26, 1936, he wrote to Dorothy Wellesley: "The doctor has stopped my creative work. I have finished Act I of my play, a scene of Act 2 and rather a good lyric." Indeed his activity was interrupted more than once. Two weeks later he reported to Margot Ruddock: "I have been ill. . . . I spend much time sitting in the sun on a terrace by the sea. . . . I have had to stop my play but I will take it up again when I am better. Before the doctor intervened I had written Act I and Scene I Act 2, and a lyric which I like."

It is difficult to see a pattern or single underlying motive for the changes Yeats made as he worked in NLI MS. 8770. The major changes are not structural, aside from the reallocation of acts I, II, and III (and their scenes) into a one-act play with six scenes. In trying to keep the story simple, laden as it is with complexities of symbolism, he deleted some allusions to the sun at NLI MS. 8770 (1), 5^r, ll. 5/6, and stars, 17^r, l. 19, as well as reference to a journey for which Attracta purportedly needs her donkey, 5^r, ll. 1–5. At 13^r, ll. 18–21, Yeats also eliminated a speech of Congal's, one line of which echoes Dorothy Wellesley's "Fire." Lines from this deleted passage of Congal's

Make a woman but no dunce
All things stood in the fire once

point to two changes in Yeats's thought. (1) The imprecations of the servant Corney urging Attracta to "burn them up" were first given to Attracta. See MS. 8770 (1), 13^v, l. 1, 14^r, ll. 2–5 and 14^v, l. 1. (Note that recto pages were written prior to the corrections or additions to them which appear on the facing versos.) (2) This eliminated speech of Congal's reveals a condescending attitude toward women: at MS. 8770 (1), 8^r, ll. 4–7 Congal objects to Attracta's

[26]Unpublished letter from Hotel Terramar, "Dec. 3 days after Christmas [1935]."
[27]Unpublished letter sent from Hotel Terramar (n.d.).

playing the flute, first because "it puts her face all crooked" and second because it turns her into a "dumb brute." (Note that Attracta's flute playing was eliminated altogether, so that Congal, or rather Corney in Congal's stead, must play the flute to summon her.) These deletions, which make Congal appear less prejudiced against the "improper" behavior of women, reinforce his "rational" image. For example, when he decides to rape Attracta as the just action of his self-styled Court of Law, he appears to be motivated less by a belief in the subordinate status of women than by a desire to make her *more* of a woman, to free her from the influence of the Herne.

The assigning of names of characters varies in two instances. The *Variorum Edition of the Plays* (p. 1012) notes that in the dramatis personae the listing of "James" a soldier is omitted in all printings, then points out that "James" appears in the stage directions after l.12 in scene 2. The three friends of Attracta—Jane, Agnes, and Mary in the manuscript: see MS. 8770 (1), 16^{r}—become Kate, Agnes, and Mary in the typescript and published texts.

It is interesting to note, finally, that Yeats eliminated an Irish colloquialism. On MS. 8770 (1), 12^{r} at ll. 8–9 he has:

> ~~He doubtless means~~ This old campaigner means
> Long headed
> ~~Being a learned~~ man of the word that he is

"Long-headed" derives from Irish parlance and may be related to the term "adz-head," which was applied to Saint Patrick, possibly because of the hat or mitre that he wore. Both "adz-head" and "long-headed" (the latter is still in use today) mean wise or learned.

The date of completion of *The Herne's Egg* can also be fixed thanks to Yeats's correspondence and collaboration with Dorothy Wellesley. A letter of June 30, 1936 reports: "To-day I am content with life again—my work has gone well. . . . To-morrow I shall finish the play, then I write the ballad of lovers, the lady and the servant." The last leaf of NLI MS. 8770 (2) has on its verso not the final lines of Corney's last speech, as one would expect, but a deleted plan for the first two stanzas of Yeats's long "ballad" "The Three Bushes." Finally, on August 5, 1936, he wrote from Riversdale: " I meant to write on Sunday but my wife offered to type my play if I would read out the MS. That took us Sunday and Monday and now I am free again." This typescript is very likely the one which is at the University of Texas with the Scribner material; it appears to be a carbon copy of Mrs. Yeats's typescript made August 3–4, 1936.

IV

The first published texts of *The Herne's Egg* were *The Herne's Egg*: *A Stage Play* (London: Macmillan, January 1938) and *The Herne's Egg and Other Plays* (New York: Macmillan, April 1938). Two of the earliest reviews were by Austin Clarke, in the *New Statesman and Nation* (January 29, 1938), and Janet Adam Smith, in the *Criterion* (April 1938). Neither was completely complimentary. Janet Smith's review concludes: "I doubt if all the point of the ending . . . would be grasped by anyone who had not heard of the belief held by certain Lamaists that the living can influence the shape into which the dead are re-born, and had not read such an account of it as Mrs. David-Neel gives. . . . Without that knowledge, the story can be understood, but the tension of the situation cannot be felt. It is hard to judge of this from a reading only . . . the whole play might be made so dream-like on the stage that we should accept anything as right." Clarke, commenting that "mists of his own past have defeated Mr. Yeats at last," concluded that "Yeats has attempted to capture the madcap spirit of the old mock-heroic tales of Gaelic tradition. . . . Synge might have succeeded, but it seems to me that Mr. Yeats succeeds merely in parodying himself rather unpleasantly."

The play was not an easy one for Yeats to put before the public after publication. He wrote to Dorothy Wellesley from Riversdale, on December 9, 1936: "The Abbey Theatre had decided not to do my new play. I am greatly relieved. I am no longer fit for riots, & I thought a bad riot almost certain." When he sent Ethel Mannin a copy of the play on February 17, 1938, Yeats wrote: "It disturbed the Abbey board until I withdrew it. An admiring member had decided that the seven ravishers of the heroine are the seven sacraments." Describing the play as "very Rabelasian," he remarked, "Do not ask me what it means."[28]

Yeats was never to see the play produced. The earliest public performances of *The Herne's Egg* were by Austin Clarke's Lyric Theatre Company at the Abbey Theatre in Dublin on October 29 and November 5, 1950. The long delay between the play's first publication and its first public performance was no doubt caused in part by its sexual content, which variously was considered outrageous and in bad taste, simply not emphasized in an effort to mask it (as in the 1950 program notes, which stress instead the theme of reincarnation), or unsuccessfully disguised as symbolic of some philosophical-religious content.

The best summary of Yeats's final attitude to the play was provided by Frank O'Connor, in his article "Quarreling with Yeats: A Friendly Recollection" (*Esquire*, December 1964):

> . . . it never dawned on me that every squabble seemed to begin and end with Higgins.
>
> There was that matter of *The Herne's Egg* for instance. Yeats had read it to me as he wrote it, and I thought it magnificent. When it came before the Board of the theatre only Ernest Blythe supported me, and he did so on the ground that the play was so obscure that no one would notice it was obscene. This was not what I felt at all, but I was glad of any support because my friend, Hayes, the Government representative, threatened to resign if the play were produced, and I was voted down. I challenged Hayes about it afterwards, and he told me that Yeats had admitted to Higgins that the seven men who rape the priestess were intended to represent the seven sacraments. Now, the play isn't very difficult. Any reader of Yeats can test that argument for himself. I feel sure that the seven men represent the sciences and the priestess revealed religion, while the rape is merely a stylization of the nineteenth-century attack on religion. . . . But Hayes was very certain about what Higgins had told him, and I knew that Yeats did get embarrassed and excited and say things he regretted next day, so that I could only reply that he didn't seem to understand his own work very well.
>
> Finally, in a fit of exasperation, I said I would produce the play myself at my own expense, with the woman I was proposing to marry as Attracta. When I told Yeats, he turned on me with real anger, and I saw that under all the good-humored detachment, he was bitterly hurt at the rejection of his beautiful play by a gang of nobodies. "And

---

[28] *The Letters of W. B. Yeats,* ed. Allan Wade (New York: Macmillan, 1955), pp. 904–905.

> why did you not insist on its being produced when you had a majority of the Board behind you?" he shouted. . . . I told him that Hayes had threatened to resign if the play were produced, because he was supposed to have said that the seven men represented the seven sacraments. Yeats blew up. "How could I have said anything so silly?" he asked, which was precisely what I had wondered myself.

V

In manuscript studies it is most illuminating to see revealed the process of struggle and the development of a writer's characteristic material as it is given its unique form. Not only can we become more conscious of the ways in which one work relates to others—its place in the writer's total production and thought—but we can follow certain steps of discovery within the work which are the manifestations of personal vision and craftsmanship that made that vision possible at given moments in the process.

Although Yeats was writing *The Herne's Egg* under pressure of ill health, failing eyesight, and imminent death (as he suspected), the play is a lighthearted treatment of a vision of death, which he was yet to deal with more seriously in *The Death of Cuchulain* and in "Cuchulain Comforted." In *The Herne's Egg*, Yeats is playing with his ultimate adversary, distancing the figures of Death and Time with irony, farce, confirmation of a belief in reincarnation, and the apparent triumph of spirituality and the natural world over mere human rationality; the natural order of beasts and the supernatural order of gods win out over the shortsighted and imperfect "law and order" of the human vision. Perhaps Yeats himself felt caught in the middle, as was his character Congal, between the growing awareness of divine caprice and a growing acceptance of nature's predictable and irresistible forces of decay, death, and renewal. In the drafts in MS. 8770 we can see Yeats continuing to explore the other side of art—the mystery of the source of power and knowledge—during the last years of his development as playwright and poet.

> As Ovid & his like have told
> That nevr knew what bird what gold
> What sun like joy laughed down that gold
> What moonlike dreams groped for pale feathr
> When Leda lay upon the grass
> For Ovid told all liter l y
>
> [MS. 8770 (1), 10^v]

He was conscious of having waited until his last years to attempt his version of divine rape and the "antithetical" challenge of Irish heathendom to "objective" Christian civilization.

The drafts and correspondence suggest that Yeats knew—perhaps for some time before going to Majorca to write—just what *The Herne's Egg* would be: a half-serious confrontation with mortality. While this is perhaps Yeats's least accepted or understood play, it attests to the imaginative powers of the "wild old wicked man" in Yeats. The changes of intention and those passages not included in the published versions offer additional evidence of Yeats's thinking in the final years of an intensely creative life and, while not "authorized" passages, they remain as part of his work—evidence of his struggle and ability to "hammer his thoughts into Unity."

Transcription Principles and Procedures

This edition provides a full transcription of the only extant manuscript version of *The Herne's Egg*: NLI 8770 (folders 1 and 2), now in the National Library of Ireland. Photographic reproductions of each manuscript page are given, facing the transcriptions. The typescript draft now in the Scribner's Archive at the Harry Ransom Humanities Research Center, Austin, Texas, is also transcribed in full.

NLI 8770 is contained in two grey manila folders, each approximately 8 by 11 inches. Folder 1 contains "Act I/24ff" and folder 2 contains "Act II/29ff." There is some doubt as to the correct number of leaves originally in folder 1. The cover reads "24ff," yet the last leaf in that folder is numbered 23 and belongs to act II, scene 1, while folder 2 reads "29ff" and does, in fact, contain 29 leaves. The contents of folder 2 begin at scene 2 of act II. Unless one of two labels or small slips of paper is counted, there may be a leaf missing from the original contents of the first folder. One of the leaves in folder 2, however, properly belongs between I, 12^v and I, 13^r. The manuscript pages are identified at the top left corner of each page of transcription in square brackets.

The play was divided differently upon publication, with the original three acts redesignated as six scenes of a one-act play. Some leaves are clean and without corrections and may not, in fact, be first drafts. Others are very worked over with much revision. All recto pages of act I are consecutively numbered; the recto pages of act II are renumbered from 1 to 10, followed by one page of text written in dark red ink with no pagination indicated. Thereafter pagination is from *a* to *f*, followed by twelve leaves that have no pagination. Yeats's page numbers, or letters, are reproduced in the transcription.

Yeats used several colors of ink, as follows in diminishing order of frequency: blue-black, black, red, and greenish-black. He also occasionally used pencil. As there is only a slight difference between the blue-black and lighter greenish-black inks, footnotes indicate changes in shade where they could be distinguished clearly. Dark blue-black ink is the norm, or first stage, for all pages except for the unnumbered page in red which follows II, 10^r.

The appearance of the manuscript has been reproduced in the transcription as carefully as possible but regularized for legibility. Many versos contain corrections and additions to the facing rectos; it is usual for arrows to run across the gap between the loose leaves from verso to the following recto to indicate where the interpolations are to be made. The present recto-verso order of this transcription does not at first sight appear to give a clear impression of the actual chronological development. The genesis of the play, however, is much easier to deduce when the text is presented in this way, with major additions for certain rectos given side by side and to the left on the previous verso, than if each interpolation were given in chronological sequence with no physically corresponding division of pages, or with a complicated set of codes which might interfere with a clear visual impression of the form of the original.

When Yeats deleted an entire passage, for example, I, 6^r, usually with a continuous curving stroke or several vertical or diagonal strokes, we have not tried to simulate his marks; rather, vertical rules in the left margin indicate a massive deletion that would have been made after any partial deletions or additions to words within that passage. Within some sectional deletions of whole passages or speeches, cancellations of individual words, lines, or short phrases frequently occur. These deletions are conventionalized throughout by the use of horizontal lines through the text in question.

Where there is no reasonable doubt that Yeats intended a word, even though letters may seem to be missing or run together at the end of that word, it is in most cases transcribed in full. In many cases Yeats's actual spelling cannot be determined although the word that is meant is recognizable; in such cases a standard spelling is given. On the other hand, Yeats's spelling is preserved in places where it is clear even if incorrect. Such deviant spellings are reproduced as faithfully as possible where meaning is obvious: for example, I, 4^r, l. 1, "tuffer." "Attracta" is spelled in a variety of ways. Some spellings are reminiscent of the Celtic pronunciations; for example, "Araght" and "Arahata." A question mark in brackets before a word indicates a conjectural reading.

Yeats frequently broke words at unusual points, or broke words not normally divided. These are joined in the transcription unless the width of the break approximates the spacing Yeats normally left between words, indicating that he considered the word in question to actually be two words or a word requiring hyphenation. A typical example found in Yeats's work is the division "to morrow."

Yeats lapses into "Hawk" or "Heron" in the early pages of the manuscript where he clearly meant to write "Herne." These lapses have been reproduced. His characteristic abbreviations (aside from his misspellings and lack of punctuation) such as "t" for "to," "up" for "upon," "-g" for "-ing" endings, "A" for "And" are, in most cases, spelled out. Some words, however, are given in a kind of shorthand: for example, "aga" for "again," "feat" for "feather," "enog" for "enough," and, in order to recreate the appearance of the manuscript yet retain readability, such shortened forms are retained unless the meaning is not immediately clear, in which case the word is expanded.

Yeats used a variety of instruments in producing the manuscripts of *The Herne's Egg*. The following typefaces have been used to designate these instruments:

roman	ink
italic	pencil
boldface	type or print

Variant colors of ink or pencil are generally described in footnotes.

Yeats's "stet" marks, and his underscorings to indicate italics, are preserved. Both the ampersand and the greek alpha are indicated in the transcription by "&." The ampersand seems to have been the initially favored symbol, since the alpha occurs most often in corrections and additions. The accompanying facsimiles, of course, provide the reader the opportunity to check such distinctions.

Symbols for illegible words and editorial conjectures:

[?]	a totally illegible word
[? ? ?]	several totally illegible words (each question mark represents one word)
~~[?]~~	a deleted totally illegible word
[?and]	a conjectural reading
[?by/?of]	alternate readings seem equally possible
i} lo} ve	an overwriting (original "love" converted to "live")

A Note on the Format of This Edition

On the principle that the record of the growth and development of a poem or play is not complete until it is carried up through the first published texts, all readings in *The Herne's Egg* (London, 1938) are presented in this edition: they are arrayed in an apparatus criticus as variants from the typed text that was prepared in 1938 and later used for the projected "Scribner Edition," never published. The apparatus also includes two other types of variant: variants found in proofs for the 1938 printing or written into an annotated volume in the possession of Anne Yeats, and variants introduced in two typed documents, one keyed to the Scribner typescript, the other keyed to a typescript or proof-sheet not located. These sources are abbreviated as follows:

Harvard	The proof sheets for the 1938 printing
HE	*The Herne's Egg* (1938)
ABY	*The Herne's Egg* (1938): annotated copy
Texas (1)	Revisions to the Scribner typescript
NLI 30,485	Revisions to unlocated typescript.

Omitted from the collations are the following:

1. Variants involving the substitution of "&" for "and"
2. Variants involving placement of punctuation inside or outside quotation marks
3. Variants involving spacing and indentation
4. Variants in punctuation or capitalization of titles and speaker identifications.

In the apparatus, the following abbreviations are used:

del	deleted or deletion
punct	punctuation
quotes	quotation marks
rev	revised or revision

S. M. Parrish
for the Yeats Editorial Board

The Herne's Egg

Transcriptions

[NLI 8770 (1), 1r; I. 1–5]

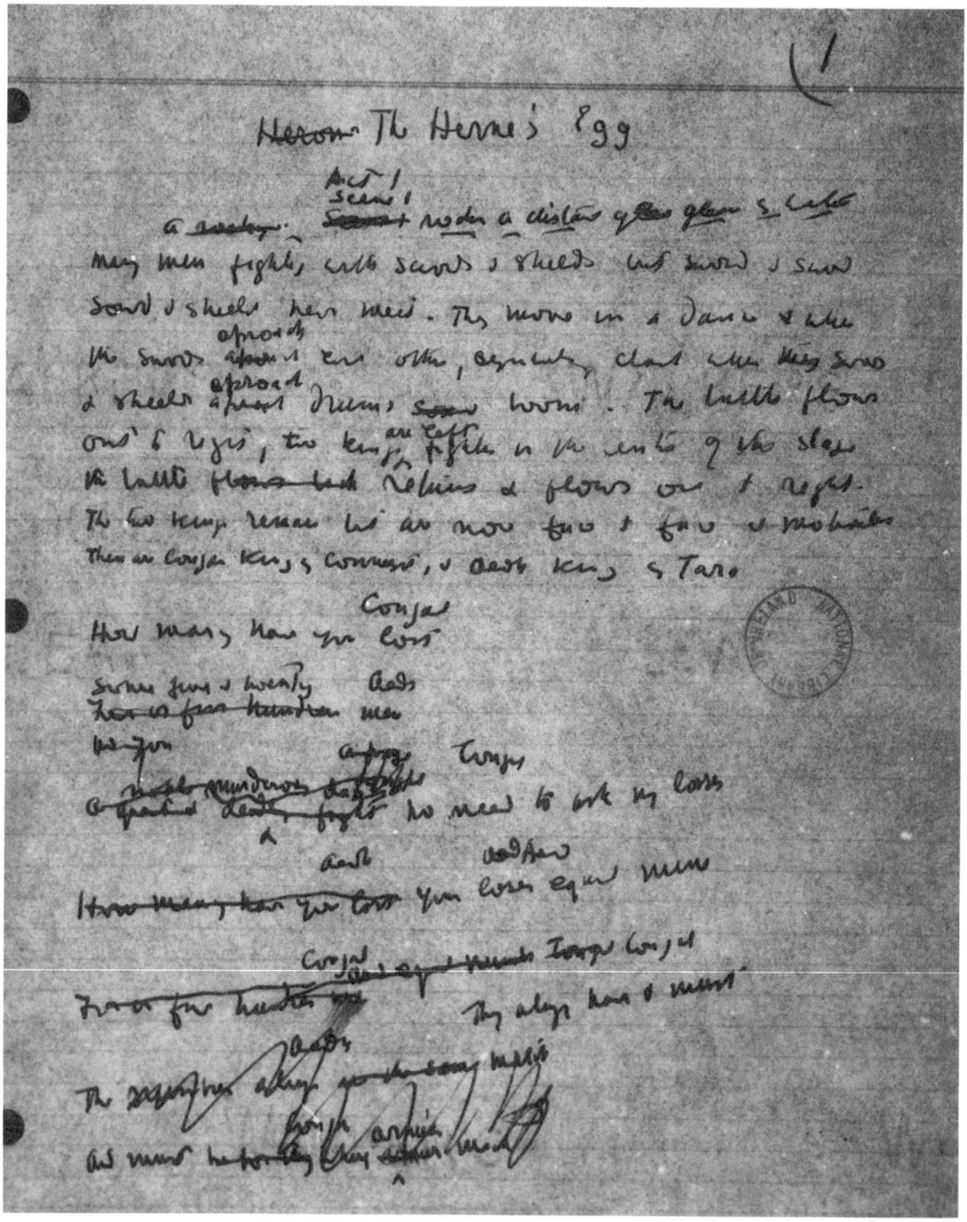
(1

~~Heron~~ The Herne's Egg

Act I
Scene I

under a distant glen

Many men fighting with swords & shields but sword & sword, sword & shield never meet. They move in a dance & when the swords approach each other, cymbals clash when the swords & shields approach drums sound. The battle flows out to right, two kings are left fighting in the centre of the stage. The battle ~~flows back~~ returns & flows out to right. The two kings remain but are now face to face & motionless. These are Congal King of Connacht, & Aedh King of Tara.

Congal
How many have you lost

Aedh
Some five & twenty men
~~Two or four hundred men~~

Congal
no need to ask my losses

Aedh
Your losses equal mine

Congal
They always have & must

[illegible]

~~Heron~~' The Herne's Egg

Act I
Scene 1

A ~~rocky.~~ ~~Scene 1~~ rocks a distant ~~glen~~ glen by water
Many men fighting with swords & shelds but sword & sword
sowrd & shield nevr meet. They move in a dance & when
aproach c
the swords ~~apoa~~ ch each other, symbals clash when ~~they~~ sword
aproach
& sheelds ~~aproch~~ drums ~~sound~~ boom . The battle flows
are left
out to right, two kings ^ fighting in the centre of the stage
the battle ~~flows back~~ returns & flows out to right.
The two kings remain but are now face to face & motionless
They are Congal King of Connaught, & Aedh King of Tara

Congal

1 How many have you lost

Aedh

2 Some five & twenty
~~Four or five hundred~~ men
~~And you~~

~~A Page~~ Congal
~~Congal~~

~~noble murderous day~~
3 ~~A great & deadly fight~~ No need to ask my losses
^

Aedh ~~Aed~~ Aed

4 ~~How many have you lost~~ Your loses equal mine

Congal

~~And equal number~~ ~~Congal~~ Congal
~~Four or five hundred men~~
They always have & must

Aedh

5 The numbers always ~~are the same~~ match

Congal

armies
6 And must ~~be for they~~ ~~Where armies ma ch~~
^

Blue-black ink, with revisions in stage directions and first revision in l. 2 in greenish-black ink.

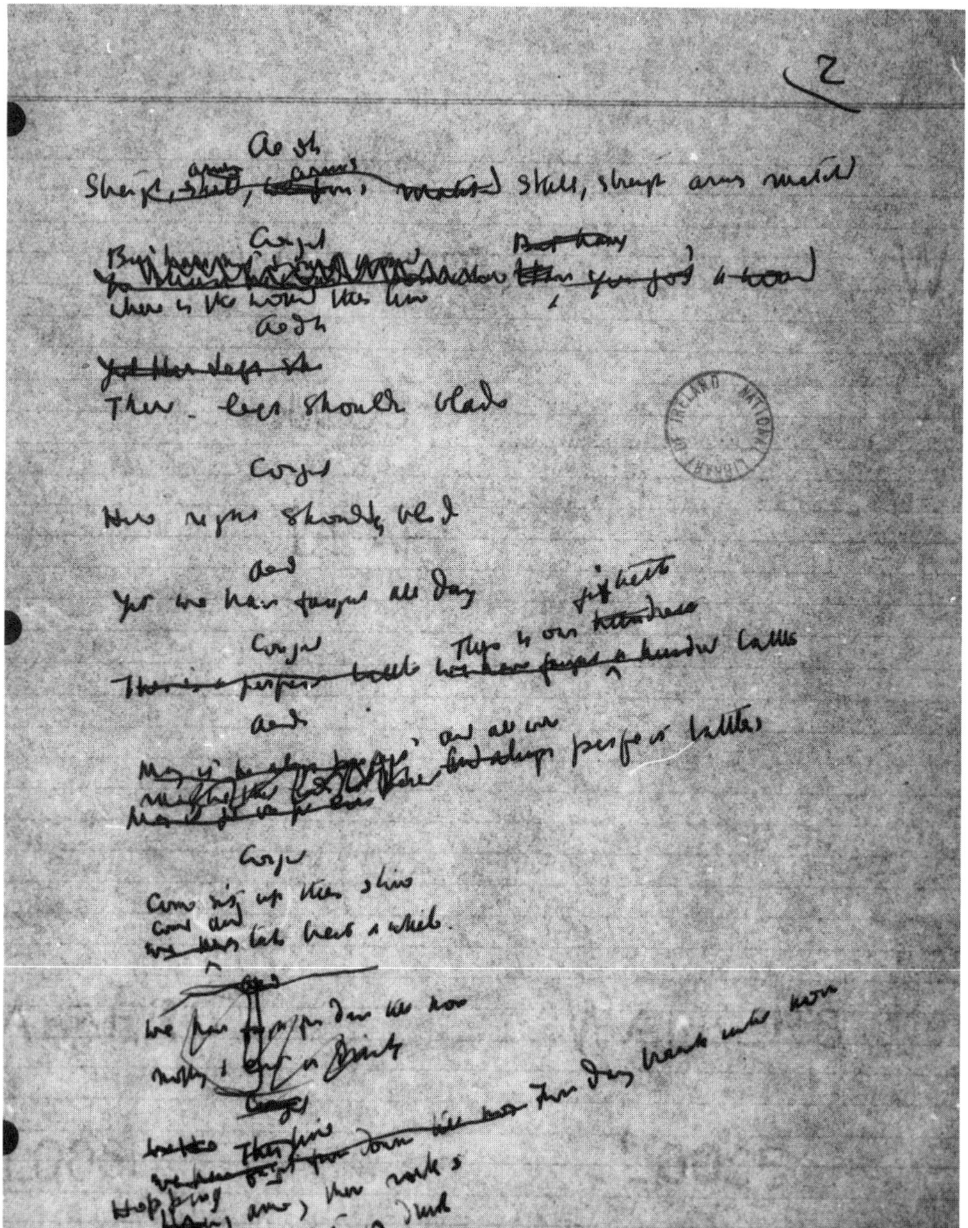

[NLI 8770 (1), 2r; I. 6–17]

2

Aedh

~~armies~~ ~~arms~~

1 Stren~~gth, skill, weapons, matched~~ Skill, strength arms matched

Congal

~~But have not some wound~~ ~~But have~~

~~You must be wounded somewhere~~ ~~Have you got~~ ~~a woun~~d ^

2 Where is the wound this time

Aedh

~~Yes Here left sh~~

3 There — left shoulder blade

Congal

4 Here right shoulder blade

Aedh

5 Yet we have fought all day

fiftieth

Congal This is our ~~hundredth~~

6 ~~This is a perfect battle~~ ~~We have fought ^ a hundred battles~~

Aedh

and all were

7 ~~May it be always perfect~~ ~~And always~~ perfect battles

~~maybe this ends not here~~

~~May it go on for ever~~

Congal

8 Come sit upon this stone

Come and

9 ~~We may~~ take breath a while.

^ ~~Aedh~~

[We have fought from dawn till noon

Nothing to eat or drink]

~~Congal~~

~~We have~~

~~This time~~

10 ~~We have fought from dawn till noon~~ From day break until noon

Hopping

11 ^ ~~Hop~~ing among these rocks

12 Nothing to eat or drink

Blue-black ink, except correction to "fiftieth", l. 6, and "Hopping", l. 11, in greenish-black.
On the verso of leaf 1, facing this, Yeats penciled the following note:

Poems in Anthology I am uncertain about

"Off the Ground" \ De la Mare

[NLI 8770 (1), 3r; I. 18–31]

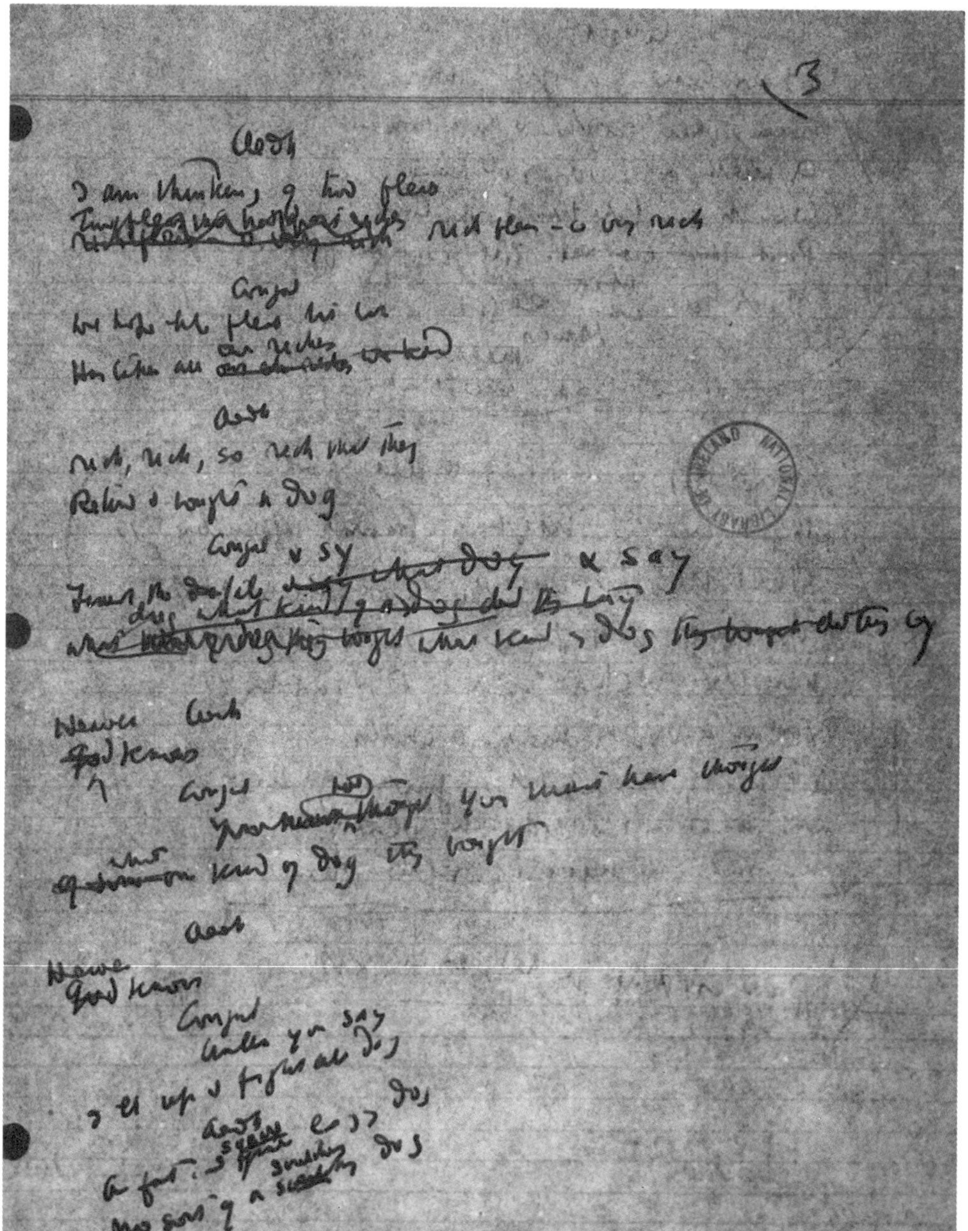

[NLI 8770 (1), 3^{r}; I. 18–31]

3

Aedh

1 I am thinking of two fleas

~~Two fleas that had great riches~~

~~rich fleas — O very rich~~ rich fleas — O very rich

Congal

2 We hope like fleas but war

our riches

3 Has taken all ~~our the riches we had~~

Aedh

4 rich, rich, so rich that they

5 Retired & bought a dog

Congal

& sy

6 Finish the ~~do~~ tale ~~& say what dog~~ & say

~~dog~~ ~~what kind of a dog did~~ ~~they buy~~

7 ~~What sort of dog they bought~~ What kind of dog ~~they bought~~ did they buy

Aedh

Heaven

8 ~~God~~ knows
^

Congal

~~have~~

~~You must~~ ^ ~~thought~~ You must have thought

What

9 ~~Of some one~~ kind of dog they bought

Aedh

Heaven

10 ~~God~~ knows

Congal

Unless you say

11 I ll up & fight all day

Aedh

square

12 A fat, squar lazy dog

scratching

13 No sort of a ~~scratchg~~ dog

Blue-black ink, with revisions in l. 6 (“dog . . . dog”) and to ll. 8–10 in greenish-black ink.

[NLI 8770 (1), 3^{v}; ll. 13–18, 1–12, 19]

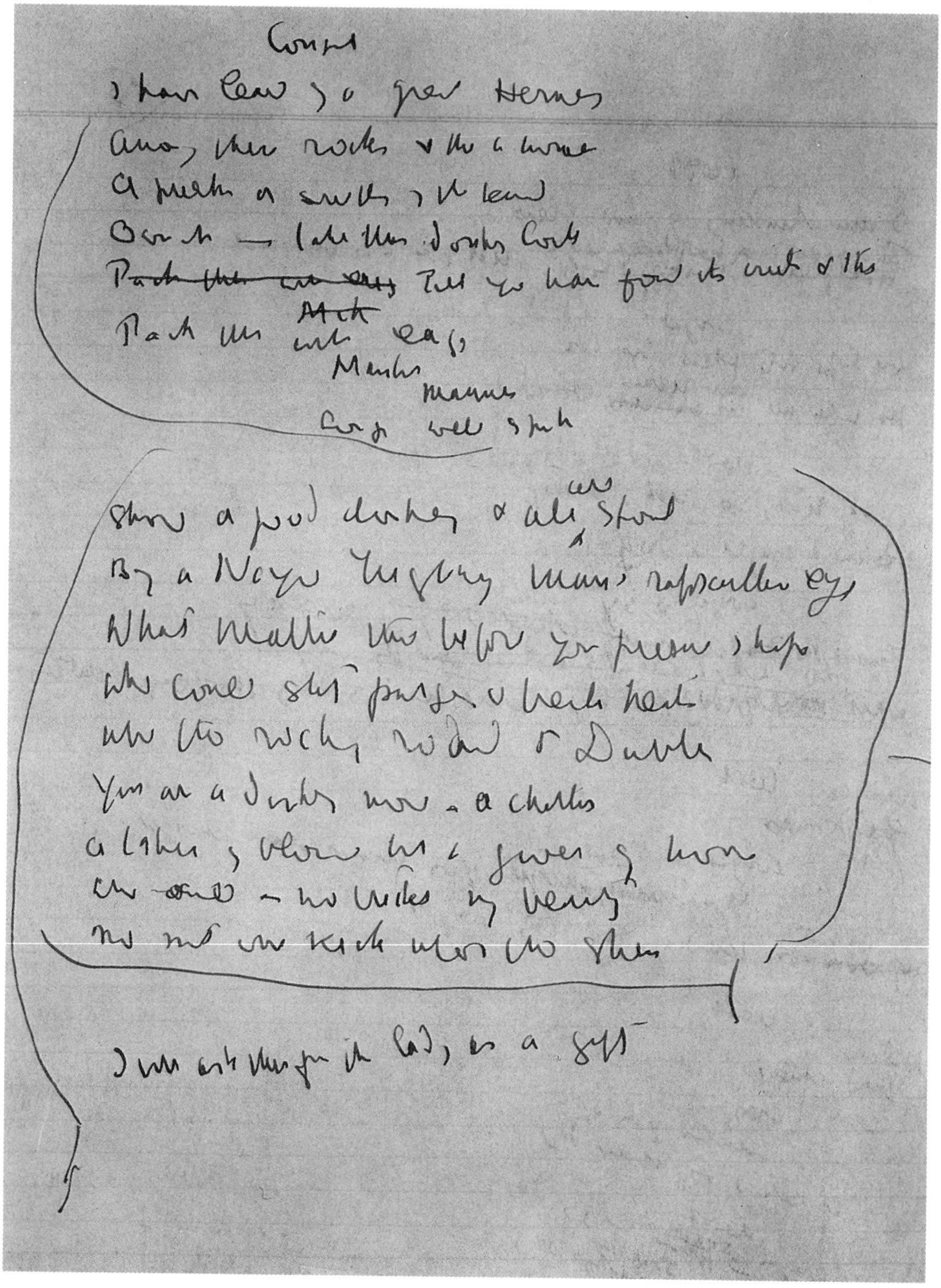

[NLI 8770 (1), 3ᵛ; ll. 13–18, 1–12, 19]

Congal
I have learned of a great Hernery
Among these rocks & that a woman
A priestess or something of the kind
Owns it — take this donkey back
~~Pack them with eggs~~ Till you have found its creels & thn
~~M ck~~
Pack them with eggs
Mantis
Manners
Cong well spoke

are
Show a good donkey & all ^ spoil
By a Mayo highway mans rapscallion eye
What matter that before your present shape
Who could slit purses & break hearts
{ad
Upon the rocky ro{d to Dublin
You are a donkey now — a [?chattel]
A taker of blows but a giver of none
Who-oah — no tricks my beauty
No not one kick upon the shin

I will ask this from the lady as a gift

Blue-black ink. Lines 7–15 replace ll. 5–10 on 4ʳ.

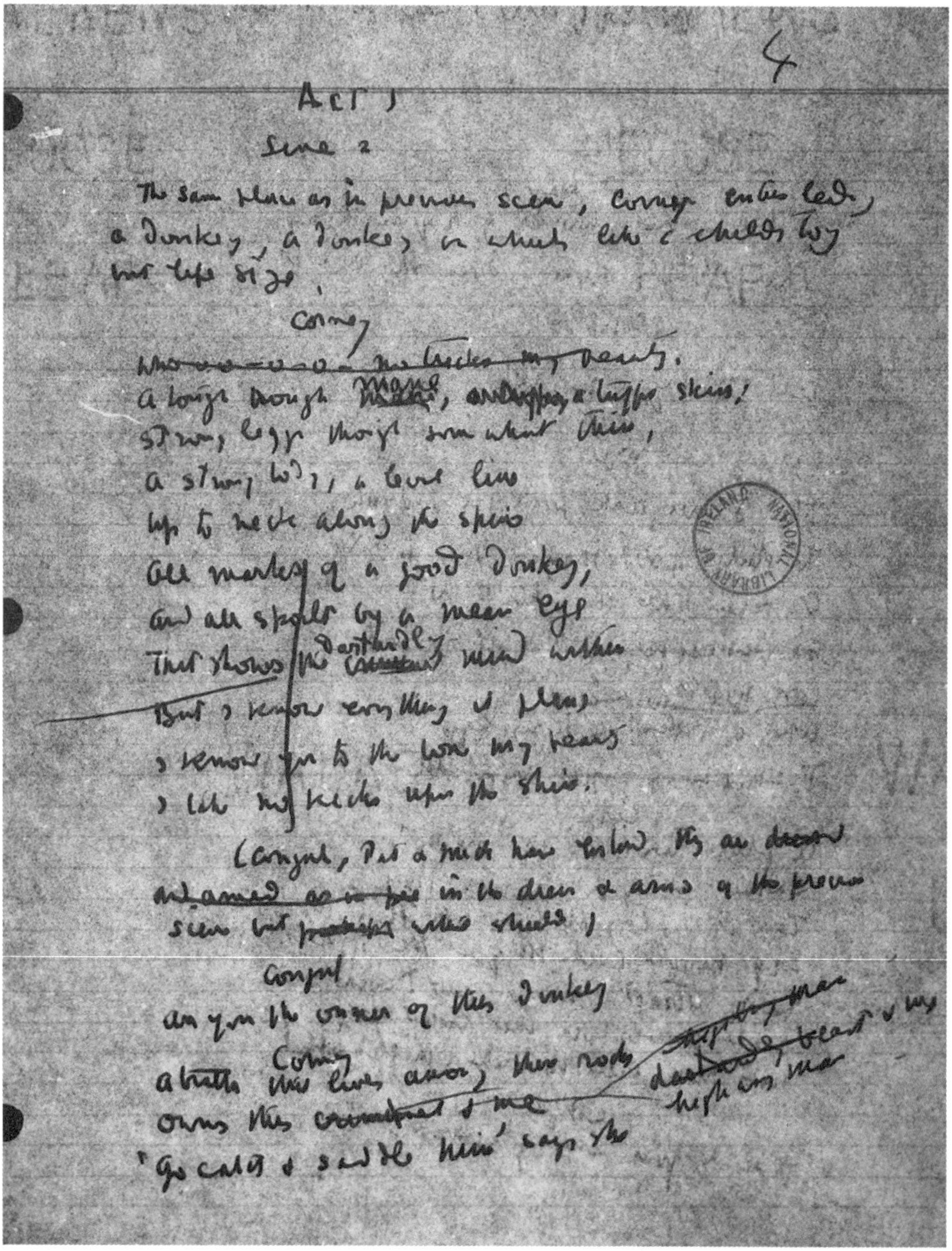

4

Act 1

Scene 2

The same place as in previous scene, Corney enters lead, a donkey, a donkey on wheels like a childs toy but life size.

Corney

~~Who [illegible] [illegible] kicks my beast.~~

A tough rough ~~[illegible]~~ mane, ~~[illegible]~~ a tough rough skin;

Strong legs though somewhat thin,

A strong body, a level line

Up to neck along the spine

All marks of a good donkey,

And all spoiled by a mean eye

That shows the ~~[illegible]~~ dastardly mind within

~~But I remove everything I please~~

~~I remove him to the town my beasts~~

~~I take my kicks upon the shins.~~

(Congal, Pat & Mike have followed. They are dressed ~~and armed as in pre~~ in the dress & arms of the previous scene but ~~[illegible]~~ without shields)

Congal

Are you the owner of this donkey

Corney

A hermit that lives among these rocks ~~[illegible] man~~ ~~dastardly, beast & my~~ high in the man

Owns this ~~[illegible] & me~~

"Go catch & saddle him" says he

[NLI 8770 (1), 4^{r}; ll. 1–15]

4

Act I
Scene 2

The same place as in previous scene, Corney enters leading a donkey, a donkey on wheels like a childs toy but life size.

Corney

~~Who o o — o — o — No tricks my beauty.~~

mane

A tough rough ~~mane, a tuffer~~, a tuffer skin;
Strong leggs though some what thin,
A strong body, a level line
Up to neck along the spine
All marks of a good donkey,
And all spoilt by a mean eye
dastardly
That shows the ~~criminal~~ mind within
But I know everything it plans
I know you to the bone my beauty
I take no kicks upon the shin.

(Congal, Pat & Mick have entered they are ~~dressed and armed as in pre~~ in the dress & arms of the previous scene but ~~perhaps~~ without shields)

Congal

Are you the owner of this donkey

Corney

Atratta that lives among these rocks
~~highway~~ man
Owns this ~~criminal & me~~ ~~dastardly be~~ast & me
highway man
'Go catch & saddle him' says she

Blue-black ink, with revisions in ll. 1, 7, and 13 in greenish-black ink.

[NLI 8770 (1), 4v; ll. 13–26]

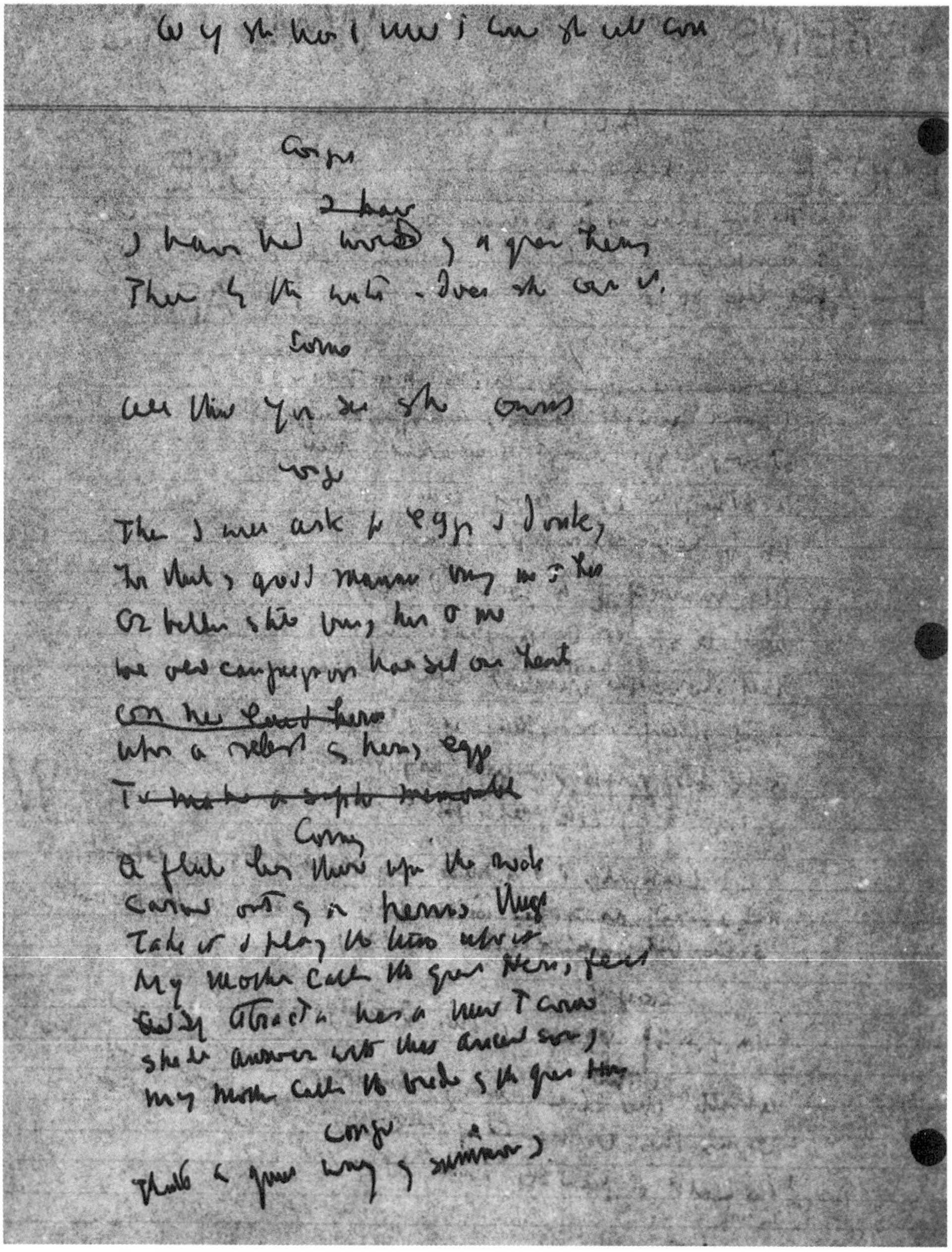

[NLI 8770 (1), 4v; II. 13–26]

And if she has a mind to come she will come

Congal
~~I have~~
I have had word of a great hernery
There by the water — does she own it.

Corny
All that you see she owns

Congl
Then I will ask for eggs & donkey
For that is good manners bring me to her
Or better still bring her to me
We old campaignors have set our hearts
~~On new laid heron~~
Upon a relesh of herns eggs
~~To make a supper memorable~~

Corney
A flute lies there upon the rock
Carved out of a hernes thigh
Take it & play the tune upon it
My Mother calls the great Herns feath
~~And~~ If Atracta has a mind to come
She ll answer with that ancient song
My Mother calls the bride of the great Hn

Congal
That's a queer way of summoning

Blue-black ink. Line at top of page is a variant of l. 13

[NLI 8770 (1), 5r; II. 13–18]

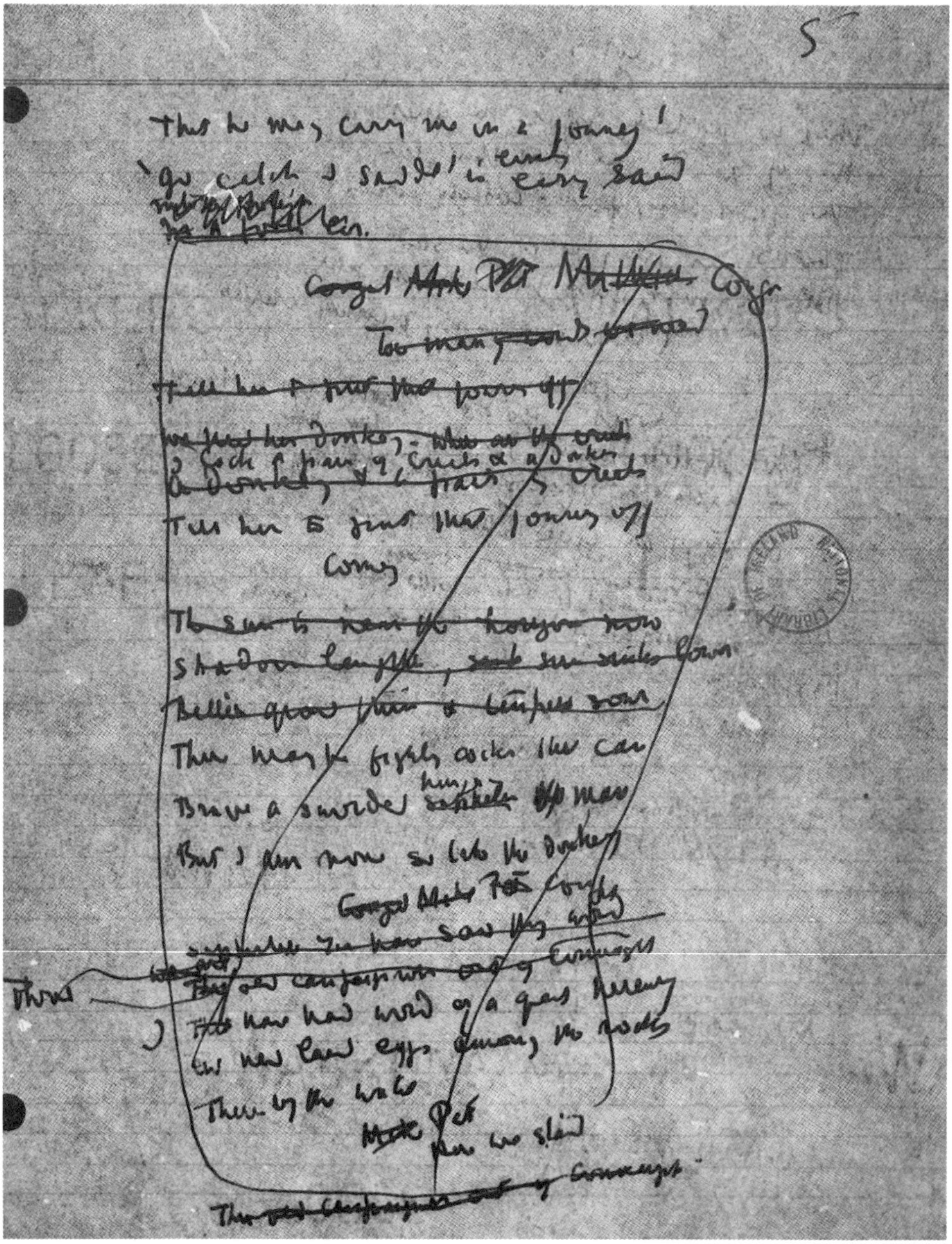

5

1 That he may carry me on a journey'
easily
2 'Go catch & saddle' is easy said
~~Into a foolish~~
~~In a fools ear.~~

~~Congal~~ ~~Mike~~ ~~Pat~~ ~~Mathias~~ Conga
~~Too many words we need~~
3 ~~Tell her to put that journey off~~
~~We need her donkey — where are the creels~~
4 I lack a pair of creels & a donkey
~~A donkey & a pair of creels~~
5 Tell her to put that journey off

Corney
~~The sun is near the horizon now~~
~~Shadows lengthen, sub sun sinks lower~~
~~Bellies grow thin & tempers sour~~
6 There may be fighting cocks that can
hungry
7 Brave a sworded ~~supperless~~ ~~wo~~ man
8 But I am none so take the donkey

~~Congal Mike~~ ~~Pat~~ Congal
~~supperless you have said thy word~~
~~We are~~
Three ~~Three old campaignors out of Connaught~~
9 I ~~That~~ have had word of a great herenry
10 And new laid eggs among the rocks
11 There by the water

~~Mike~~ Pat
here we stand
12 ~~Three old campaigners out of Connaught~~

Blue-black ink.

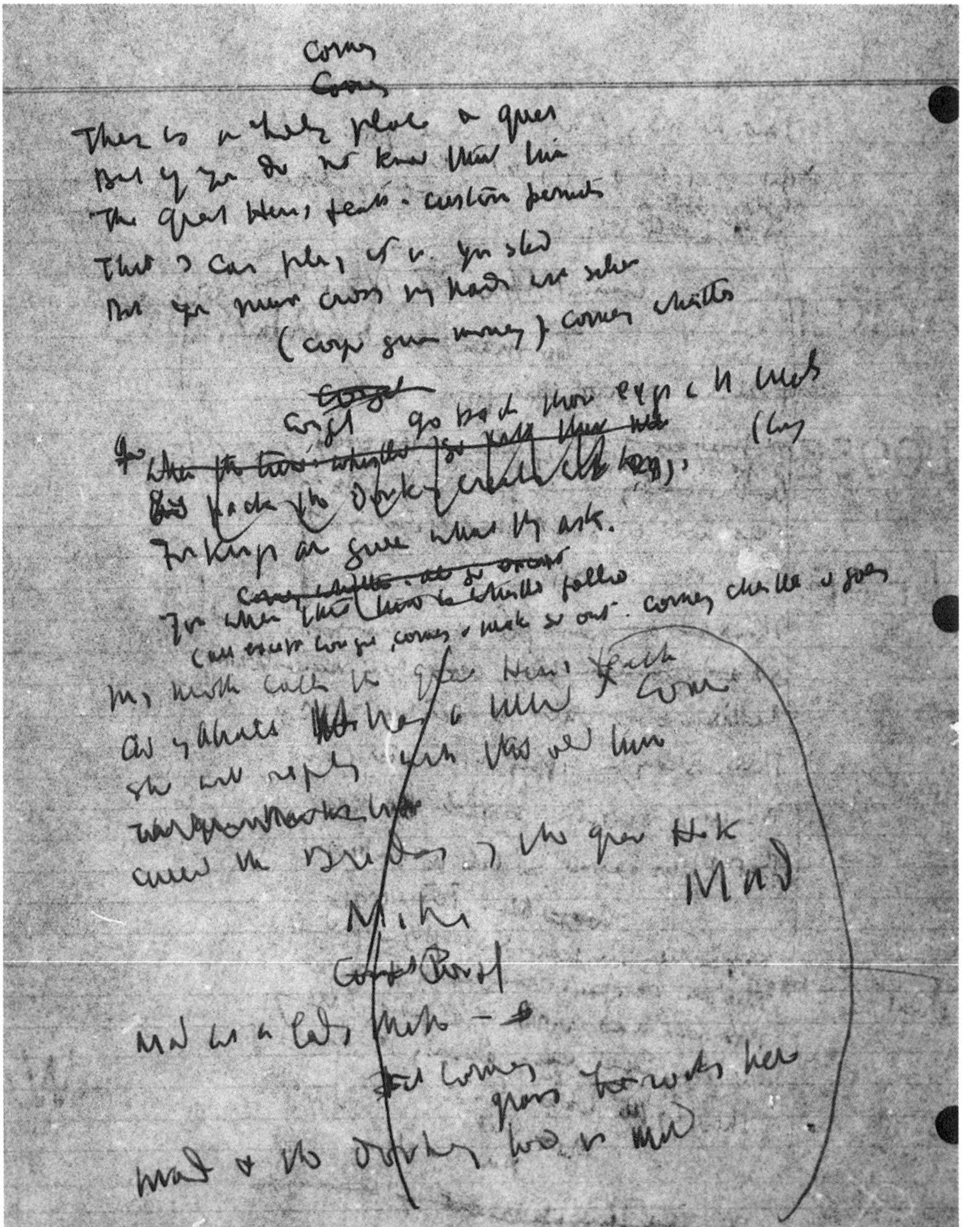

Corney
~~Corney~~
This is a holy place & queer
But if you do not know that tune
The Great Herns feather — custom permits
That I can play it in your sted
But you must cross my hands with silver

(Congal gives money) — Corney whistles

~~Congal~~
Congl
~~Go~~ go pack those eggs in the creels
When the tune's whistled go with these men
Go [?]
~~And~~ pack the donkey creels with eggs
For Kings are given what they ask.

~~Corney whistles — all go except~~
For when that ~~tune is~~ whistled follow
(all except Congal, Corney & Mike go out. Corney whistles & goes

My mother calls the great Herns feath
And if Atratta ~~her~~ has a mind to come
She will reply with this old tune
~~the great hawks bride~~
Called the Brides of the great hak

Mike Mad
~~Congal~~ {C / pongl}
Mad but a lady Mike — a

~~Pat~~ Corney
grass ~~he~~ rocks here
Mad & the donkey too is mad

Lines 1–8 and stage directions in blue-black ink, the remainder in light red except vertical deletion stroke in blue-black. Lines 9–14 replaced ll. 14–17 on 6r before being deleted.

[NLI 8770 (1), 6r; ll. 45–46, 13–16, 21–25]

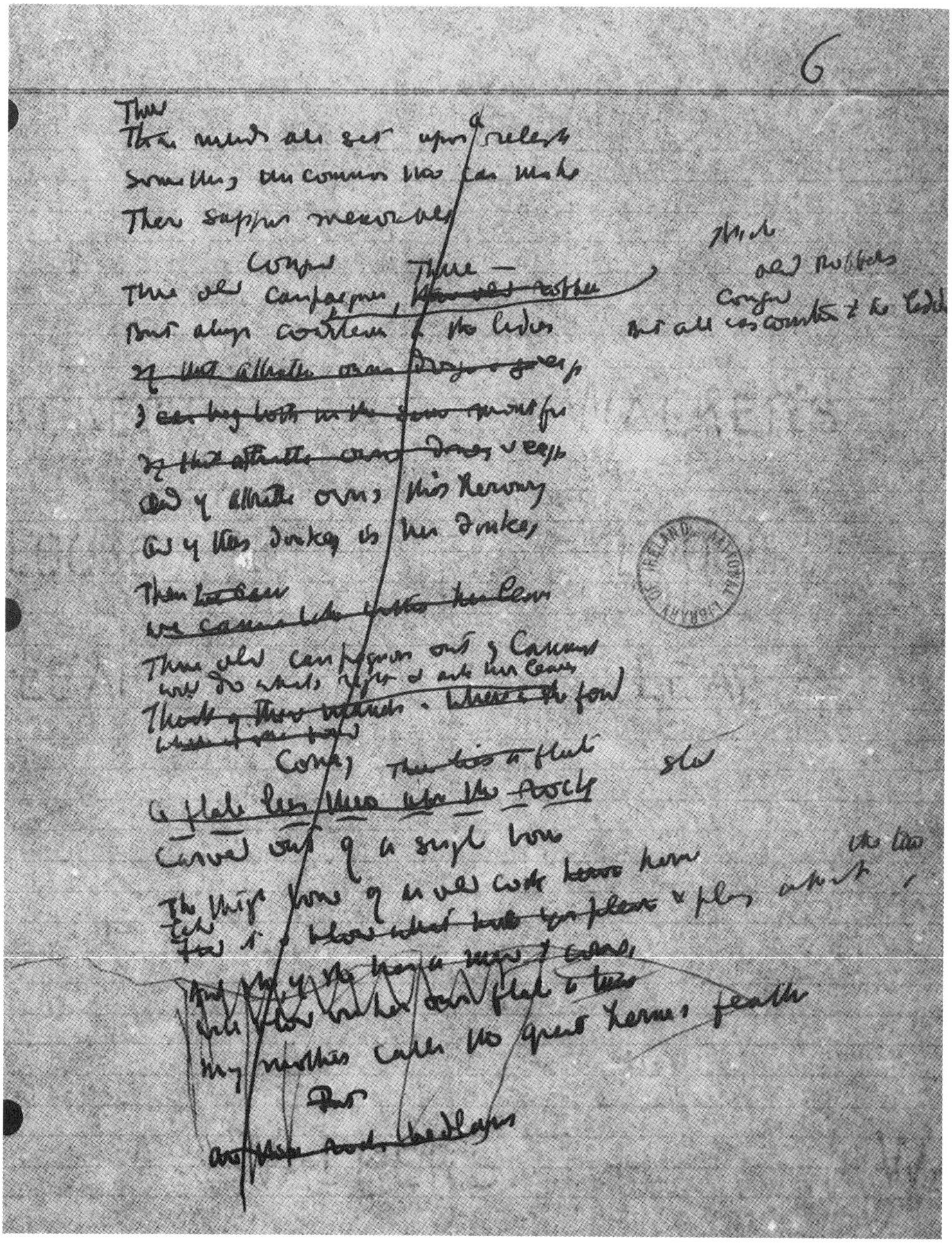

[NLI 8770 (1), 6r; II. 45–46, 13–16, 21–25]

6

Three a
1 ~~Three~~ minds all set upon relesh
2 Something un common that can make
3 There supper memorable

Congal
Three Mike
Three old campaigners, ~~three old robbers~~ old robbers
Congal
4 But always courteous to the ladies But all ways courteous to the ladies
~~If that Attratta owns donkey & g eggs~~
~~I can beg both in the same mouthful~~
~~If that Attratta owns doney~~ & eggs
5 And if Attratta owns this heronry
6 And if this donkey is her donkey
~~Then We can~~
~~We cannot take without her leave~~
7 Three old campaigners out of Connaught
8 Will do whats right & ask her leave
~~Think of there manners — where is she~~ found
9 Where is she found
Corney
~~There lies a~~ flute
10 ~~A flute lies there upon the ro~~ck stet
11 Carved out of a single bone
12 The thigh bone of an old cock ~~heron~~ herne
Take the tune
13 ~~Find~~ it & ~~blow what notes you please~~ & play what ^
14 And she, if she has a mind to come,
15 Will blow on her own flute a tune
16 My mother calls the great hernes feathr

~~Pat~~
17 ~~Are these rocks the Hernes~~

Blue-black ink, with ll. 13–17 deleted in light red ink and "& play what the tune" added in light red ink.

[NLI 8770 (1), 7^{r}; ll. 60–61]

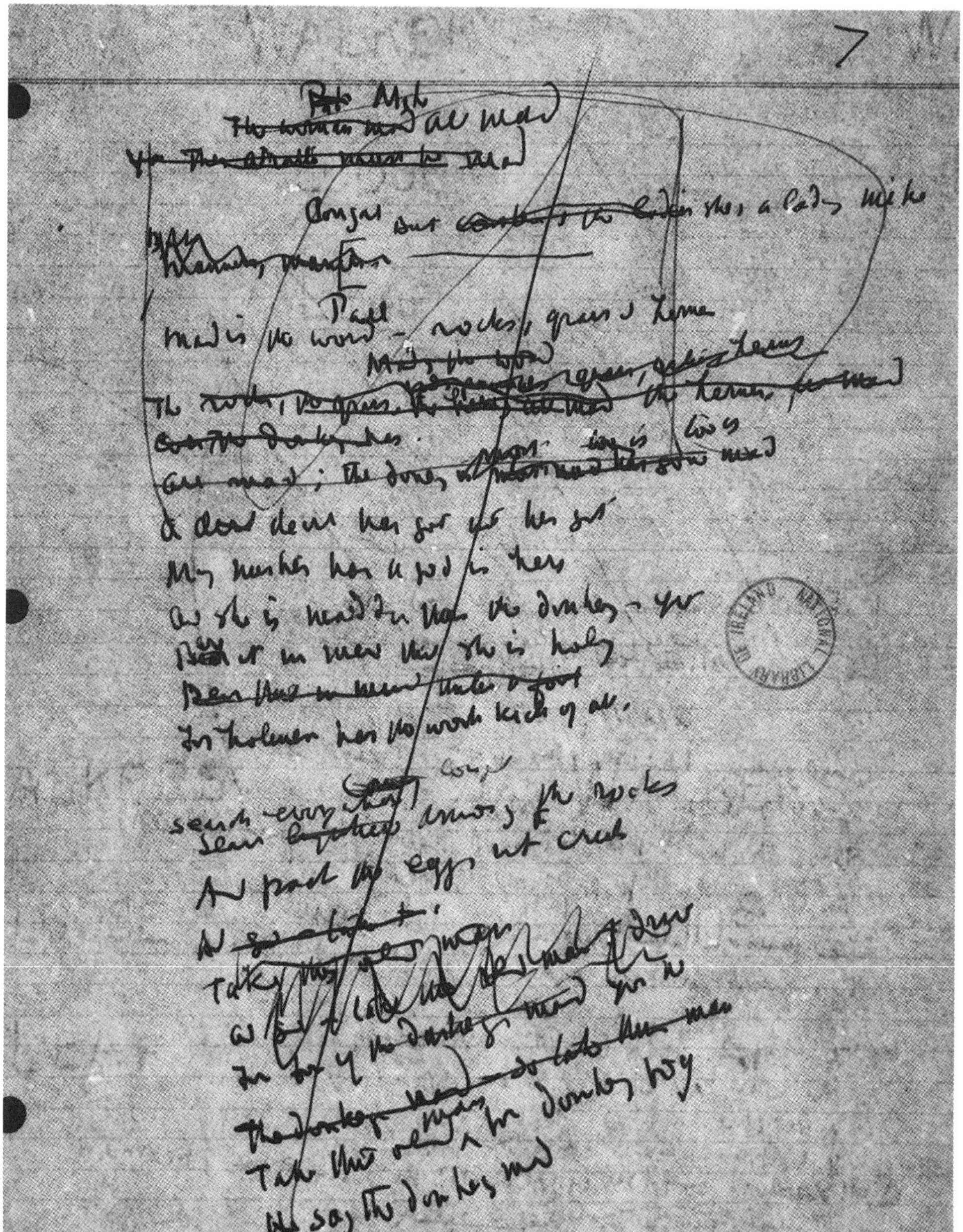

7

~~Pat~~ Mike
~~The woman mad~~ all mad
~~You Then Attratta must be mad~~

Congal
~~But~~ ~~But courteous to the ladies~~ She s a lady Mike
~~Manners, manners~~ ————————

Patt
Mad is the word — rocks, grass & hernes
~~Mad s the word~~
~~birds, animals, grass, water, hernes~~
The ~~rocks, the grass, the hern, & all mad the hernes, all mad~~
~~Even the donkey has~~
~~most~~ ~~too~~ is too is
~~All mad; the doney is most mad has gone mad~~
A ~~devil~~ devil has got into his gut
My mistress has a god in hers
And she is madder than the donkey — yet
are
~~Bear~~ it in mind that she is holy
~~Bear that in mind unles a fool~~
For holiness has the worst kick of all.

~~Corney~~ Congal
Search everywhere
Searc ~~evywhere~~ among the rocks
the
And pack the eggs into creels
And ~~go — take this~~
~~Take this old man~~
And go — take this old man to drive
For for if the ~~donkeys mad~~ you ne
~~The donkeys mad — so take this man~~
man
Take this old ^ for donkey boy
He say the donkey mad

Blue-black ink. Separate deletion of ll. 1–10 and the deletion of "Corney" and addition of "Congal" above l. 17 are in light red ink.

[NLI 8770 (1), 7v; II. 29, IV. 158–63, II. 32–37]

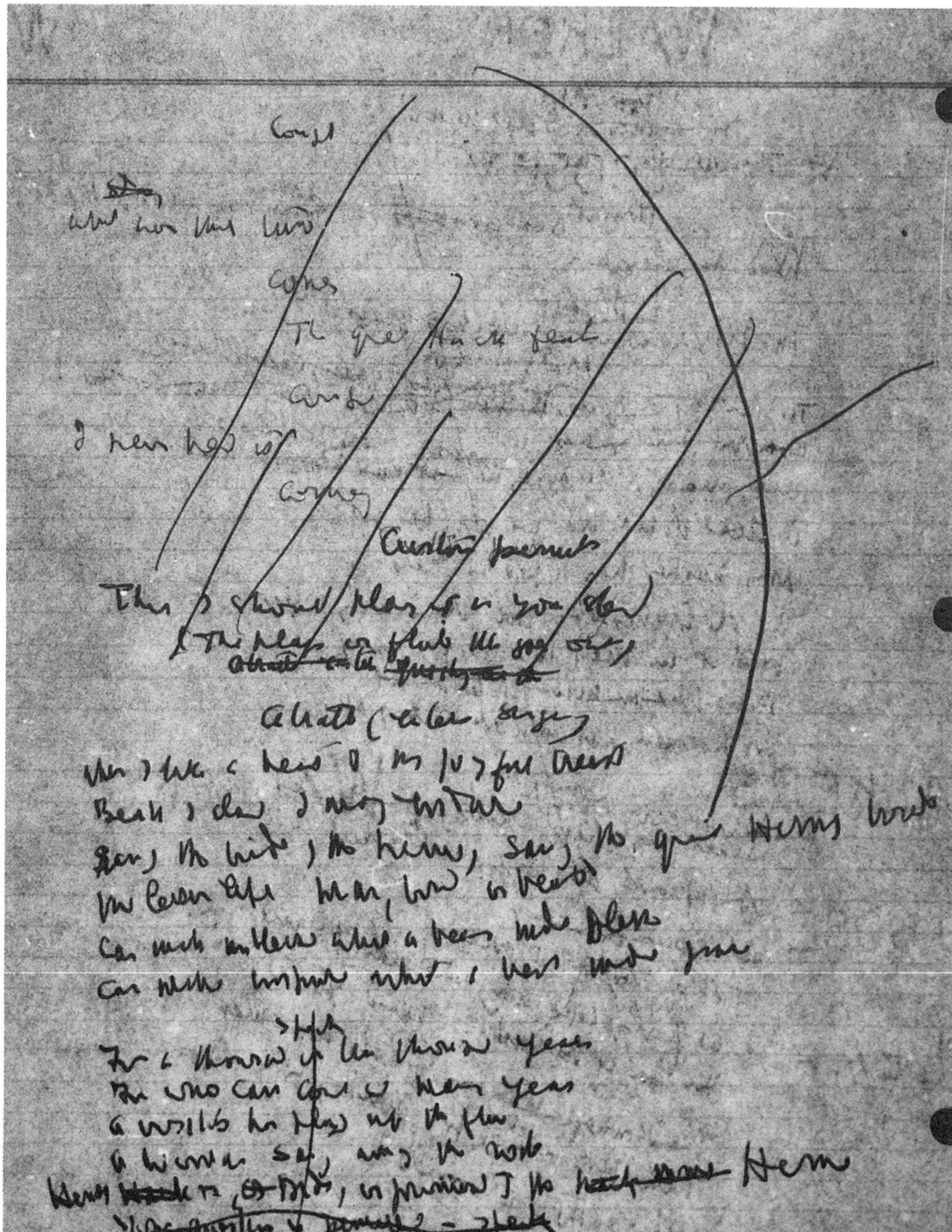

[NLI 8770 (1), 7^{v}; II. 29, IV. 158–63, II. 32–37]

Congal

~~Stay~~

1 What was that tune

Corney

The gre Hawk feathr

Congal

2 I nevr herd it

Corney

Custom permits

3 That I should play it in you sted

(The plays on flute then goes out)

~~Atratta enters quickly as the~~

Attratta (enters singing

4 When I take a beast to my joyful breast
5 Beak & claw I may endure
6 Sang the bride of the herne, sang the great Herns bride
7 No lesser life man, bird or beast
8 Can make unblessd what a beas made Blessd
9 Can make impure what a best mde pure

Speaks

10 For a thousand or ten thousand years
11 For who can count so many years
12 A visitor has played upon the flute
13 A Woman sang among the rock
14 Hernes ~~Hawk~~ s, ~~or~~ Bride, or promised to the ~~hawk herne~~ Herne
15 ~~Your question is permitted — speak~~

Lines 1–2 in light red ink; "Custom permits" in light red reinforced in dark red ink; remainder in dark red. Speeches by Congal and Corney and last line of Attracta's speech deleted in blue-black ink with "Herne" at end of l. 14 added in blue-black ink. Arrow from ll. 1–5 interpolates them below l. 3 on 8^{r}.

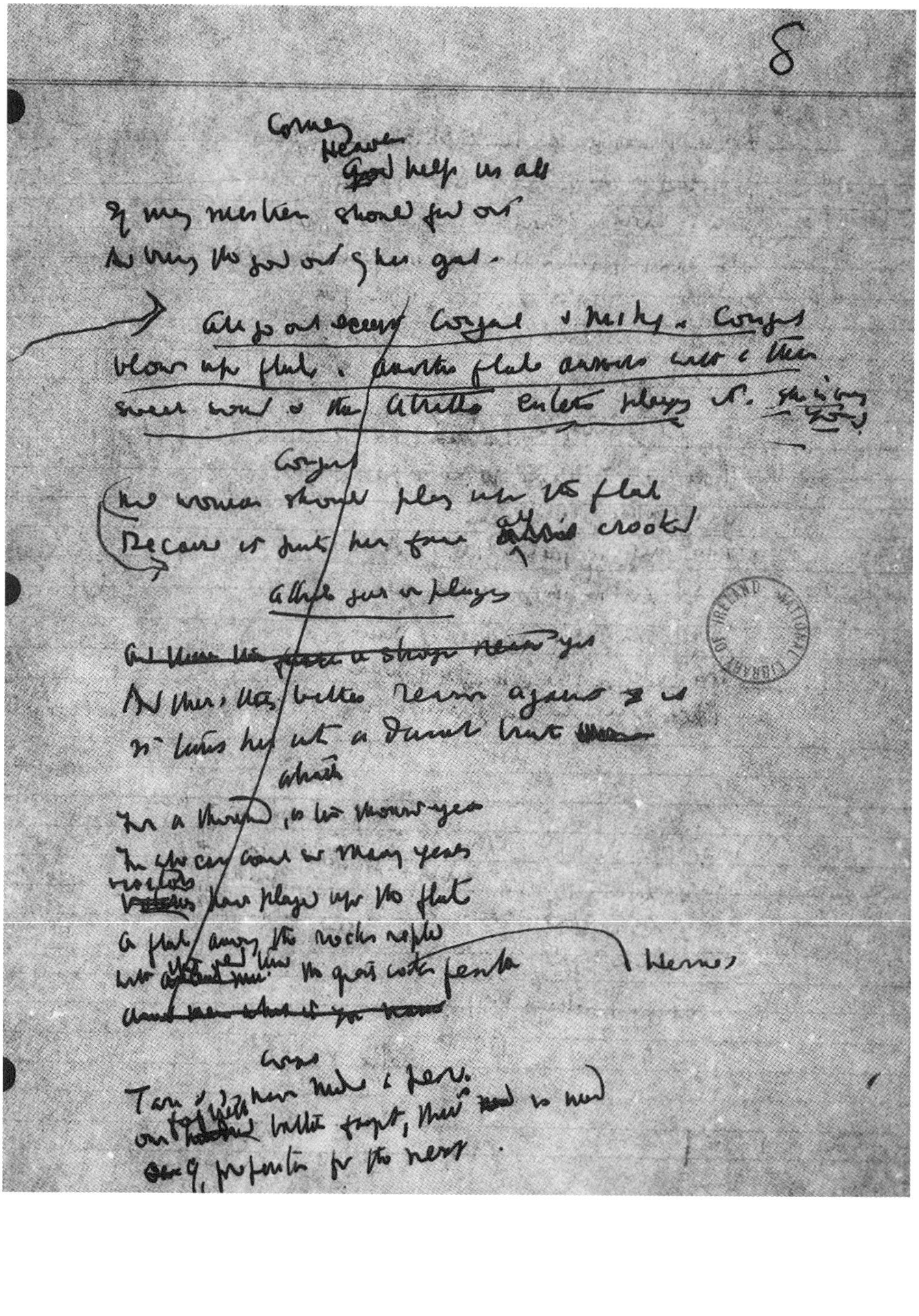

8

Corney
Heaven
~~God~~ help us all
If my master should find out
And bring the god out of her gut.

All go out except Congal & Mike. Congal
blows upon flute. Another flute answers with a
sweet sound & the Attracta enters playing it. [illegible]

Congal
No woman should play upon the flute
Because it puts her face all crooked

Attracta puts [illegible] plays

~~[illegible]~~ [illegible]
And there's little better reason against it
[illegible] a [illegible]
[illegible]
For a thousand, [illegible] thousand years
[illegible] many years
[illegible] have played upon the flute
A flute among the rocks [illegible]
[illegible] the great [illegible] Hernes
~~[illegible]~~

Corney
[illegible]
[illegible]
[illegible]

Corney
Heaven
~~God~~ help us all
If my mistress should find out
And bring the god out of her gut.

All go out except Congal & Mike. Congal blows upon flute. Another flute answers with a thin sweet sound & then Attratta enters playing it. She is very young.

Congal
No woman should play upon the flute
all
Because it puts her face ~~awrie~~ crooked
^

Attratta goes on playing

~~And then this further a stronger reason yet~~
And there s this better reason against ~~y~~ it
It turns her into a dumb brute ~~beast~~

Atratta
For a thousand, or ten thousand years
For who can count so many years
visitors
~~Voteries~~ have played upon the flute
A flute among the rocks replied
that old tune
With ~~ancient mu~~ the great cocks feather Hernes
~~Armed man what it your name~~

Congal
Tara & I have made a peace.
fiftieth is
Our ~~hundred~~ battle fought, there ~~need~~ is need
~~[?]~~ Of preparation for the next.

Blue-black ink. Single deletion stroke between ll. 3–12, arrows at ll. 4–5 transposing these two lines, and "is need" at end of l. 14 are in red ink.

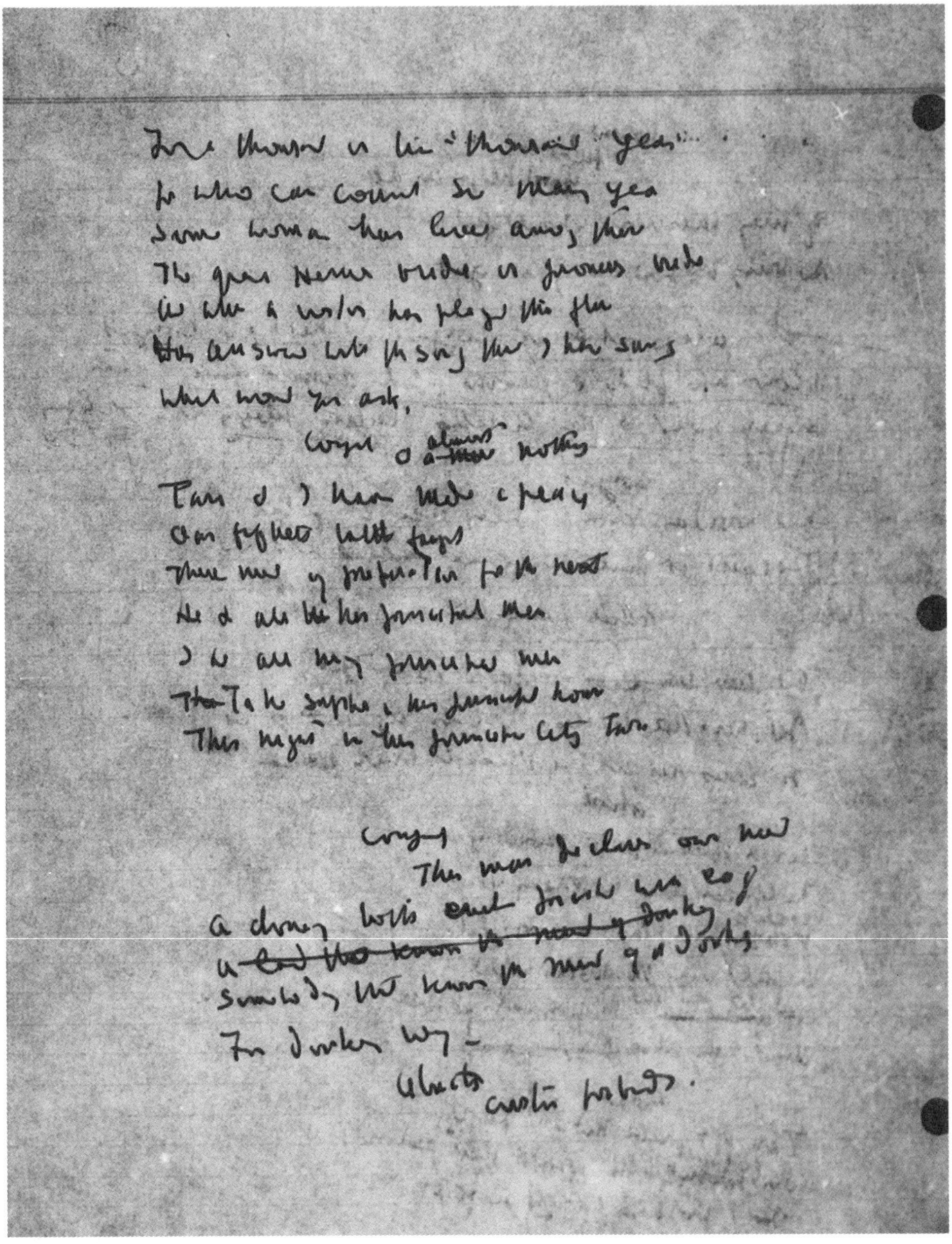

[NLI 8770 (1), 8^{v}; II. 32–44, 47–50]

For a thousand or ten thousand years
for who can count so many yea
Some woman has lived among these
The great Hernes bride or promised bride
And when a visitor has played this flu
Has answered with the song that I have sung
What would you ask

Congal almost
O ~~a mere~~ nothing
Tara & I have made a peace
Our fiftieth battle fought
There need of preparation for the next
He & all ~~th~~ his principal men
I & all my principal men
~~Thi~~ Take supper in his principal house
This night in his principal City Tara

Congal
This man declares our need
A doney with creels packed with eggs
~~A lad that knows the mind of don~~key
Somebody that knows the mind of a donkey
For donkey boy —

Atracta
Custom forbids.

Blue-black ink.

[NLI 8770 (1), 9r; ll. 41–48, 51–54]

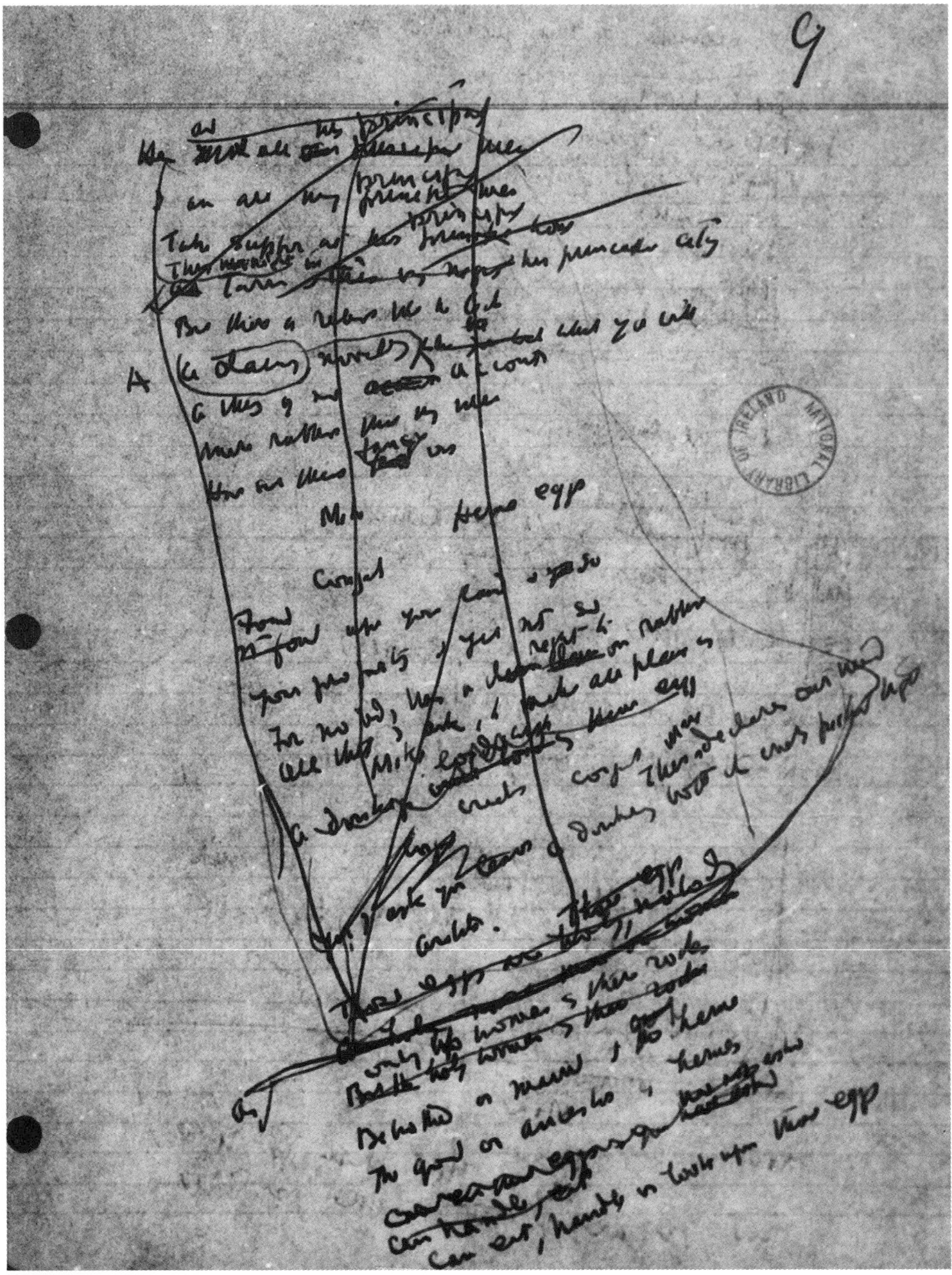

Blue-black ink, except l. 4 revised in red-black ink, ll. 14–17 revised partly in dark red, last line added in greenish-black, and ll. 17–18 deleted in red.

9

~~and~~ ~~his principal~~
1 He ~~with all his principal men~~
principal
2 I and all my principal men
principal
3 Take supper at his ~~principle~~ house
This ~~nig~~ night in
4 ~~At~~ Tara, ~~this very night~~ his principal city
5 But thers a relesh that we lack
~~We~~
6 A A dainy novelty ~~what you wish~~ what you will
7 A thing of no ~~accont~~ a c cont
8 Mere rubbish that my men
fancy
9 Have set their ~~fanc~~ on
Mike
Herne eggs
Congal
Found
10 ~~Its found~~ upon your land & ~~you~~ so
11 Your property & yet not so
right to
12 For nobody has a ~~claim claim~~ on rubbish
13 All that I ask, to make all plain is
Mike
loaded with
14 ~~A donkey creel load of Herns eggs~~
creels
~~Congal~~ Congal man
15 This ^ declares our need
~~Yet I ask your leave~~
16 A donkey with its creels packed tight
Arahta
~~Those eggs~~
17 ~~Those eggs are holy, nobody~~
18 ~~Are holy not a man or woman~~
19 Or/ only the women of these rocks
~~But the holy women of these rocks~~
~~gre~~
20 Betrothed or married to the herne
21 The god or ancestor of hernes
hav not asked
~~Can eat these eggs [?&] you have asked~~
~~Can handle, eat~~
22 Can eat, handle or look upon those eggs

[NLI 8770 (1), 9v; ll. 32–61]

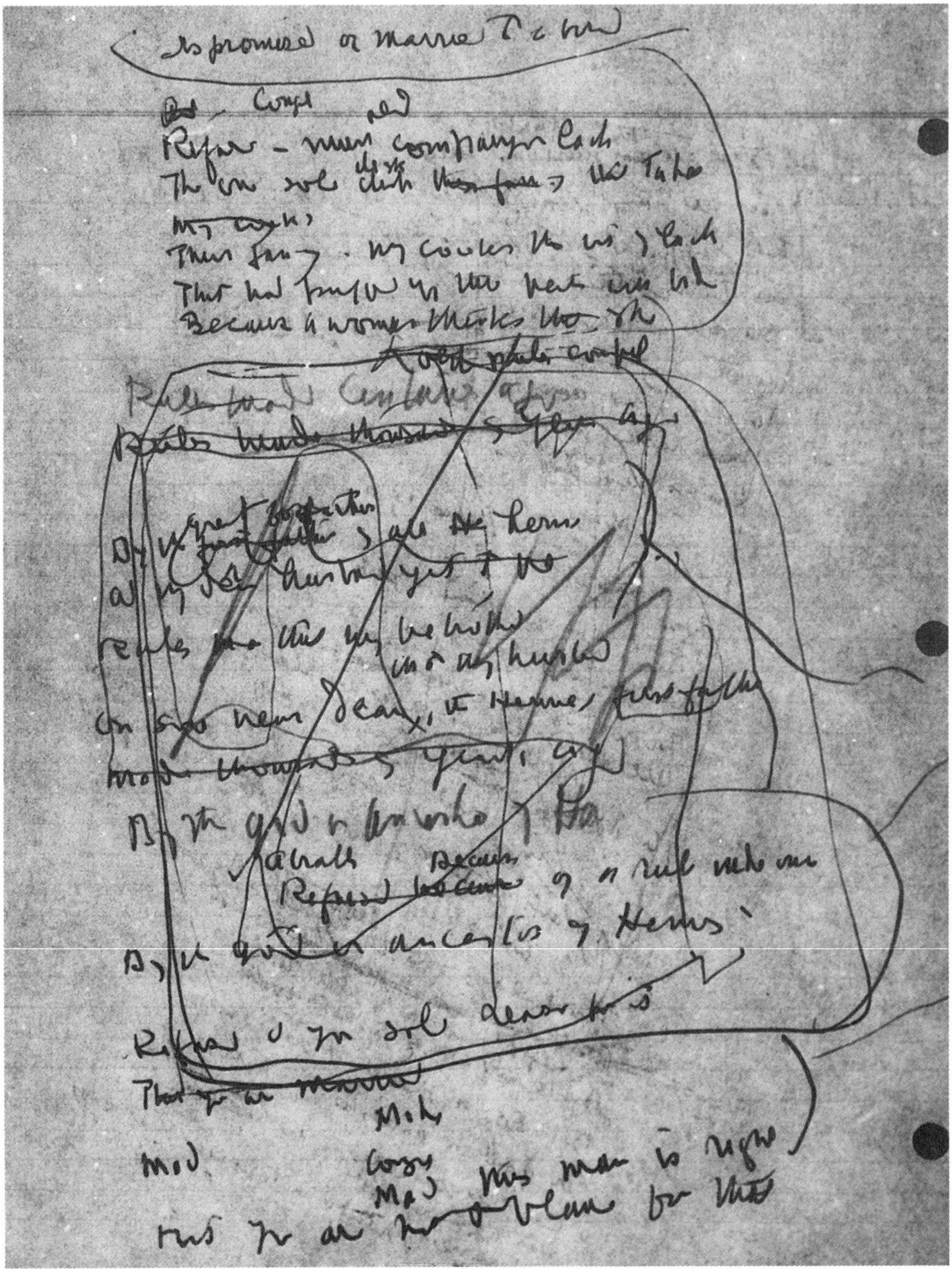

Is promised or married to a bird

Congal

~~But~~ old
Refused — must compaigners lack
dish
The one sole dish ~~they fancy~~ that takes
~~My cooks~~
Their fancy. My cooks then out of luck
That had puffed up their herts with prid
Because a woman thinks that she
old rules compel
Rules made centuries ago
Rules made thousands of years ago
great fore-father
By the ~~first father~~ of all He herns
And my dear husband yet to be
Rules ~~ma~~ that my betrothed
that my husband
On some near day, , the Hernes first father
Made thousands of years ago
By the God or Ancestor of Her

Atratta

Because
~~Refused because~~ of a rule made once
By the god or ancestor of Herns

Refused & you sole reason for it
That you are married

Mike

Mad

Congal

Mad this man is right
But you are not to blame for that

Blue-black ink, except “Atratta” and ll. 14–15 in red ink. Deletions to ll. 7–17 are multicolored, with main diagonal strokes in red, wavy strokes in pencil, and smaller deletions in blue-black. Arrows transpose l. 1 to between ll. 6–7, ll. 14–15 to follow l. 8 on 10^{r}, and ll. 18–19 to replace ll. 14–16 on 10^{r}.

[NLI 8770 (1), 10r; ll. 55–65]

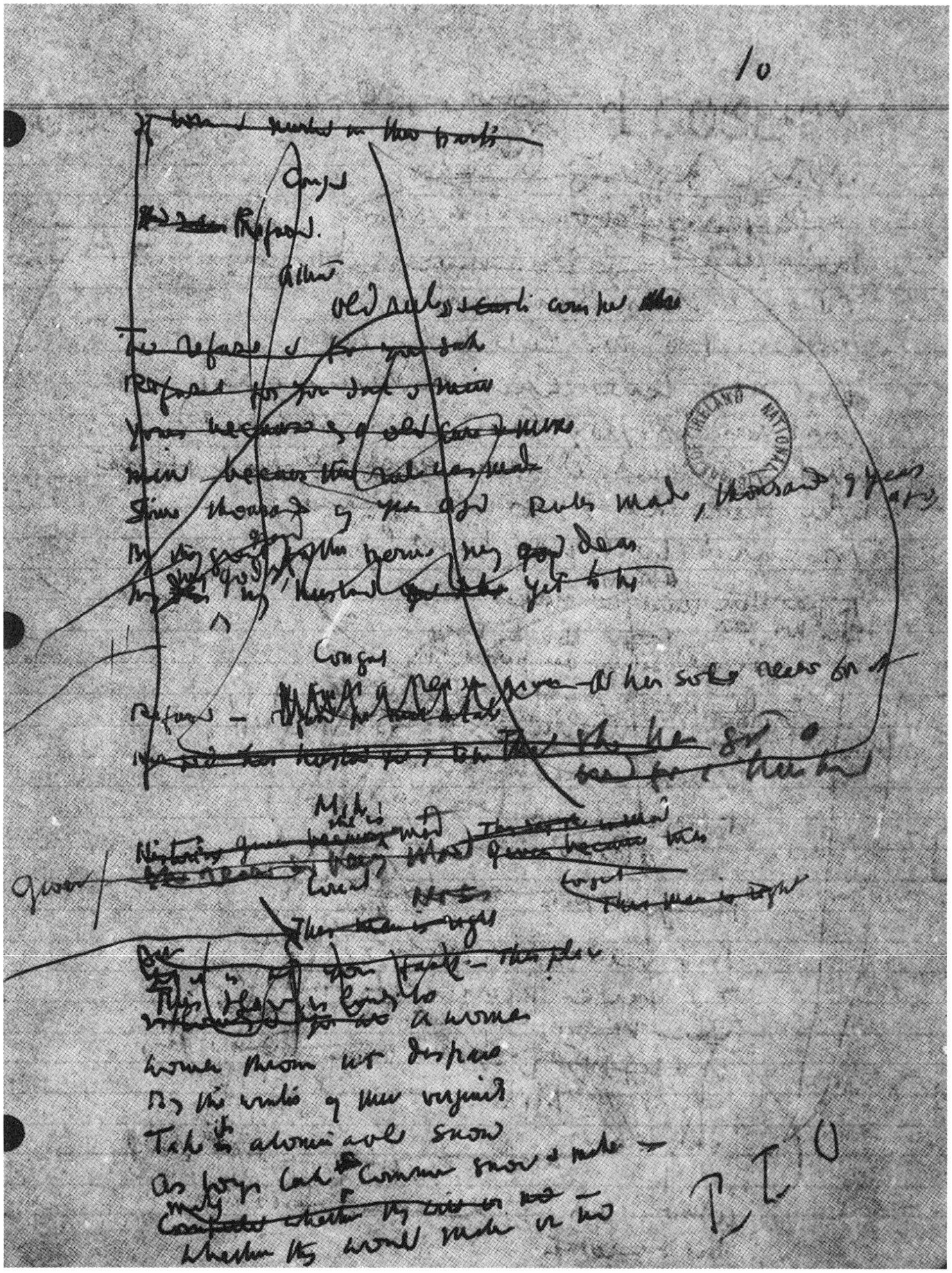

[NLI 8770 (1), 10r; II. 55–65]

10

1 ~~If born & nurtured in these parts~~
Congal
R
2 ~~We~~ ~~I am~~ refused
Attrat
Old rules ~~& customs~~ compel ~~me~~
To refuse & for your sake
3 Refusal for your sake & mine
4 Yours because of an old Curse & mine
5 Mine because this rule was made
6 Some thousands of years ago Rules made, thousands of years
grand ago,
7 By the great^father herne my ~~god~~
my god dear
8 My ~~dear~~^my husband ~~yet to be~~ ~~yet to be~~
Congal
9 & such a reason given — And her sole reason for it
10 Refused — ~~refused for such a tale~~
11 ~~Her god her husband yet to be~~ ~~*That she has got a*~~
~~*bird for a husband*~~
Mike
she is
12 ~~Histerics, given because~~^mad They say she is mad
13 Given ~~*She [??] for being Mad*~~ ~~Given because mad~~
Congal
Mad ~~Congal~~
14 ~~This man is right~~ ~~This man is right~~
~~But~~
15 ~~Yet it is not your fault~~ — ~~this place~~
16 This place is lonly too
~~Is lonely & you are~~ a woman
17 Women thrown into despair
18 By the winter of their virginity
its
19 Take ~~a~~ abominable snow
~~the~~
20 As boys take^common snow & make —
~~Making~~
21 ~~Compelled whether they will or no~~ —
22 Whether they would make or no

P .T. O

Blue-black ink, with deletions and additions as follows: l. 2 deletion and capital in red ink; l. 6 "Rules . . . ago,", l. 7 "grand", and l. 8 "dear" added in greenish-black ink; ll. 9–10 deletion and addition in red ink; l. 12 deleted in pencil; ll. 12–14 additions at right entered in red ink, pencil additions deleted in both pencil and red ink; ll. 20–21 dashes added in red ink.

[NLI 8770 (1), 10^{v}; ll. 64–74, 34–5, 95–7]

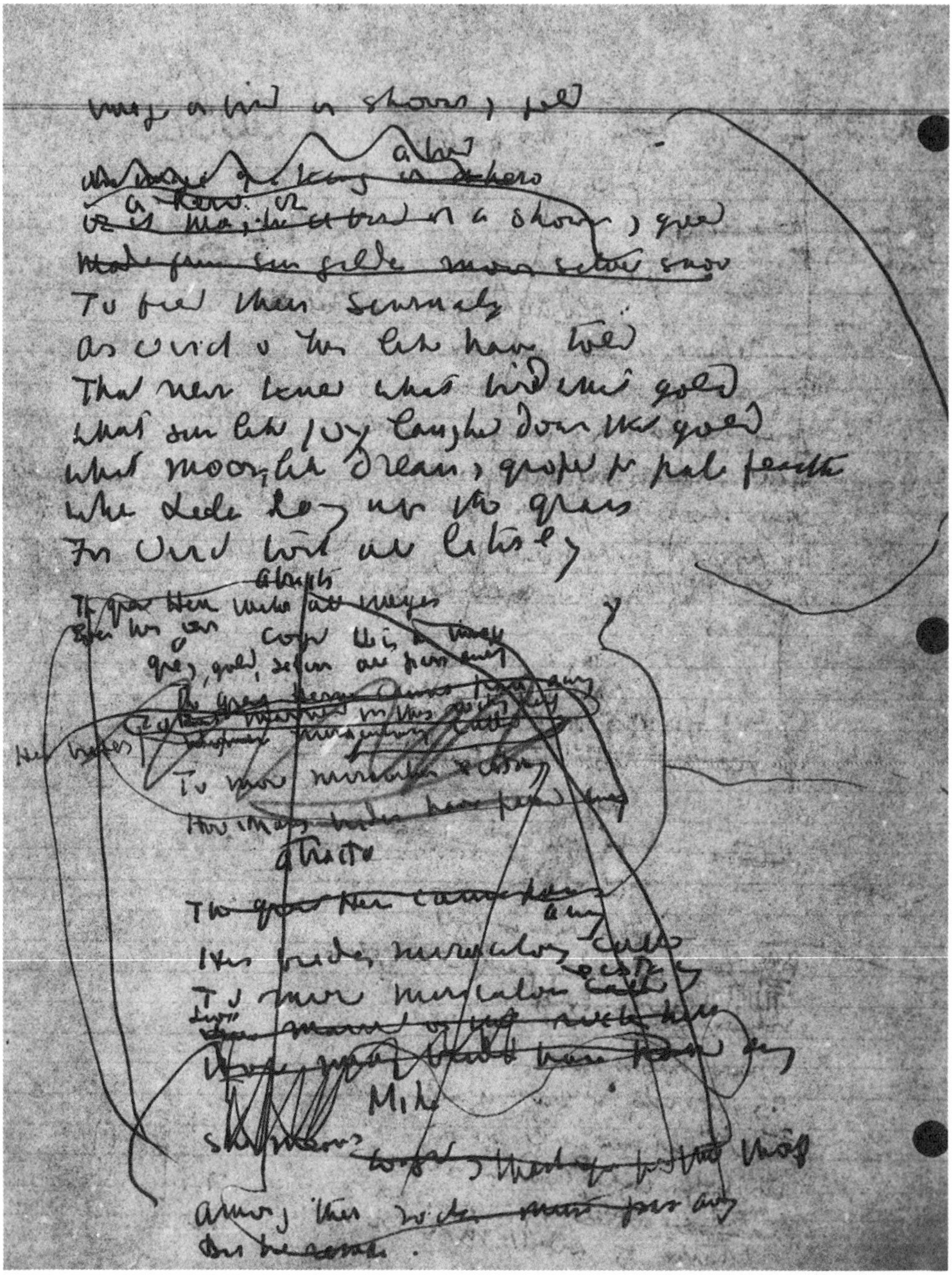

[NLI 8770 (1), 10^{v}; II. 64–74, 34–5, 95–7]

1 Image or bird or shower of gold
a bird
An image of a king or a hero
a hero or
~~Or it may be a bird o~~r a shower of gold
~~Made from sun gilde moon silverd snow~~
2 To feed their sensualy
3 As Ovid & his like have told
4 That nevr knew what bird what gold
5 What sun like joy laughed down that gold
6 What moonlike dreams groped for pale feathr
7 When Leda lay upon the grass
8 For Ovid told all liter l y
Atracta
9 The great Her makes all images
10 Even his own
Congal
He is an image
11 grey, gold, silver all pass away
12 The Great herne cannot pass away
13 & But Married on this rocky hill
14 His brides ~~Women~~ miraculously called
15 To more miraculous ecstasy
16 How many brides have passed away

Atracta
17 ~~The great Hern cannot pass~~
away
18 His brides miraculous called
ecstacy
19 To more miraculous ~~calld~~
Living
20 ~~Were married on this rock~~ hill
21 ~~How many brides have passd away~~
Mike
22 She means
~~Congal~~
~~I thank you for this~~ thought
23 ~~Among these rocks must pass away~~
24 ~~But he remai~~.

Blue-black ink, except l. 6 touched up in red ink, ll. 9–16 revised in greenish-black ink, then deleted in pencil.

[NLI 8770 (1), 11r; ll. 66–73, 32–5, 62–3]

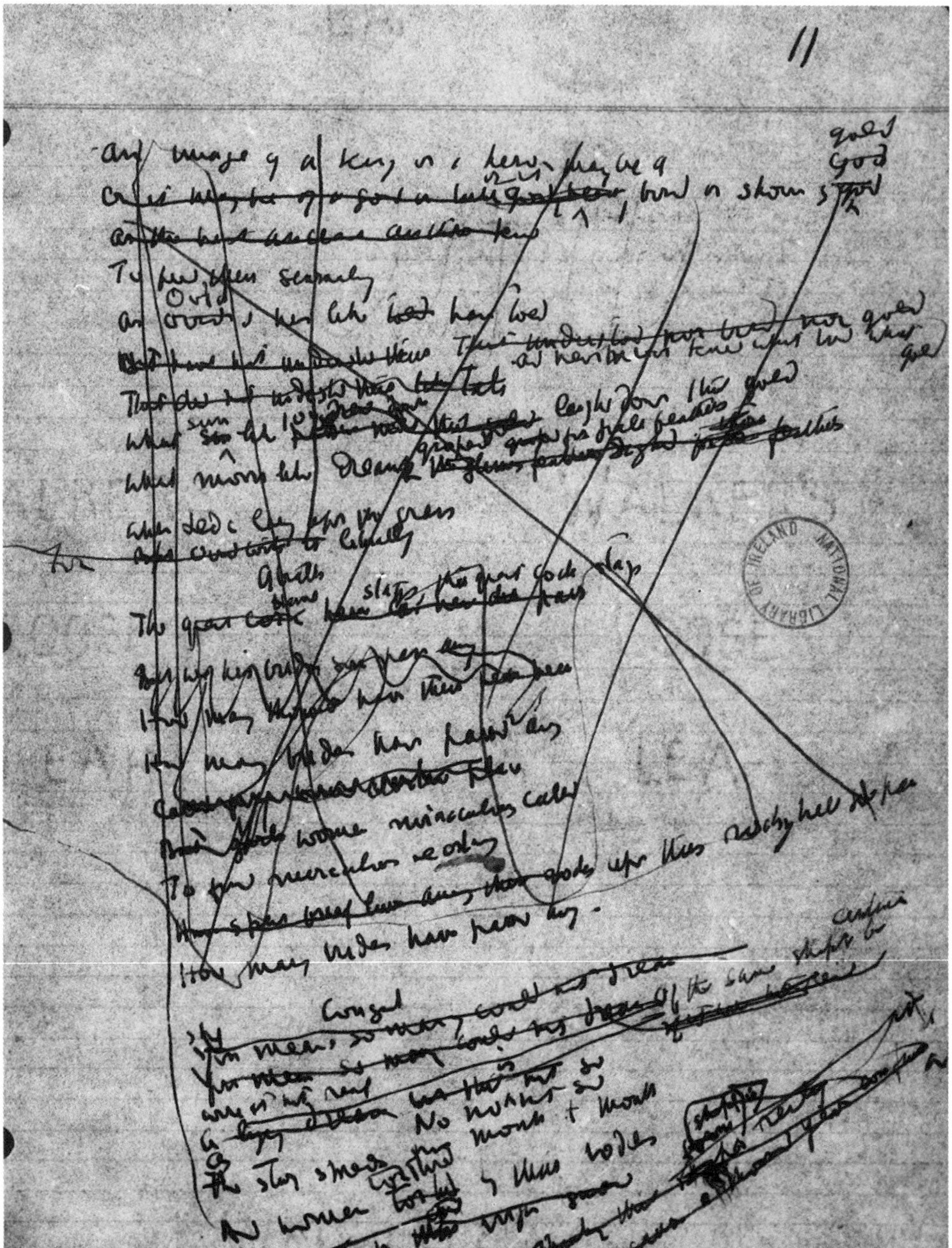

[NLI 8770 (1), 11[r]; ll. 66–73, 32–5, 62–3]

11

1 An image of a king or a hero gold
or it may be a ~~God~~
2 ~~Or it may be of a god or bull God, beast,~~ bird or shower of ~~god~~
3 ~~As the best ancient authors knew~~ ^ ^
4 To feed their sensualy
Ovid
5 As ~~Ovid~~ & his like ~~told~~ have told
~~But have not understood thei~~rs ~~That understood nor bird nor~~ gold
and nevr ~~nevr~~ knew what bird what
6 That did not understand their ~~tak~~ tale gold
sun joys ~~drew~~ down
7 What ~~sun~~ like ~~passes never that gold~~ laughs down that gold
^ groped ~~groped~~ for pale feathers ~~those~~
8 What moon like dreams ~~the gleaming feathers Sighed for su feathers~~
9 When Leda lay upon the grass
10 ~~For But Ovid told it literally~~
Atratta
Herne stays this great cock stays
11 The ~~great cock herne can nevr die pass~~
12 But we his brides soon pass away
How many thousand have there been been
13 How many brides have passed away
~~Called from some other place~~
14 ~~But girls~~ women miraculously called
15 To find miraculous ecstasy
~~Have spent brief lives among these r~~ocks upon this rocky hill side passed
16 How many brides have passed away.
Congal
~~She~~
~~You mean so many could not dream~~ certain
17 ~~You mean so many could not dream~~ Of the same shape be
were it not real is ~~If it was not cert~~
18 ~~A lying dream~~ ~~But that not~~ so
A No no ^ not so
19 ~~The~~ story spreds from mouth to mouth
tortured
20 And women ~~tor mt~~ by their bodies
~~that~~ ~~shape is~~
21 ~~Copy it in their virgin snow~~ ~~form~~
~~Thinking this shape realy it~~
~~Because a thousand years confirmed~~ ^

Blue-black ink, with deletion of ll. 1–16 in red ink. Final revisions of l. 2 and additions at right, ll. 5–6, in greenish black. Corrections "She" above l. 17, "were it not real" and "If it was not cert" above l. 18 also in red ink, along with deletion of "lying dream."

[NLI 8770 (1), 11v]

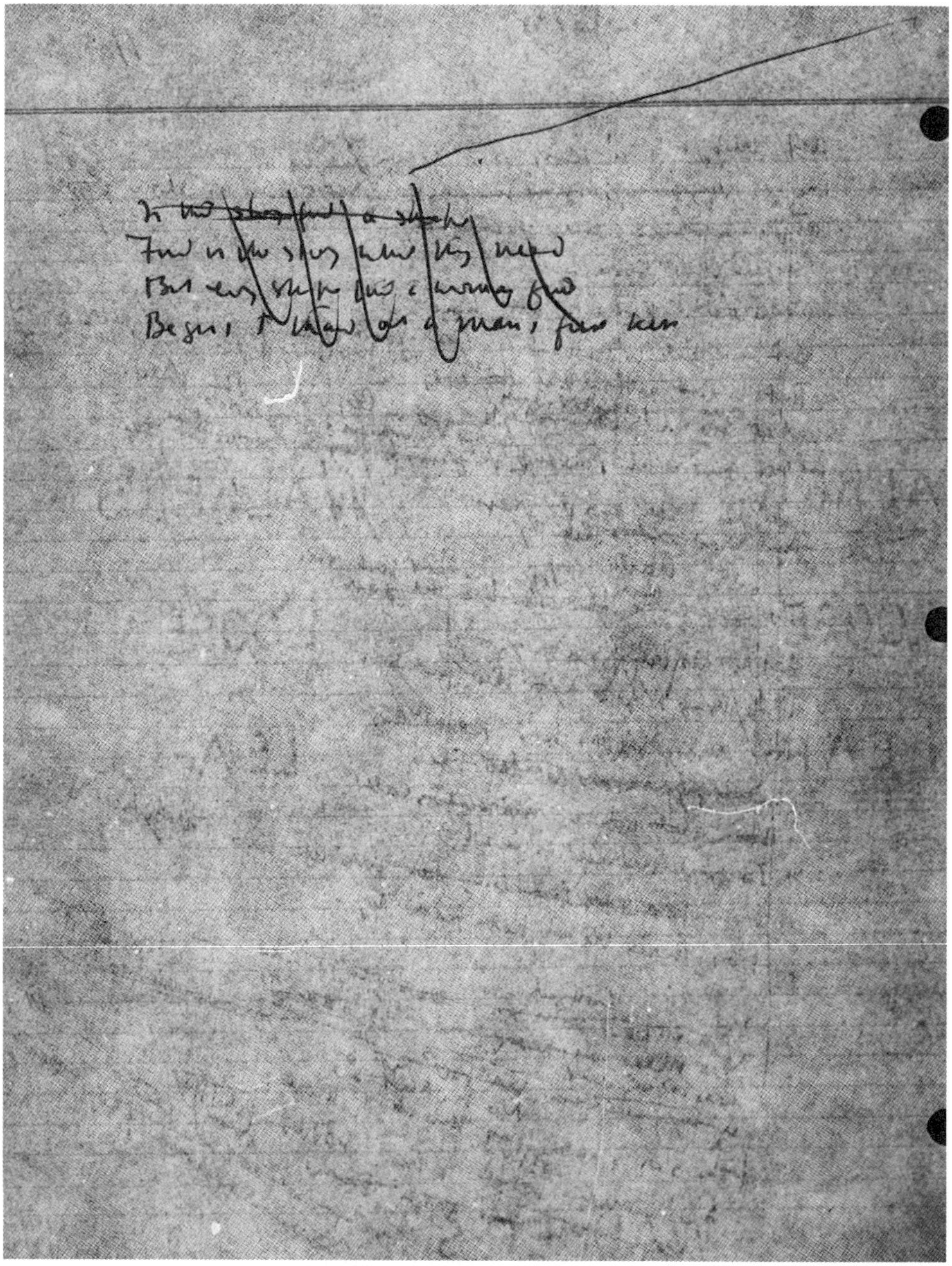

[NLI 8770 (1), 11v]

~~In that story find a shape~~
Find in the story what they need
But every shape that a woman finds
Begins to thaw at a man s first kiss

Red ink, with deletion in blue-black. Correction line points to ll. 1–7 on 12r.

[NLI 8770 (2), unnumbered page; ll. 66–79]

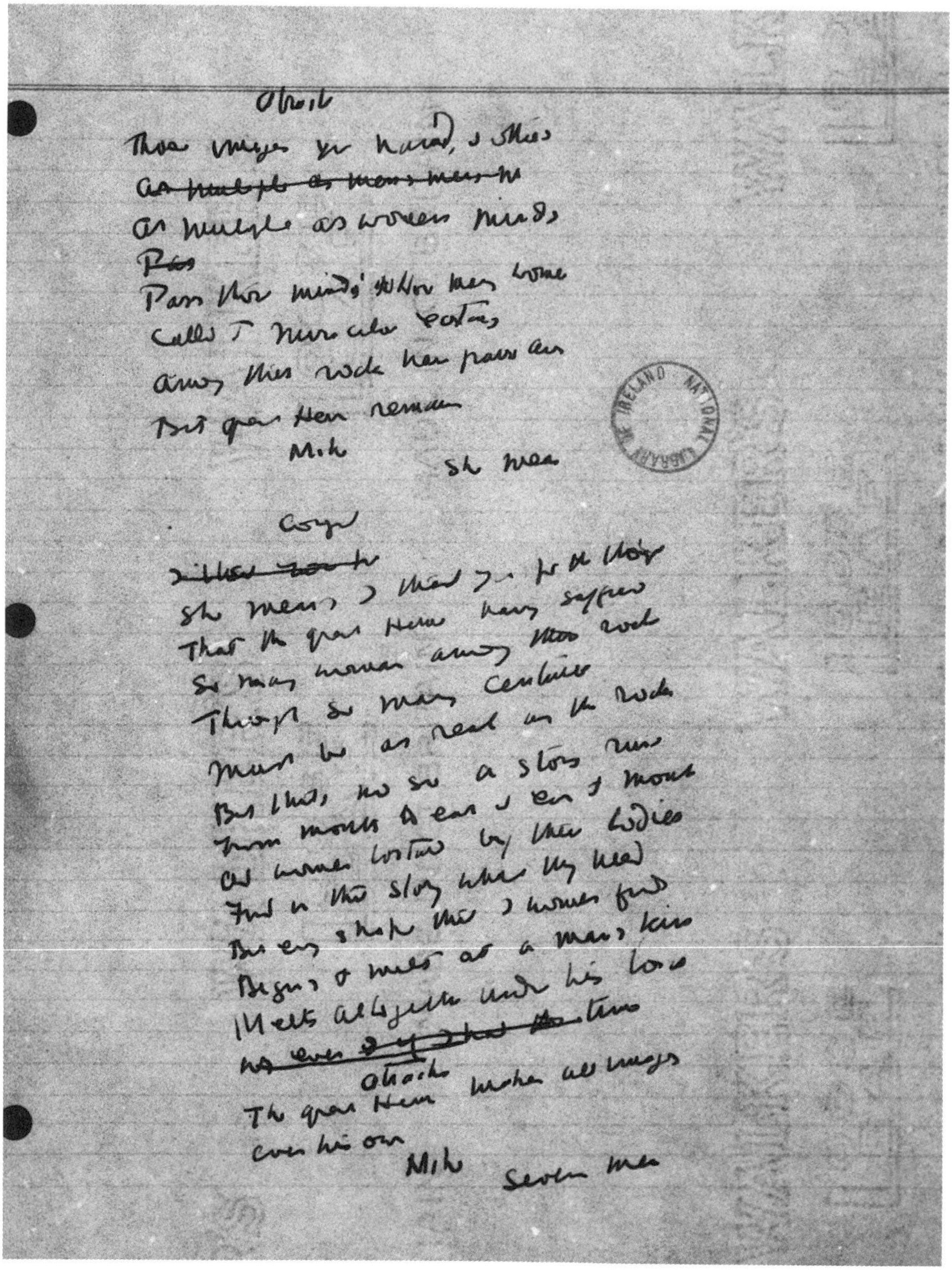
Attracta
Those images you named, & others
~~as multiple as mens minds~~
As multiple as womens minds
~~Pass~~
Pass those minds' [illegible] some
Called the [illegible]
Among these rocks have passed away
But great Herne remain
Mike
Sh men

Congal
~~[illegible]~~
She means, & I thank you for the thought
That the great Herne having supped
So many women among these rocks
So many centuries
Though so many
Must be as real as the rocks
But that's no so a story runs
From mouth to ear & ear to mouth
Old women lost by their bodies
Find in that story what they need
But every shape that a woman finds
Begins to melt at a man's kiss
Melts altogether under his touch
~~no ever [illegible]~~ time
The great Herne Attracha makes all images
over his own
Mike
Seven men

Atracta

1 Those images you named, & others
~~As multiple as men s mens~~ w
2 As multiple as womens minds
~~Pas~~
3 Pass throu minds; ~~h~~ How many women
4 Called to miraculous ecstacy
5 Among thes rock hav passd away
6 But great Hern remains

Mike

She means

Congal

~~I thank you fr~~
7 She means I thank you for the thoght
8 That the great Herne having suffered
9 So many women among these rocks
10 Through so many centuries
11 Must be as real as the rocks
12 But thats no so a story runs
13 From mouth to ear & ear to mouth
14 And women torturd by their bodies
15 Find in this story what they need
16 But evry shape that a woman finds
17 Begins to melt at a mans kiss
18 Melts altogether under his touch
19 ~~Why even if I had the~~ time

Atracta

20 The great Hern makes all images
21 even his own

Mike

Seven men

Blue-black ink. Found in 8770 (2), these lines revise the exchange on 10^{v} and 11^{r} of 8770 (1).

[NLI 8770 (1), 12r; ll. 65–89]

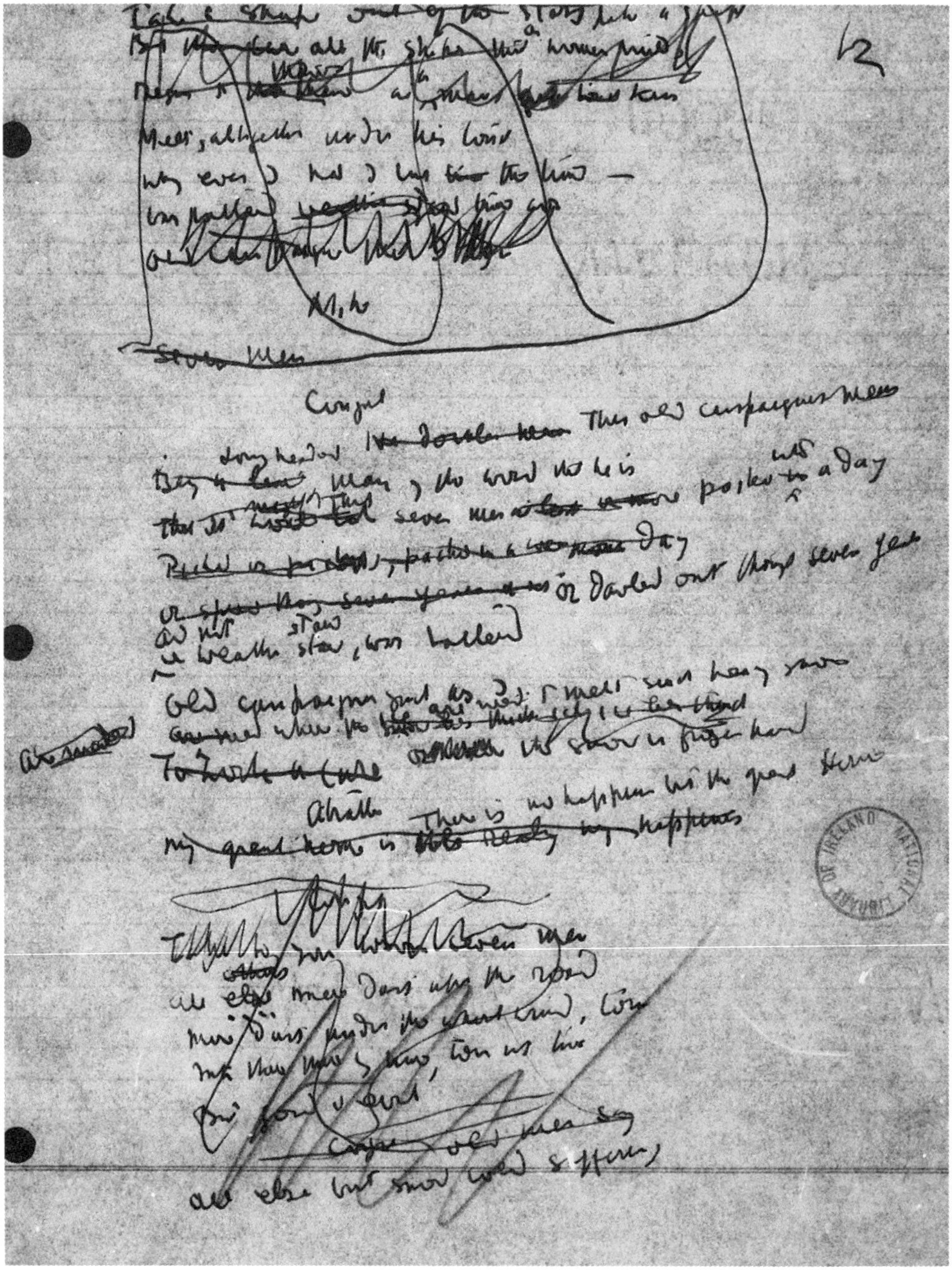

[NLI 8770 (1), 12^{r}; II. 65–89]

1 ~~Take a shape~~ ~~out of the story~~ take a shape
a
2 But ~~number~~ all the shapes that woman [?makes] 12
thaws a
3 Begin to ~~thaw thaw~~ at ^ mans ~~first~~ touch kiss
4 Melt s altogether under his touch
5 Why even I had I but ~~time~~ the time —
6 War battered ~~weather stained~~ time worn
7 ~~Old campaigner that I am~~

Mike
~~Seven men~~

Congal
8 Long headed ~~He doubtless means~~ This old campaigner means
9 ~~Being a learned~~ man of the word that he is
might That into
10 ~~That it would take~~ seven men ~~at least or more~~ packed ~~in~~ a day
11 ~~Picked or picking, packed in a yea~~ ~~month day~~ ^
~~Or spred through seven years & not~~
12 And not staind Or dawdled out through seven years
13 ^A weather ~~stai~~, war batterd
14 Old campaigner such as I
ice are need to melt such heavy snow
15 ~~Are marked~~ ~~Are need~~ where the ~~snow lies thick~~ ~~ice~~ ice ~~lies thick~~
~~Or where the snow is frozen~~ hard
16 ~~To work a cure~~
Atratta
17 There is no happiness but the great Herne
18 ~~My great herne is sole realy~~ ~~my happines~~
Congal
19 ~~Take to you bosom seven men~~
~~others~~
20 All ~~else~~ mere dust upon the road
21 Mere dust under the whirl wind, torn
22 Into that [?] thaw by time, torn upon time
23 But good & evil
~~Congal~~
~~Old men say~~
24 All else but snow cold suffering

Lines 1–3 revised and then deleted in red ink, except "first", l. 3, deleted in pencil. Line 4 "s" added to "melt" in red. Line10 "into" and l. 12 "staind" added in red. Lines 15–16 revised in red and l. 17 is entirely in red. Line 18 deleted in red, with "my happiness" added and deleted in red. Lines 19–24 deleted in greenish-black ink and pencil. Additions at right of ll. 8, 10 are also in greenish-black ink.

[NLI 8770 (1), 13^r; ll. 87–99]

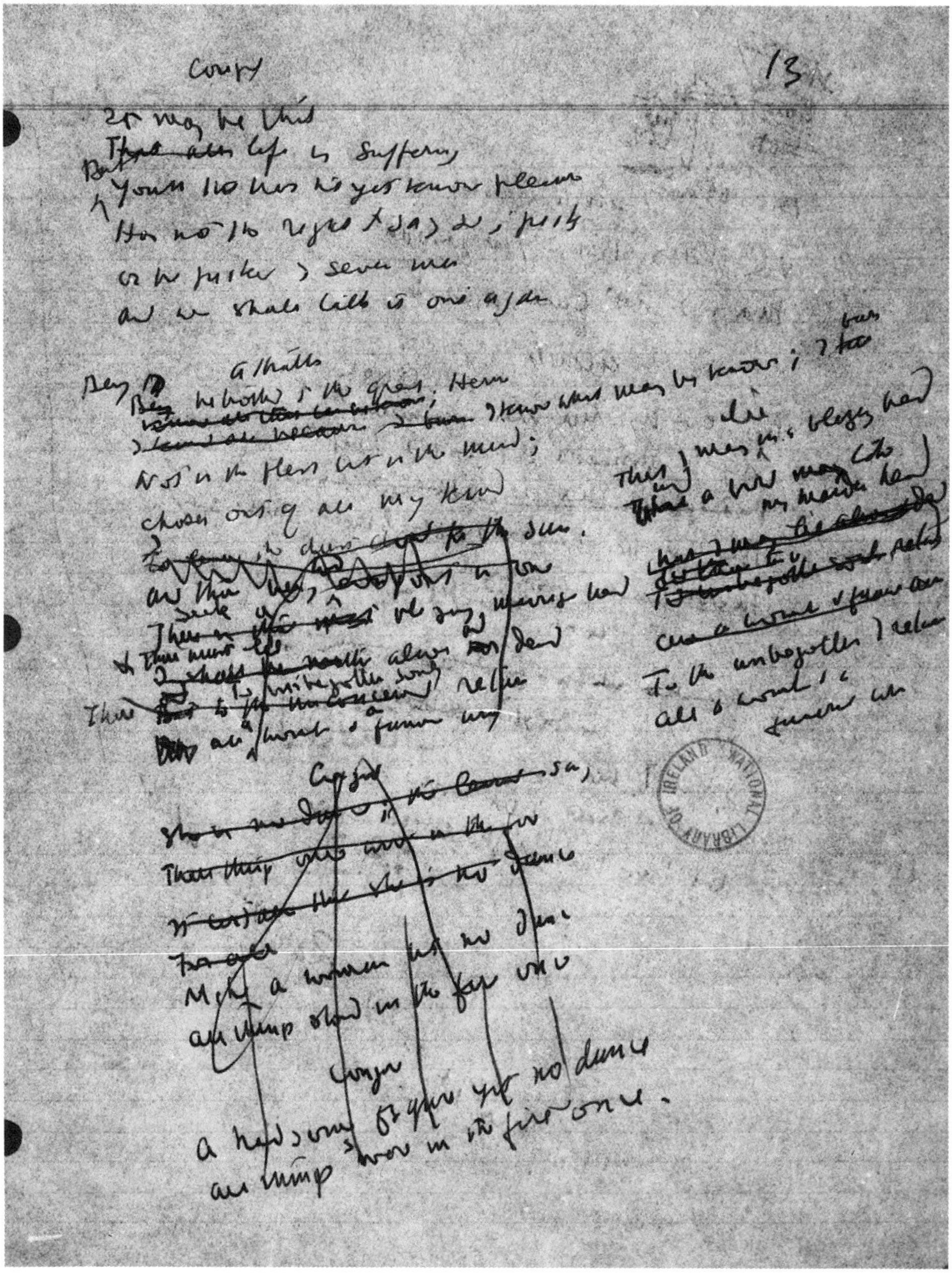

[NLI 8770 (1), 13r; ll. 87–99]

Congal

It may be that 13

1 ~~That all~~ life is suffering

But

2 ^Youth that has not yet known pleasure

3 Has not the right to say so; pick

4 Or be picked by seven men

5 And we shall talk it out again

Being ~~to~~ Attratta

6 ~~Being~~ betrothed to the great Herne

~~Know all that can be known~~; burn

7 ~~I know all because~~ ~~I burn~~ I know what may be known; I ~~kn~~

8 Not in the flesh but in the mind;

lie

9 Chosen out of all my kind

10 That I may ^ in a blazing bed

and

11 That a bird may take

my maiden head

~~That I may lie alive & ded~~

~~when~~

~~And there to u~~

~~To unbegotten souls return~~

~~All a womb & funeral urn~~

>

12 To leave the dust cloud for the sun.

had

13 And there being ^ ever [?joy] in one

Seek a

14 ~~There in that most~~ blazing marrage bed

& there must lie and

15 ~~I shall be nei~~ther alive ~~nor~~ dead

And To unbegotten souls

There ~~But to the unconceived~~ return

a a

~~There~~ all ^ womb & funeral urn

16 To the unbegotten I return

17 All a womb & a

funeral urn

Congal

~~She is no dunce; the learned~~ say

~~These things once were in the fire~~

~~Its certain that she is no dunce~~

~~For all~~

18 Make a woman but no dunce

19 All things stood in the fire once

Congal

20 A handsome figure yet no dunce

s

21 All things were in the fire once.

Blue-black ink, except "lie", l. 10, added in pencil.

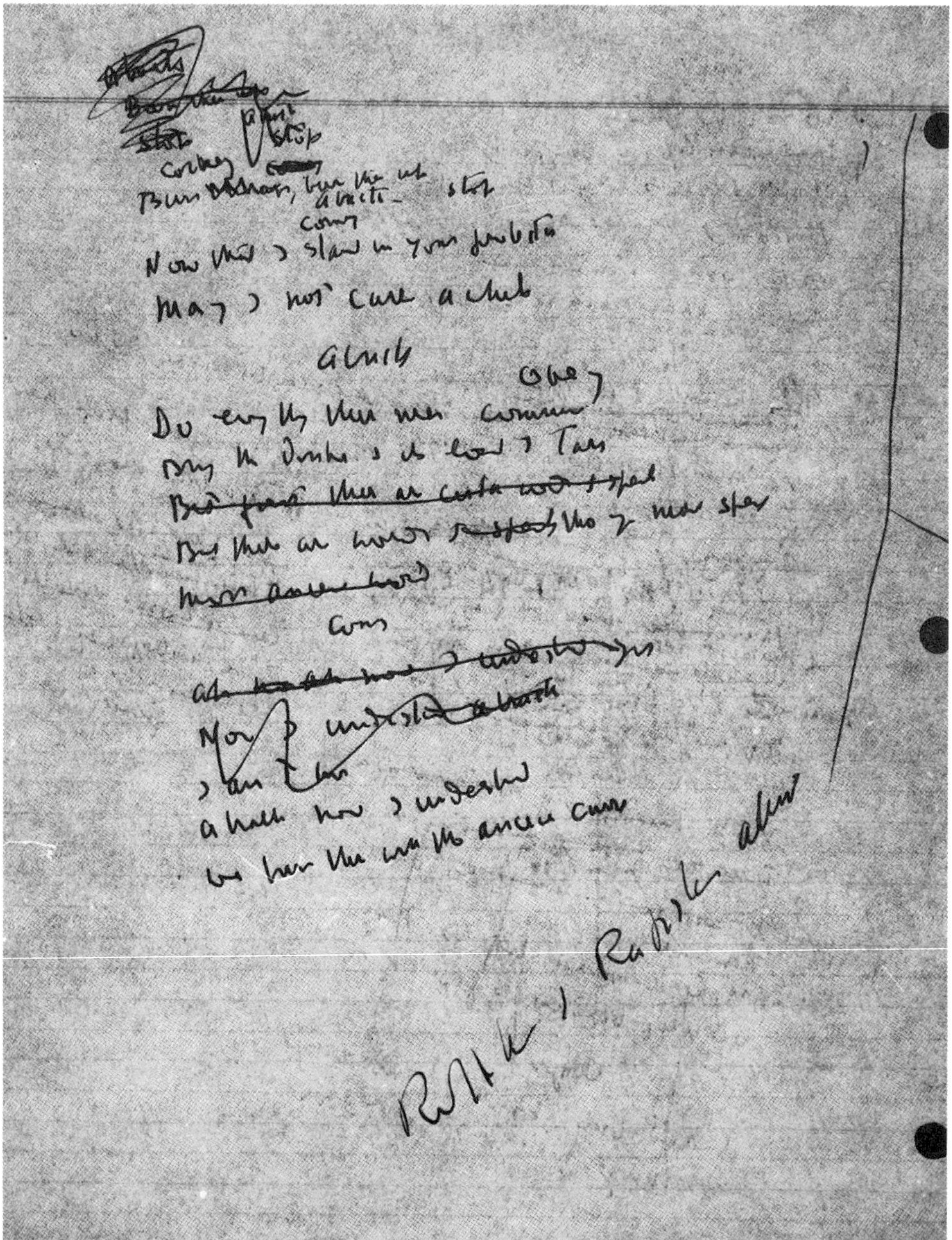

[NLI 8770 (1), 13v; II. 100–116]

Atracta

~~Burn them up~~

Atract

~~Stop~~ ~~Stop~~

Corney ~~Corney~~

1 Burn ~~the up~~, burn them up

Atracta — stop

Corney

2 Now that I stand in your protection

3 May I not curse a while

Atractt

Obey

4 Do evry thing these men command

5 Bring the donke & its load to Tara

~~But first there are certain words to speak~~

6 But there are words to speak tha you must speak

~~Most ancient word~~

Corney

~~Ah now Ah now I understand you~~

Now I understand Atracta

I am to cur

7 Atratta now I understand

8 We burn the with the ancient curse

Robbers & Rapsk alions

Blue-black ink. Arrow from “Robbers & Rapsk alions” inserts text on this page below “Stop” on 14r, l. 5.

[NLI 8770 (1), 14r; II. 100–116]

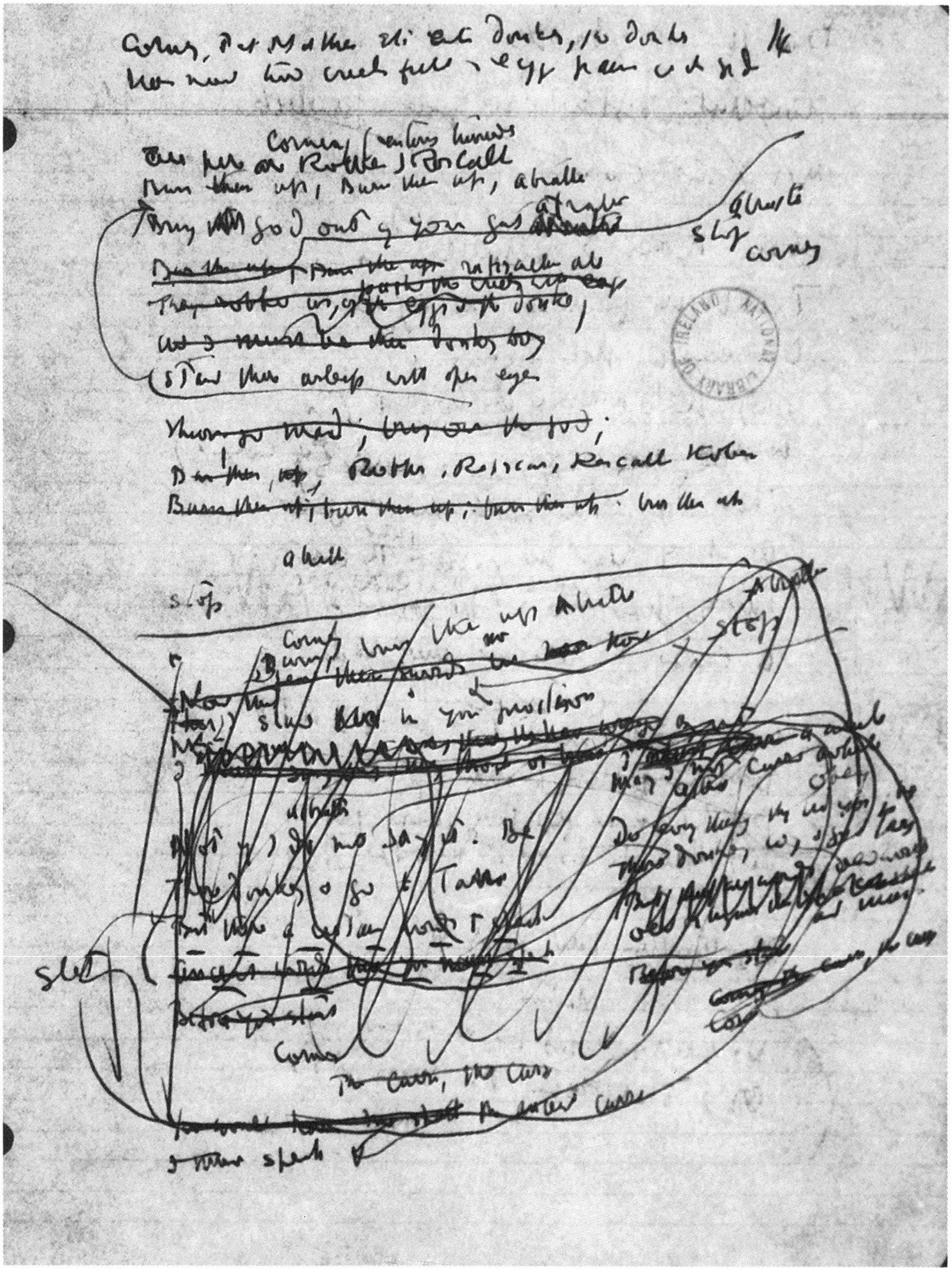

[NLI 8770 (1), 14r; II. 100–116]

Corney, Pat Mathis etc enter donky, the donky 14
has now two creels full of eggs pain on its side

Corney (enters hurriedly

1 All here are Robbers & Rascalls

2 Burn them up, Burn them up, Atratta

Atratta Atracta

3 Bring ~~that~~ god out of your gut ~~Attratta~~ Stop

Corney

~~Burn them up, Burn them up~~ rapscallions all

~~packed the creels with eggs~~

~~They robbed us, of the eggs & the donkey~~

~~And I must be their donkey boy~~

4 Stand there asleep with open eyes

~~Shiver, go mad, bring out the god;~~

~~Burn them up~~, Robber , Rapscal , Rascalls Robers

~~Burn them up; burn them up; burn them up;~~ burn them up

Atratta

5 Stop

Corney

Burn, burn them up Atratta

I no Atracta

~~fear their swords but never now~~ Stop

~~Now that~~

There I stand ~~here~~ in your protection

Make

[?~~time stand still~~] ~~those they have wronged us~~

~~I must sing out my thoughts or burst my gut~~

I ~~must curse~~ a while

May I not curse awhile

Attratta Attrct

Not if I do no say it. Be

Obey

Do evry thing they ask you, be

There donkey & go to Tara There donkey boy & go to Tara

But there ar certain words to speak ~~But there are words, old words~~

stet ~~Old & begun [? ? can speak]~~

Ancient words that you must speak and [? man]

~~Before you start~~ ~~Before you start~~

~~Corney the curse, the curse~~

Corney ~~Corn~~

~~The curse, the curse~~

~~You would have me speak the ancient curs~~e

6 ~~I must~~ speak

Blue-black ink. Arrow inserts l. 4 above l. 3.

[NLI 8770 (1), 14^{v}; ll. 100–116]

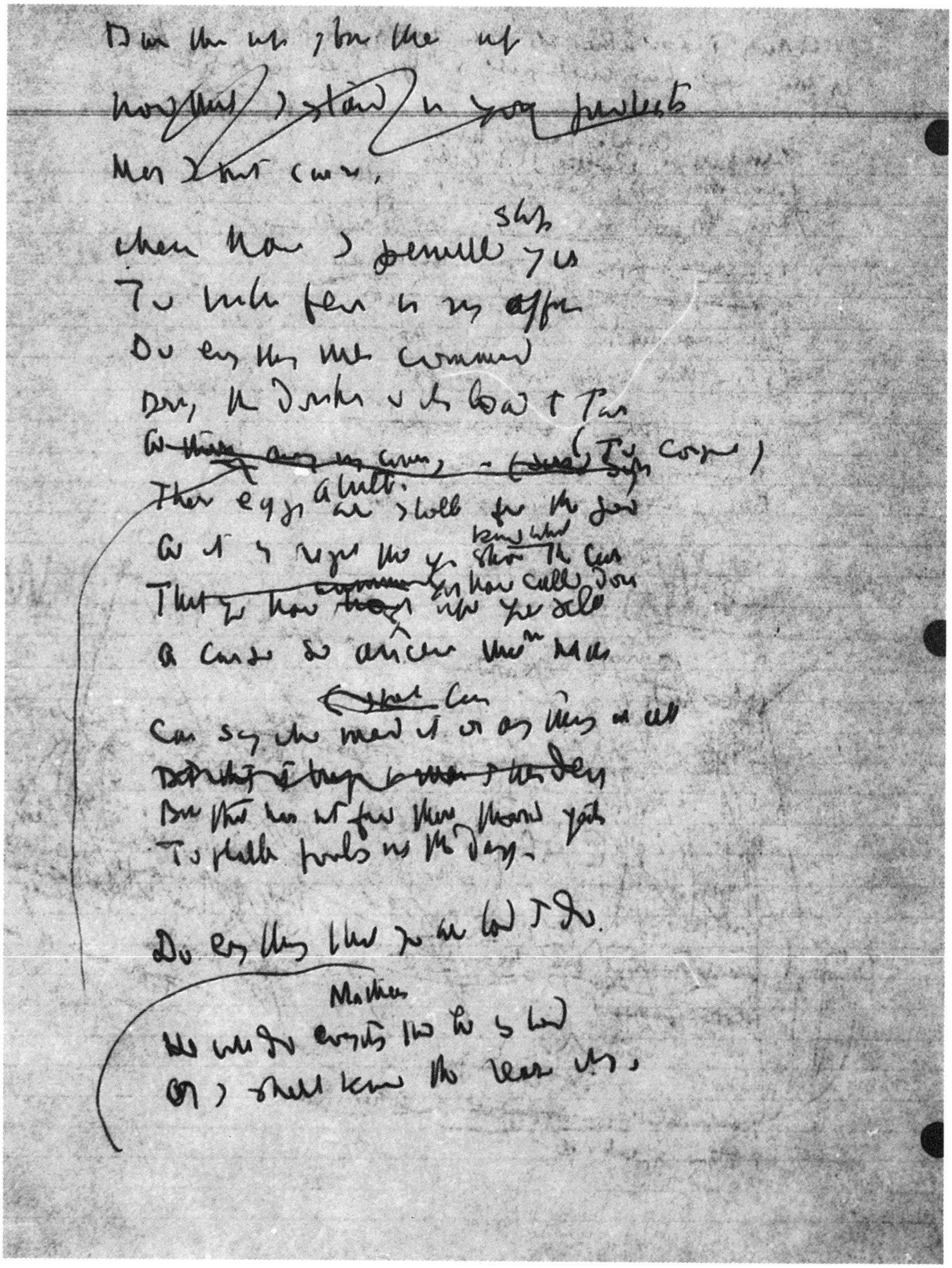

[NLI 8770 (1), 14ᵛ; II. 100–116]

Burn them up ; bu the up
[Now that I stand in you protectn
[May I not curse.

Stop

When have I permitted you
To inter fere in my affirs
Do evry thing they command
Bring the donky & its load to Tar

(To Congal)

~~And there away my coming — (Sirs) Sirs~~

Atratta

These eggs are stolle from the god

know what

And it is right that you shou the cur

~~commanded~~ you have calld down

~~That you have broug~~ upon your self

^ no

A Curse so ancien that man

~~(Shall~~ Can

Can say who made it or any thing at all
~~But that it bring a man to his death~~
But that has not faild these thousnd years
To flatter fools up the day.

Do evry thing that you are told to do.

Mathias

He will do evry thing that he is bid
Or I shall know the reason why.

Blue-black ink. Arrow inserts ll. 14–15 between ll. 5–6.

[NLI 8770 (1), 15r; ll. 36–7, 109–112, 120–30]

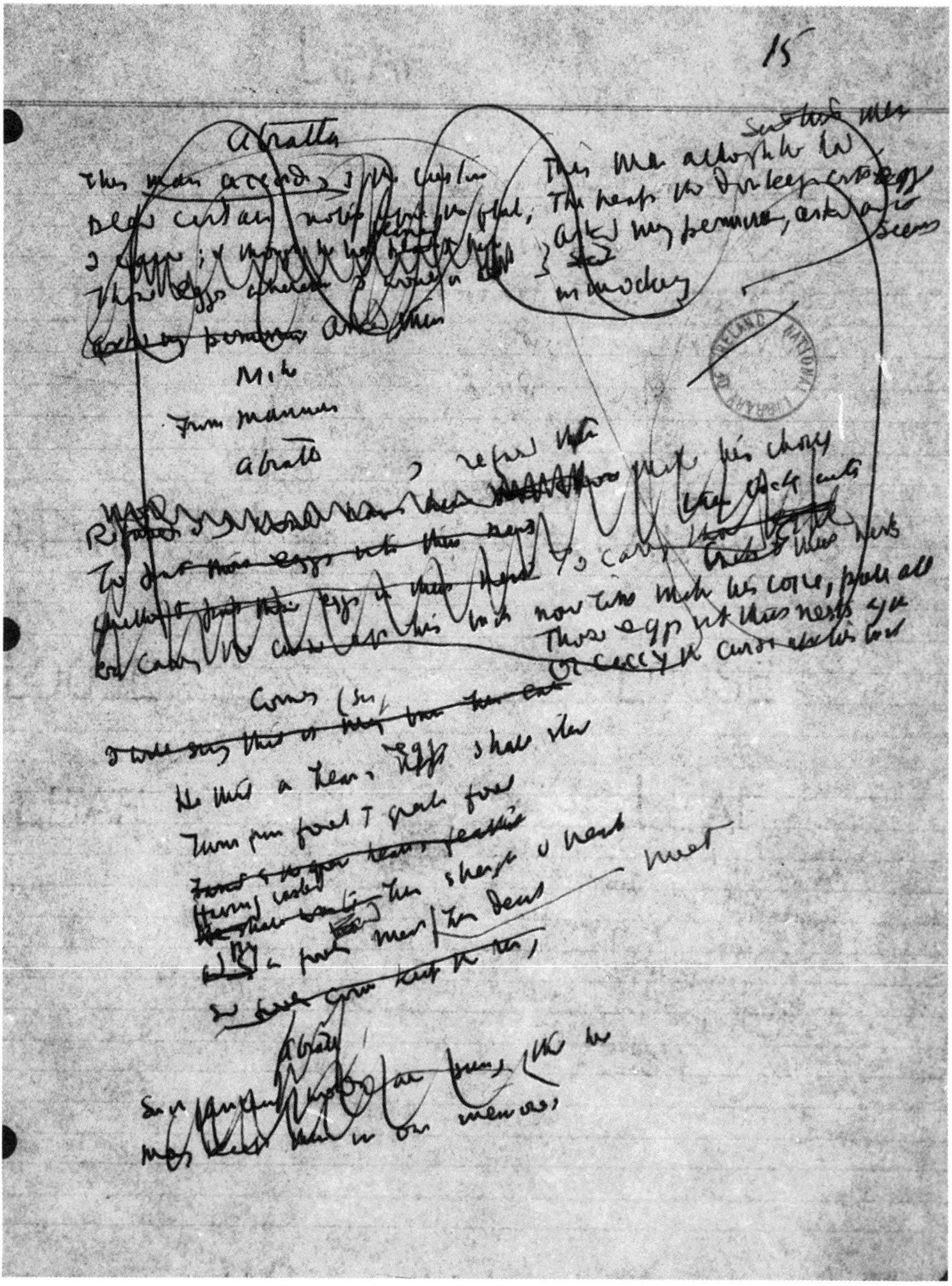

15

Atratta

1 This <u>man according to</u> the custom

2 Blew certain notes upon the flute;

planed

3 I came; & though he had ~~plot~~ to take

4 Those eggs whether I would or no

5 ~~Asks my permission~~ Asked them

Mike

6 From manners

Atratta

~~Now~~ I refused this

7 ~~Refused & I would have him now choose~~

To ~~put those eggs in their nests~~

8 ~~Whether to put those eggs in their nest~~

9 Or carry the curse upon his back

sent his men
This man although he had
The heap the donkey with eggs

Asked my permission, asked as it
[?] seems
in mockery

Make his choice
they lack wits
To carry ~~those eggs~~
back to their nests
Now he'll make his choice putt all
Those eggs into their nests agin
Or carry the curse upon his back

Corney (Sings

10 ~~I will sing that it may burn his ear~~

eggs

11 He that a hearns ~~nest~~ shall steal

12 Turns from fool to greatr fool

13 ~~Turned by the great hearns feather~~

14 Having wasted

15 ~~He shall waste~~ his strength & breath

By ~~hand~~

16 ~~And by~~ a fools meet his deat meet

17 ~~So fools come keep the rest~~

Atratt

18 Such ancient words are sung that we

19 May keep them in our memory

Blue-black ink, with Attracta's speeches, ll. 1–5, 7–9, deleted and revised in dark red. "From" in l. 6, "(Sings" above l. 10, and "eggs" above l. 11 are also in red ink.

[NLI 8770 (1), 15v; II. 135–40, IV. 158–75]

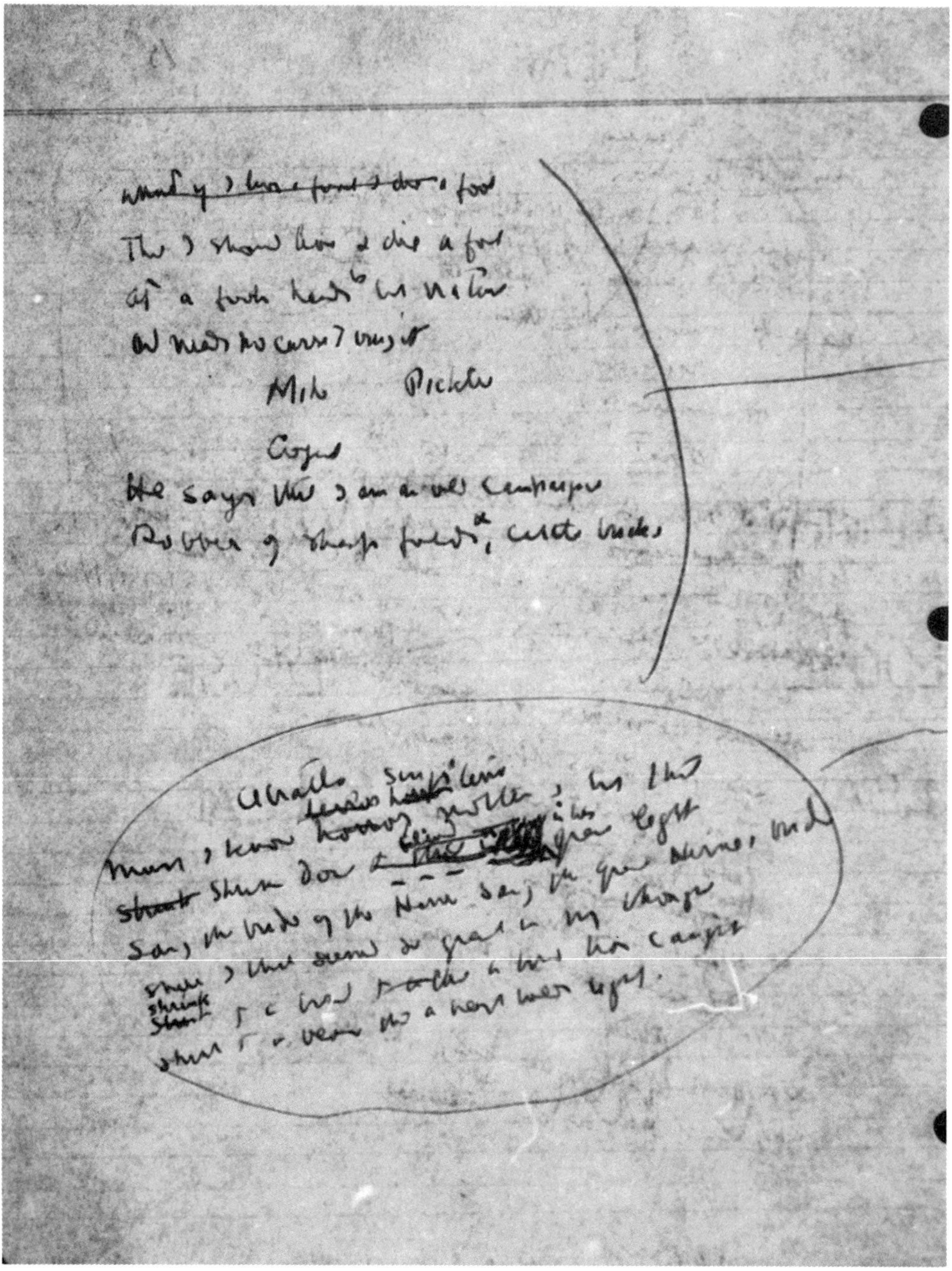

[NLI 8770 (1), 15^{v}; II. 135–40, IV. 158–75]

~~What if I live a fool & die a~~ fool

That I should live & die a fool
is
At a fools hands but nature
And needs no curse to bring it

Mike Pickled

Congal
He says that I am an old campaigner
&
Robber of sheep folds, cattle trucks

Atratta
Sings
~~terror~~ ~~horror~~ terror
Must I know ~~horror~~ nothin g but that
blind ~~in this~~ in his
~~Shrink~~ Shrink down ~~to these rocks~~ ^ great light
Sang the bride of the Herne Sang the great Hernes bride
Shall I that seemd so great in my thought
Shrink
~~Shrunk~~ to a bird ~~to a~~ that a bird has caught
Shrink to a beast that a beast holds tight.

Red ink. Arrows insert ll. 1–5 above l. 1, ll. 6–11 above l. 9 on 16^{r}.

[NLI 8770 (1), 16r; ll. 139–52]

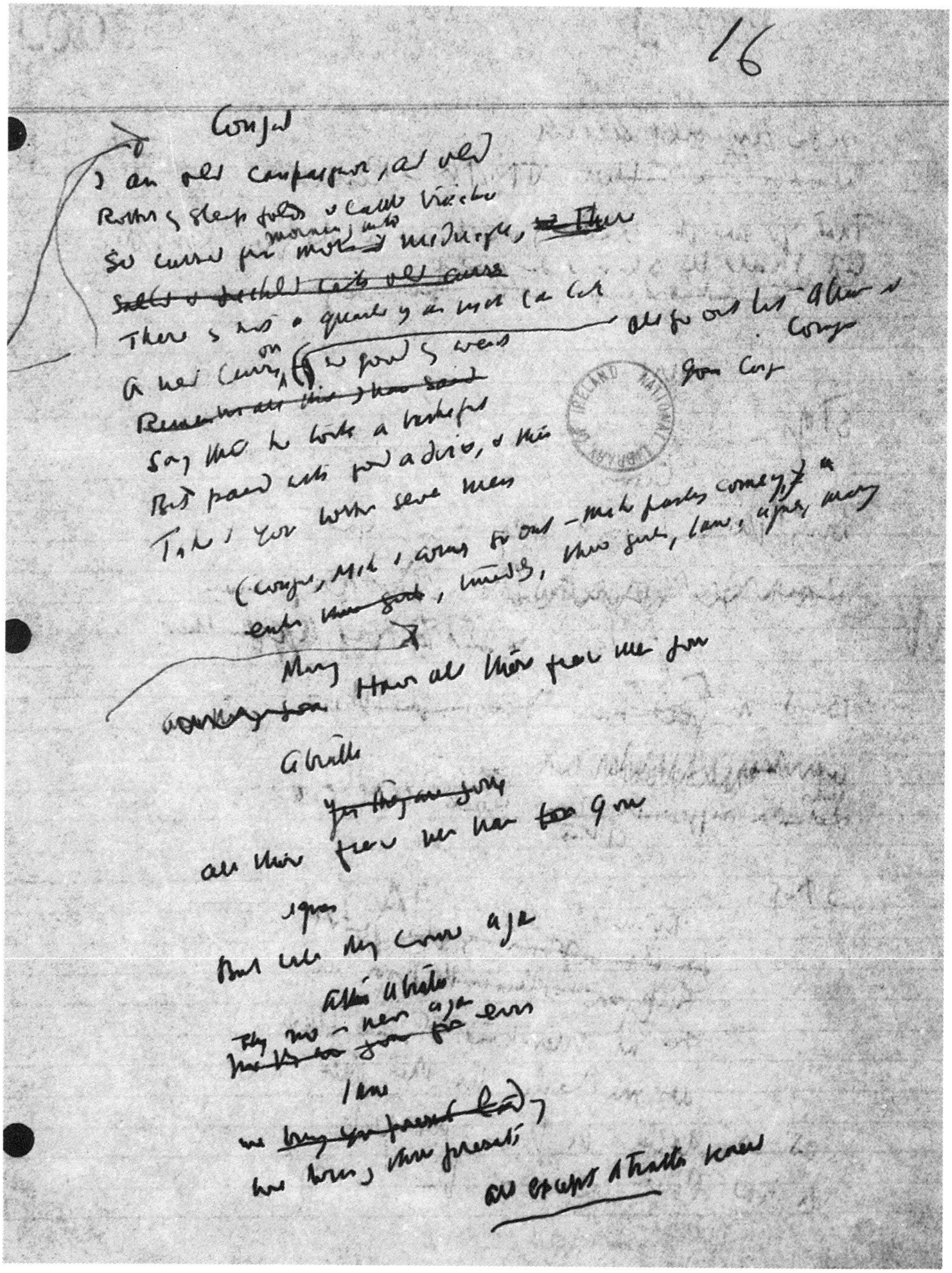

16

Congal

1 I an old campaigner, and old
2 Robber of sheep folds & cattle trucks
morning until
3 So cursed from ~~morn to~~ midnight, ~~so there~~
~~Salted & pickled with old curses~~
4 There is not a quarter of an inch can take
on
5 A new Curse^ so good by wench — All go out but Atract & Congal
~~Remember all that I have said~~
6 Say that he took a baskeful — ~~Con~~ Congal
7 But paid with good advice, & then
8 Take to your bosom seven men

(Congal, Mike & Corney go out — Mike pushing Corney,~~)~~ ~~a~~ enter ~~three girls~~, timidly, three girls, Jane, Agnes, Mary

Mary

9 ~~Are they gone~~ Have all those fierce men gone

Atratta

~~Yes they are gone~~
10 All those fierce men have ~~fon~~ Gone

Agnes

11 But will they come aga

~~Attra~~ Atrata

12 ~~They~~ No — nevr again
~~No they hav gone for~~ ever

Jane

~~We bring you presents lady~~
13 We bring three presents

All except Atratta kneel

Blue-black ink. Arrows linking material from 15v, deletions and revisions to ll. 3–4, and the deletion stroke through "Remember . . . said" are in red ink.

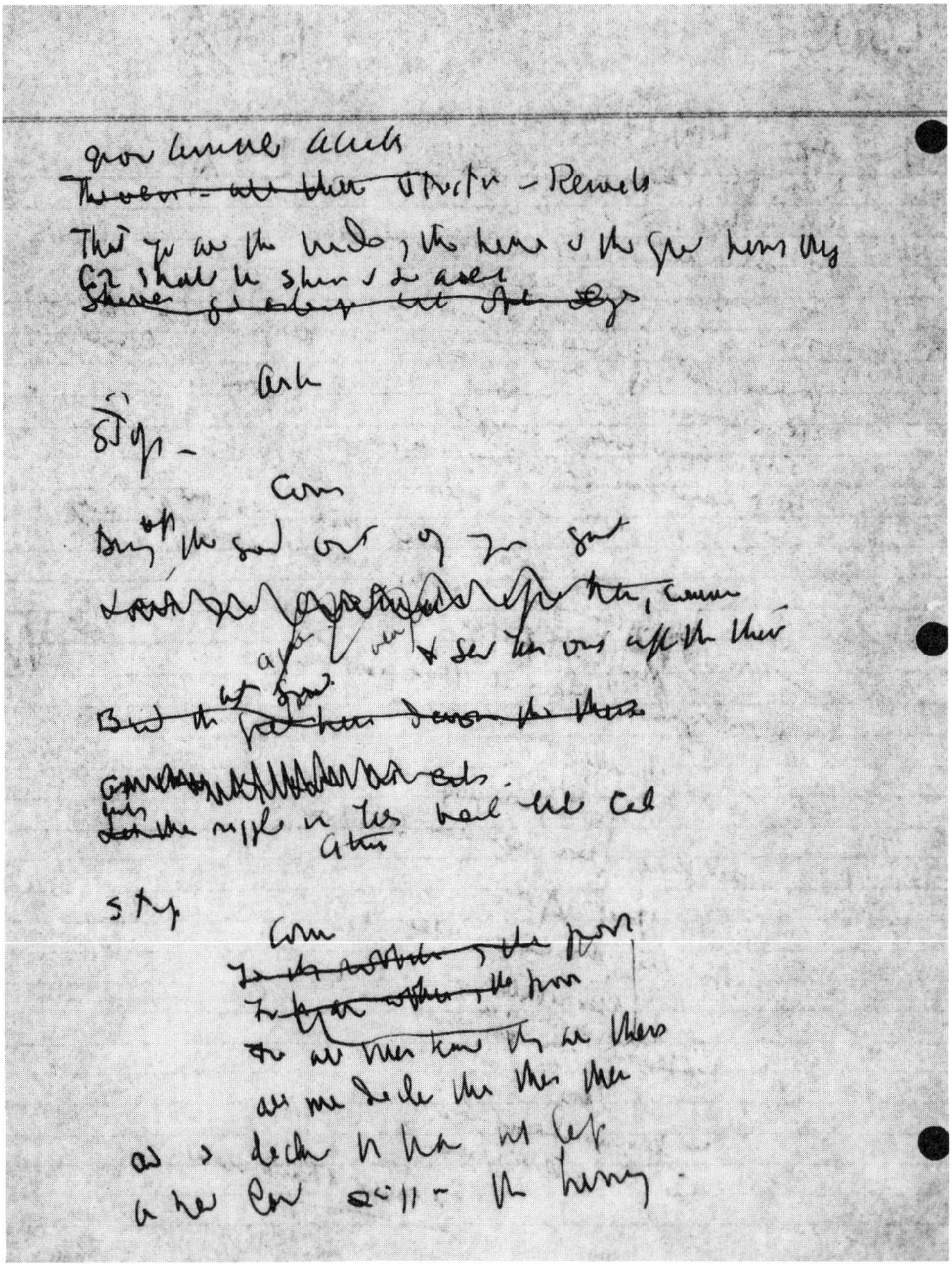

[NLI 8770 (1), 16^{v}; ll. 101–108]

1 Grow terrible Atratta
~~Theeves — all theives Atracta~~ — Reveele
2 That you are the bride of the herne & the Gret herns brid
3 Or shall he shivr & go aslee
~~Shiver go asleep with open eyes~~

Artr
4 Stop —

Corny
up
5 Bring the god out of your gut
6 ~~Lay your commands [?] upon hi~~m, cursing
7 & send him out after the theives
but god
8 ~~Bid the gret hern devour the thieves~~
9 ~~As though they were but eels~~
make
10 ~~Let~~ them riggle in his beak like eels.
Atract
Stop
Corn
~~For they robbers of the~~ poor
~~For th are robbers of~~ the poor
11 For all men know they are theivs
12 All men declare tha ther theivs
13 And I declare they have not left
14 A new laid egg in the hernery

Blue-black ink.

[NLI 8770 (1), 17r; ll. 153–67]

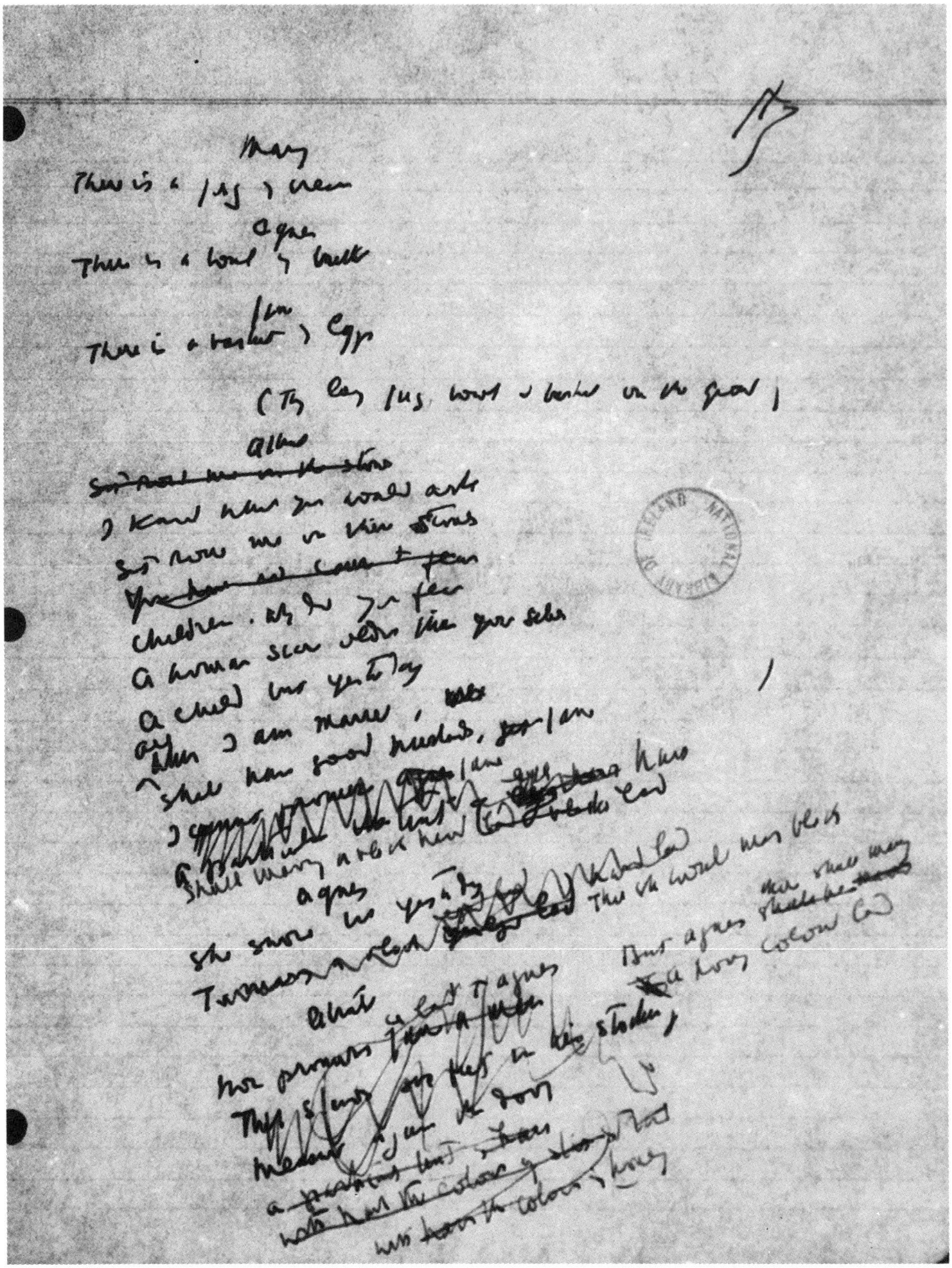

[NLI 8770 (1), 17r; II. 153–67]

Mary 17
1 There is a jug of cream
Agnes
2 There is a bowl of buttr
Jane
3 There is a basket of eggs
(They lay jug, bowl & basket on the ground)
Attract
~~Sit round me on the stones~~
4 I know what you would ask
5 Sit roun me on these stones
6 You have no cause to fear
7 Children. Why do you fear
8 A woman scarc older than your selves
9 A child but yesterday
All
10 ^When I am married, ~~will~~
11 Shall have good husbands, ~~Yes~~ Jane
I cannot promise ~~Agnes~~ Jane
eye
A particular ~~the~~ tint of ~~eye & hair~~ hair
12 Shall marry a black head ~~lad blacks~~ lad
Agnes
13 She swore but yesterday
~~eyed lad haired lad~~
14 ~~To marry a black yes eyed lad~~ That she would mary black
Atrata
a lad to Agnes there shall marry
15 Nor promised ~~Jane a man~~ But Agnes ~~shall be married~~
16 ~~To~~^A honey colourd lad
17 That stands six feet in his stockings
18 Measurd agains the door
~~A particular tint of hair~~
19 ~~With hair the colour of stars Straw~~
~~with hair the colour of honey~~

Blue-black ink. Written underneath ll. 6–8 on the facing verso, evidently toward ll. 11–14 here, are two partial lines: "Agnes [?] / Jane black [?]."

[NLI 8770 (1), 18^{r}; II. 168–80]

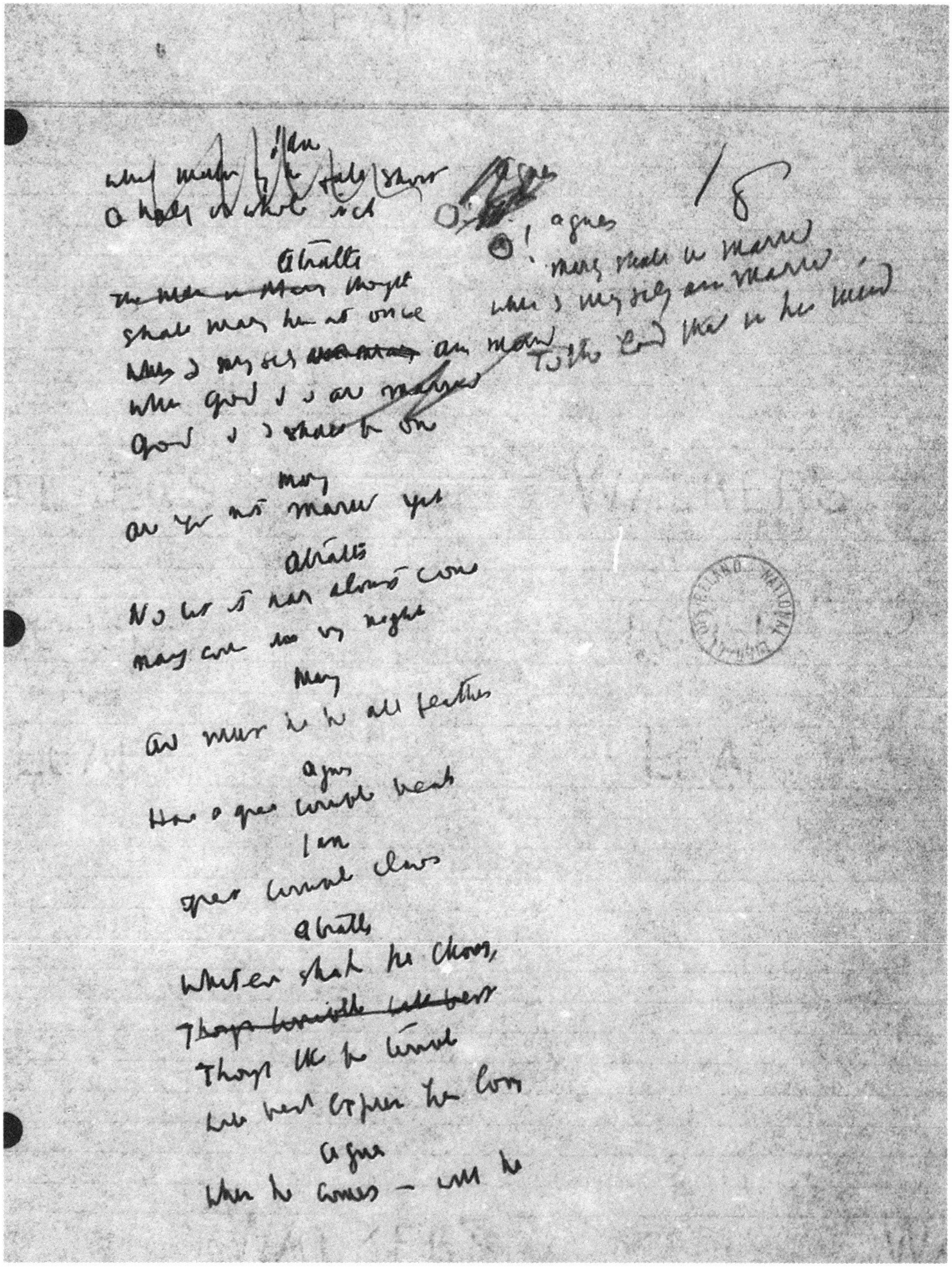

[NLI 8770 (1), 18r; II. 168–80]

Jane
What matter if he fall short
A half or whole inch

~~*Agnes*~~
~~*O O*~~ 18

Agnes
O!
Mary shall be married
When I myself am married
To the lad that in her mind

Atratta
1 ~~The man in Mary~~ thought
2 Shall marry her at once
3 When I myself ~~am mary~~ am married
4 When God & I are married
5 God & I shall be one
Mary
6 Are you not married yet
Atratta
7 No but it has almost come
8 May come this very night
Mary
9 And must he be all feathers
Agnes
10 Have a great terrible beak
Jane
11 Great terrible claws
Atratta
12 Whatever shape he chooses,
~~Though terrible will best~~
13 Though that be terrible
14 Will best express his love
Agnes
15 When he comes — will he

Blue-black ink, except deletion strokes through ll. 1, 3, 5 and Attracta's speech, ll. 2–4, in pencil.

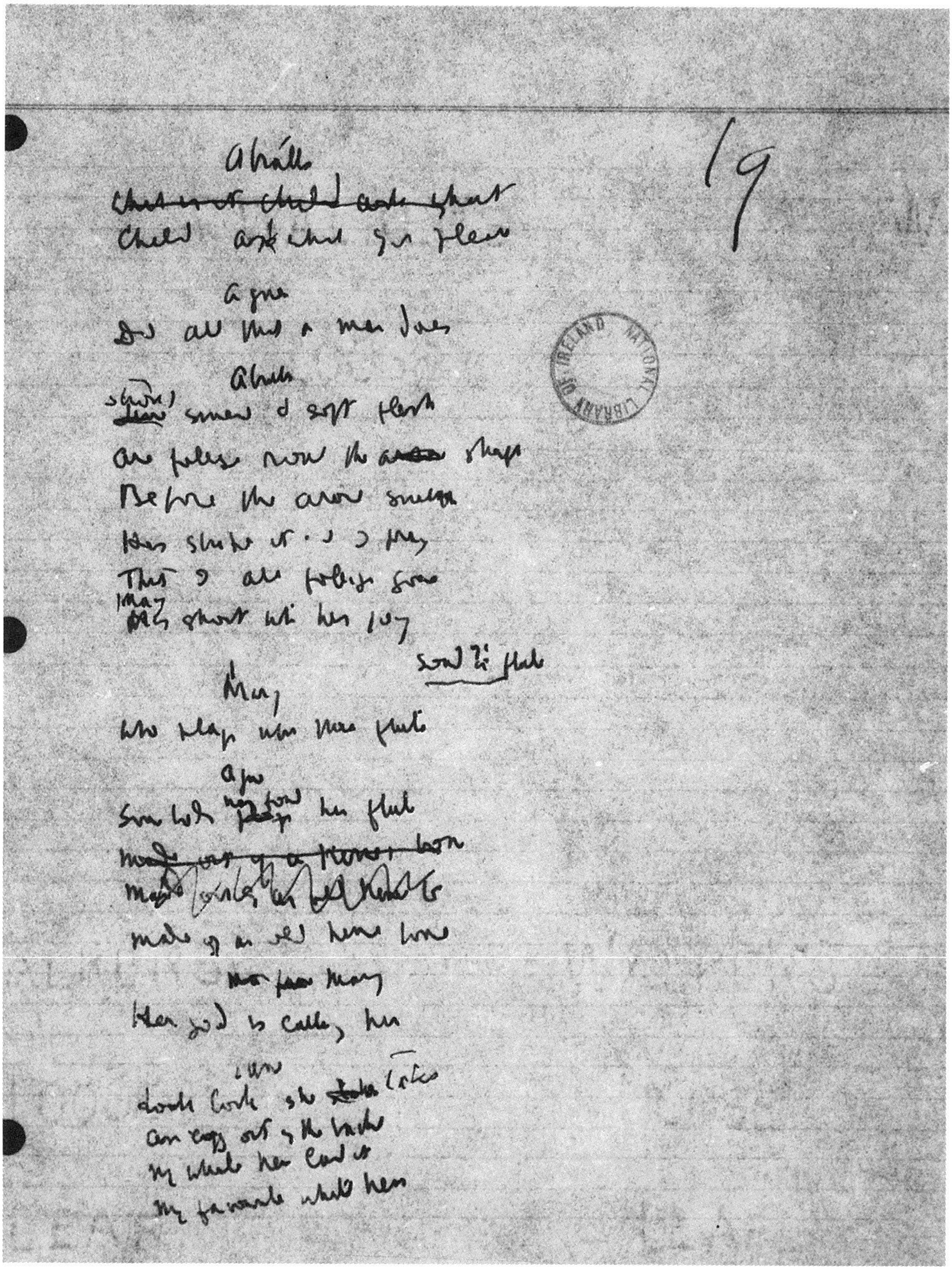

[NLI 8770 (1), 19^{r}; ll. 181–94]

Atratta
~~What is it child ask what~~ 19
Child   ask what you please
Agnes
Do all that a man does
Atrata
Strong
~~Sine~~ sinew & soft flesh
are folege round the ~~arrow~~ shaft
Before the arow smith
Has stript it. & I pray
That I all foliege gone
May
~~May~~ shoot into his joy
of
Sound a flute
Mary
Who plays upon that flute
Agnes
has found
Some body ~~plays~~ his flute
~~Made out of a hernes bone~~
~~Made out of an old herns bo~~
Made of an old herne bone
~~Ma~~ ~~Jane~~ Mary
Her god is calling her
Jane
Look look she ~~stakes~~ taks
An egg out of the basket
My white hen laid it
My favourite white hen

Blue-black ink, with revisions in ll. 3–4, 8, and 13 apparently in darker ink.

[NLI 8770 (1), 20^r; ll. 195–212, 219–20]

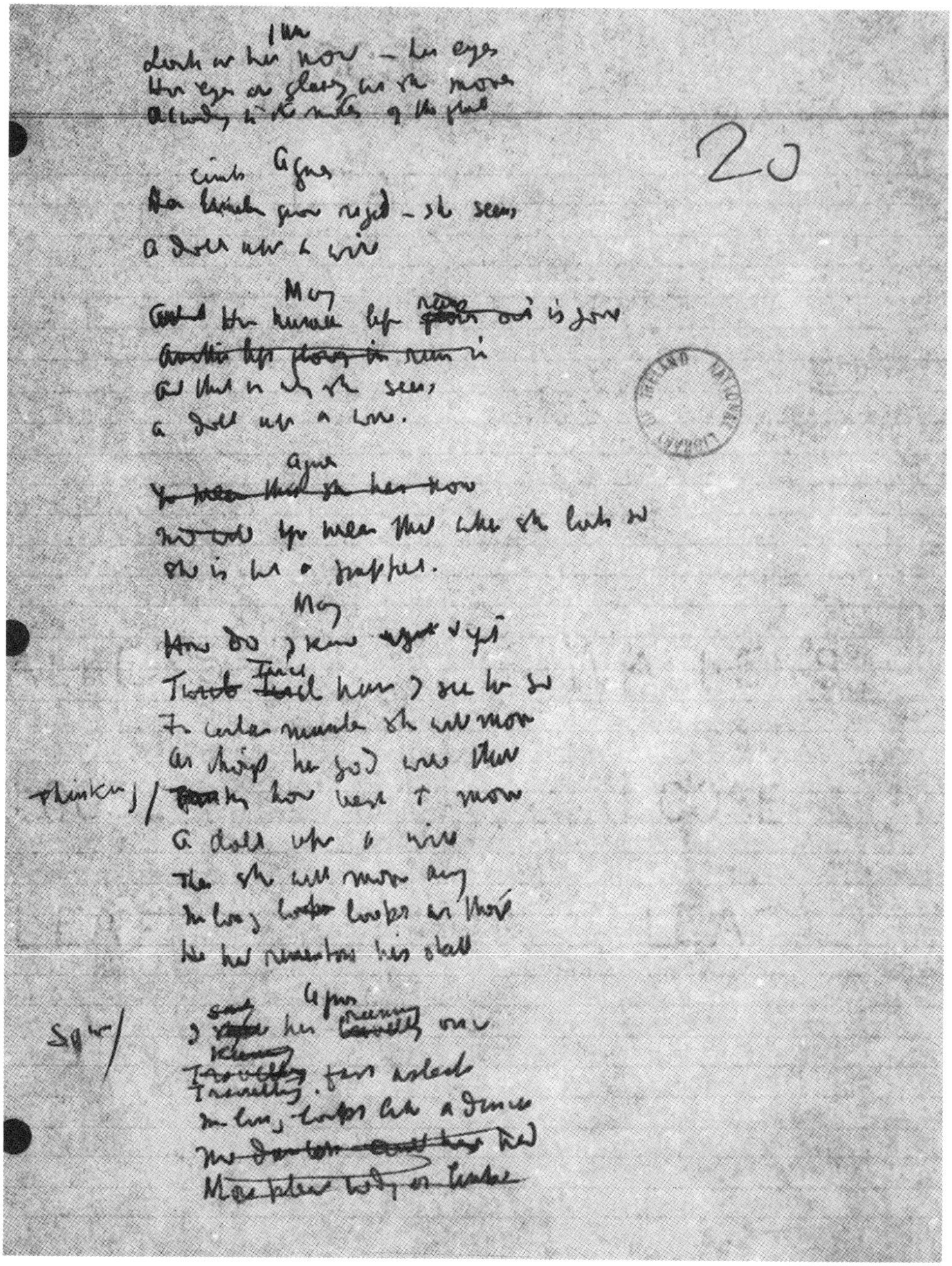

Jane
Look at her now — her eyes
Her eyes are glassy but she moves
According to the notes of the flute

Agnes 20
limbs
Her ~~limebs~~ grow rigid — she seems
A doll upon a wire
Mary
~~runs~~
~~And h~~ Her human life ~~flows out~~ is gone
~~Another life flows in runs in~~
And that is why she seems
A doll upon a wire
Agnes
~~You mean that she has now~~
~~No will~~ You mean that when she looks so
She is but a puppet.
Mary
How do I know ~~& yet~~ & yet
Twice
~~Twice Twice~~ have I see her so
For certain minutes she will move
As though her god were there
Thinking/ ~~Thinking~~ how best to move
A doll upon a wire
Then she will move away
In long ~~loops~~ loops as though
He had rememberd his skill
Agnes
~~saw~~ running
Saw/ I ~~shall~~ her ~~travelling~~ once
~~Running~~
~~Travelling~~ fast asleep
Travelling
In long loops like a dancer
~~No dancers could have had~~
~~More pliant body or limbs~~

Blue-black ink, with revisions in ll. 4, 11–12, 15, and "saw" above l. 20 in darker ink.

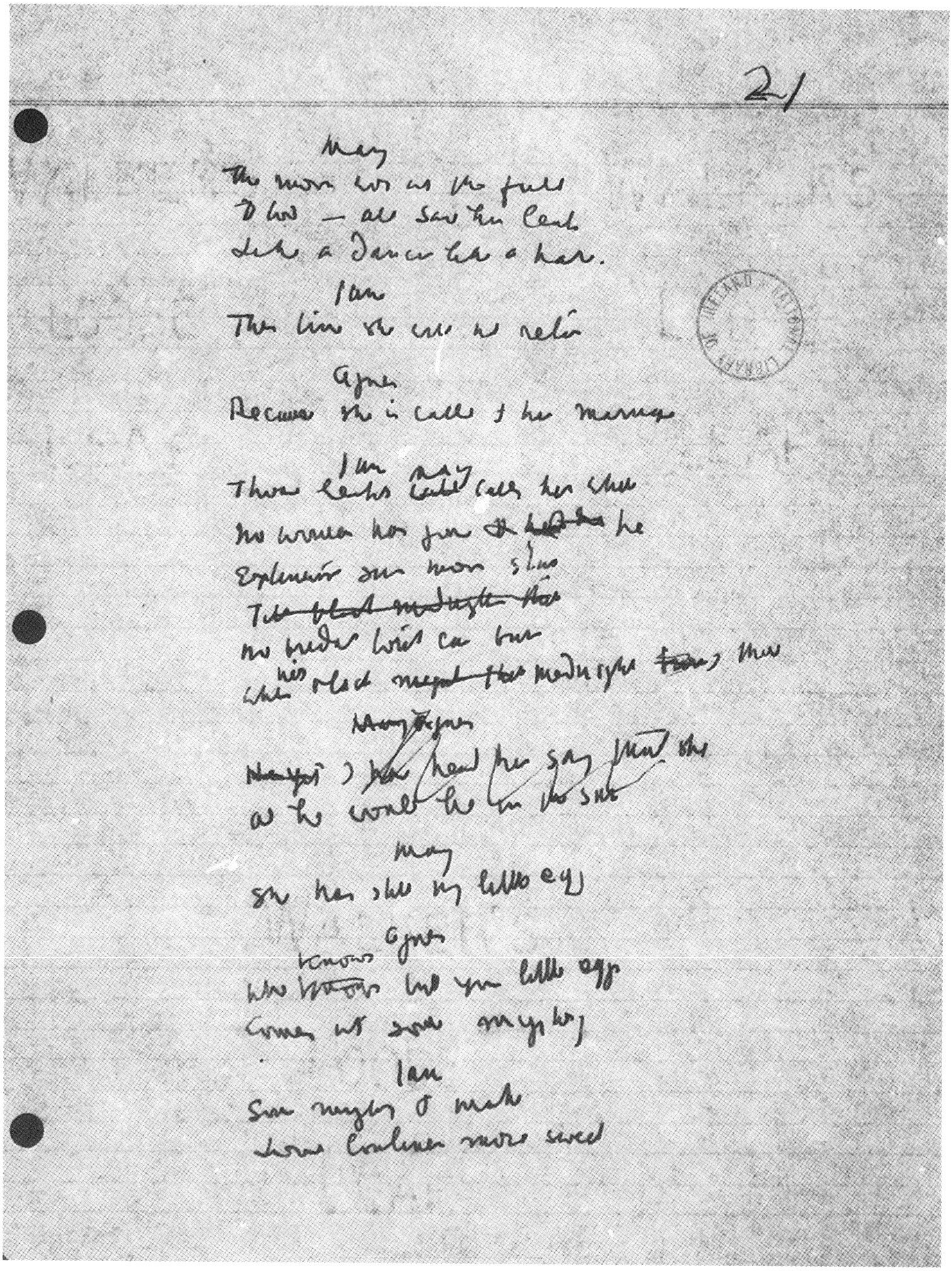

[NLI 8770 (1), 21^{r}; ll. 221–31, 213–17]

21

Mary
The moon was at the full
I too — all saw her leap
Like a dancer like a hare.
Jane
This time she will not return
Agnes
Because she is calld to her marriage
Jane may
Those leaps ~~call~~ call her where
~~she~~
No woman has gone ~~&~~ ~~her~~ he
Extinguish sun moon stars
~~Till black midnights there~~
No bridal torch can burn
his
When black ~~might there~~ midnight ~~burns~~ there
~~Mary~~ Agnes
~~Have Yet~~ I have heard her say that she
And he would be in the sun
Mary
She has still my little egg
Agnes
knows
Who ~~knows~~ but your little egg
Comes into some mystery
Jane
Some mystery to make
Love lonliness more sweet

Blue-black ink.

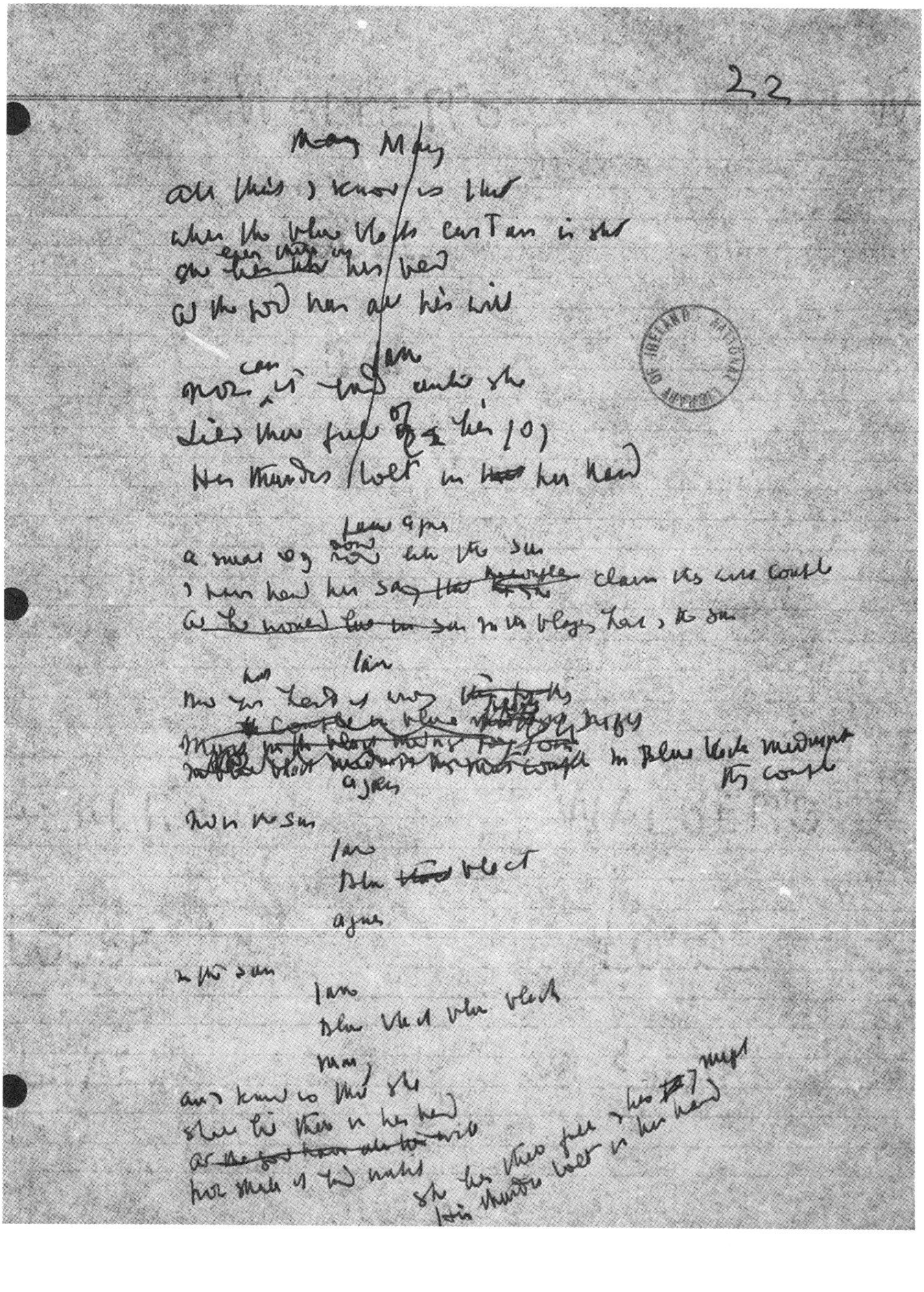

[NLI 8770 (1), 22^{r}; II. 232–42]

22

~~Mary~~ Mary
All that I know is that
When the blue black curtain is shut
lies there on
She ~~lies upon~~ his bed
And the god has all his will
Jane
can
Nor ^ it end until she
of
Lies there full ~~of s~~ his joy
His thunder bolt in ~~his~~ her hand
~~Jane~~ Agnes
rond
A smal eg rou like the sun
~~he couple~~
I have heard her ~~say that & she~~ claim they will couple
~~And he would live in sun~~ In the blazing heat of the sun
Jane
have
But you heard it wrong ~~then for they~~
black
~~Th Couple in blue midnight~~ night
Must ~~in the black midnight joy~~ ~~join~~
~~In blue black midnight they must couple~~ In Blue black midnight
they couple
Agnes
No in the sun
Jane
Blue ~~black~~ blact
Agnes
In the sun
Jane
Blue black blu black
Mary
All I know is that she
Shall lie there in his bed
~~And that god have all his~~ will
Nor shall it end until
She lies there full of his ~~joy~~ might
His thunder bolt in her hand

Blue-black ink.

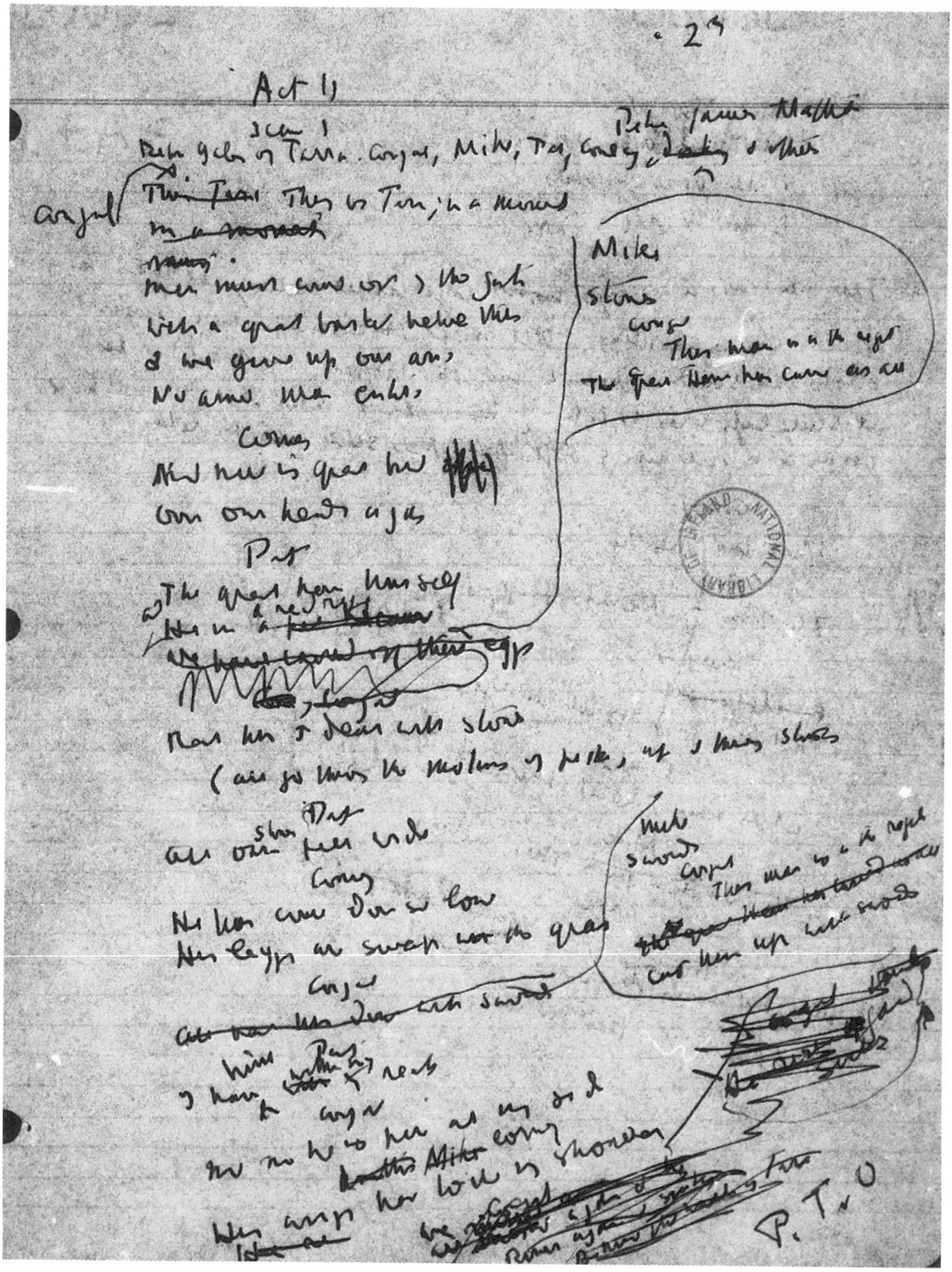
Act II

P. T. O

[NLI 8770 (1), 23r; III. 1–22]

23

Act II
Scene 1 — Peter, James Mathis

Before Gates of Tarra. Congal, Mike, Pat, Corney~~, donkey~~ & others

1 ~~This Tara~~ This is Tara; in a moment
Congal
~~In a moment~~
~~Must~~
2 Men must come out of the gate
3 With a great basket between them
4 & we give up our arms
5 No armed man enters
Corney
6 And here is Great bird ~~upon~~
7 Over our heads again
Pat
8 The great hern him self
And a red rage
9 ^He in a ~~fret because~~
~~We have carried off those eggs~~
~~Corney Congal~~
12 Beat him to death with stones
(All go through the motions of picking up & throwing stones
Pat
stones
13 All our fell wide
Corney
14 He has come down so low
15 His leggs are sweep ~~wa~~ the grass
Congal
~~All beat him down with swords~~
Pat
him within my
18 I have ^ ~~with my~~ reach
Congal
19 No no he is here at my side
~~Mathis Mike~~ Corney
20 His wings have touche my shoulder
~~We are~~ Congal
~~We missed again~~
~~All missed again & he~~
~~Rises again & sinks~~
~~Behind the wall of Tara~~

Mike
10 Stones
Congal
This man is in the right
G
11 The g}reat Herne has cursd us all

Mike
16 Swords
Congal
This man is in the right
~~The great Hearn has cursed us all~~
17 Cut him up with swords

~~Congal sinks~~

~~He rises again~~
~~Sinks~~

P. T. O.

Blue-black ink. This sheet is filed with 8770 (2).

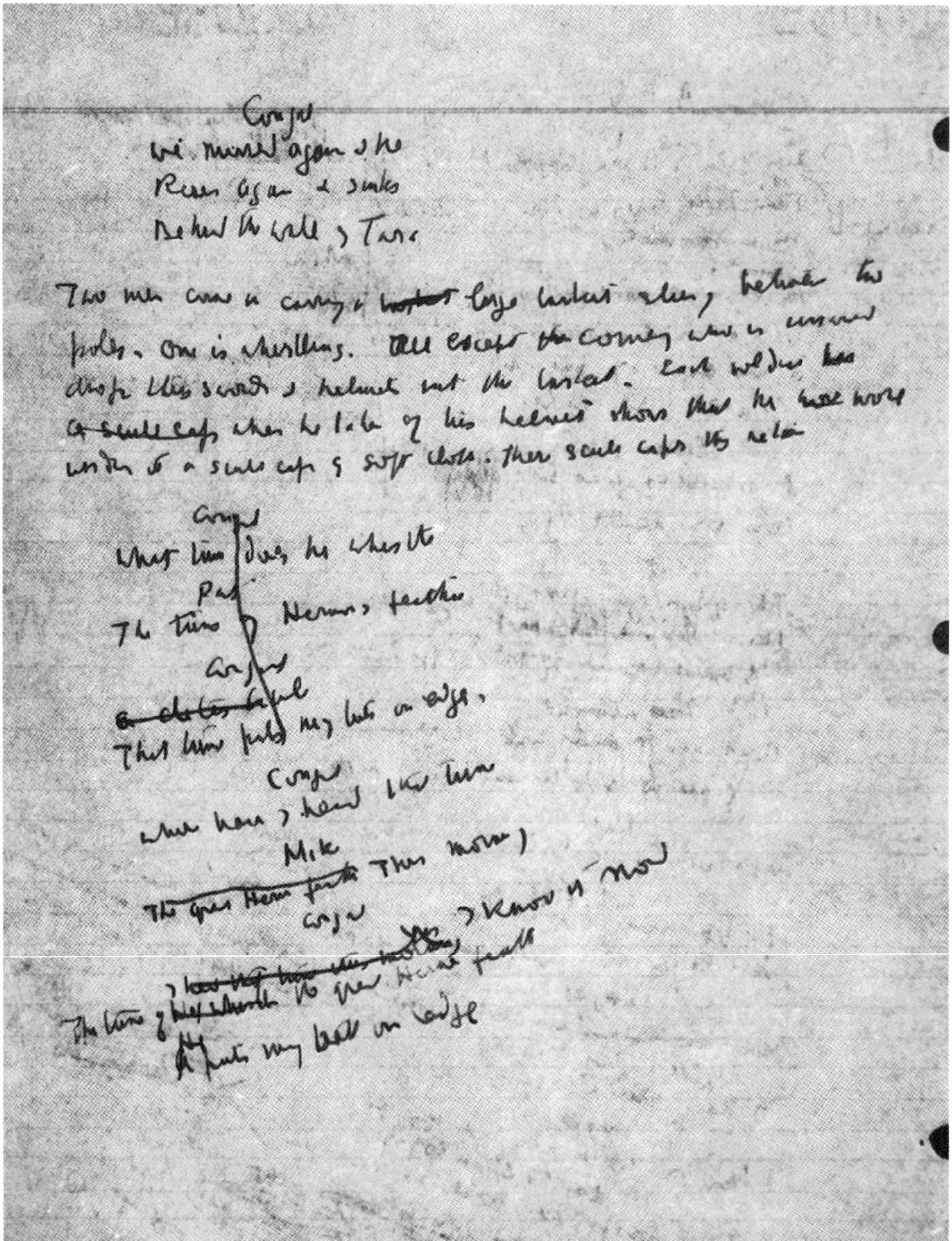
Congal
We must again & he
Rises again & sinks
Behind the wall of Tara
Two men come in carrying a ~~bottle~~ large basket slung between two poles. One is whistling. All except the corner who is unarmed drop their swords & helmet into the basket. Each soldier has ~~a scull cap~~ when he take off his helmet shows that he had worn under it a scull cap of soft cloth. These scull caps they retain
Congal
What tune does he whistle
Pat
The tune of Herne's feather
Congal
~~a clothes~~ [illegible]
That tune puts my teeth on edge.
Congal
Where have I heard that tune
Mike
~~The great Herne feather~~ This morning
Congal I know it now
~~[illegible]~~
The tune of ~~[illegible]~~ the great Herne feather
It puts my teeth on edge

[NLI 8770 (1), 23^{v}; III. 20–26]

Congal
1 We missed again & he
2 Rises again & sinks
3 Behind the wall of Tara

Two men come in carry a ~~basket~~ large basket slung between two poles. One is whistling. All except ~~the~~ Corney who is unarmed drop their swords & helmets into the basket. Each soldier ~~has a scull cap~~ when he takes of his helmet shows that he ~~wore~~ wore under it a scull cap of soft cloth. These scull caps they retain

Congal
What tune does he whistle
Pat
The tune of Herons feather
Congal
~~A detestible~~
That tune puts my teeth on edge
Congal
4 Where have I heard that tune
Mike
~~The great Hern feath~~ This morning
Congal
Yes I know it now
I ~~herd that tune this morning~~
5 The tune of ~~He Whistles~~ the great Herne feathr
He
6 ~~A~~ puts my teeth on edge

Blue-black ink.

[NLI 8770 (2), 1r; IV. 1–12]

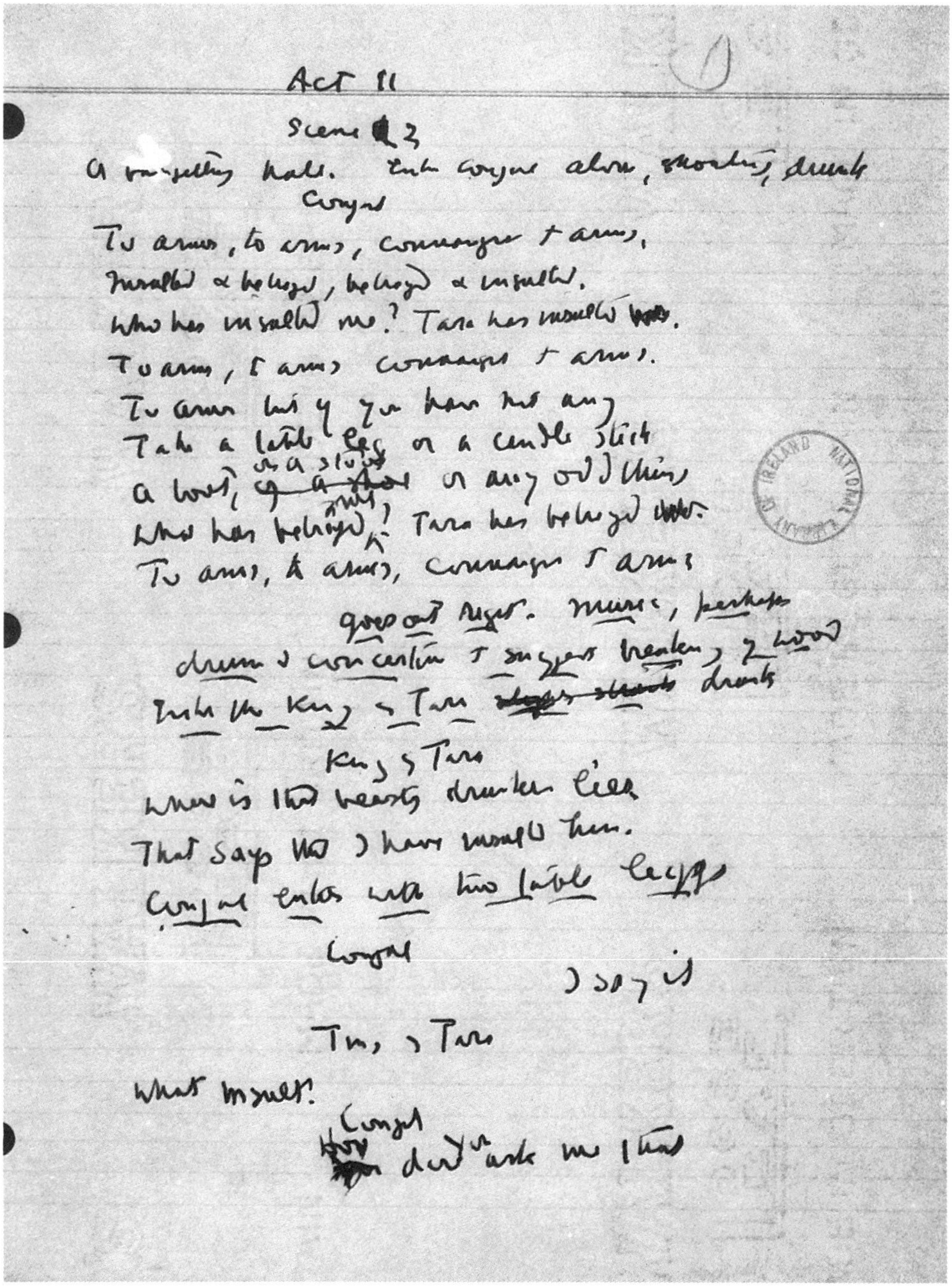
Act II

Scene 2

A vaulting hall. Enter Congal alone, shouting, drunk

Congal

To arms, to arms, Connaught to arms,
Insulted & betrayed, betrayed & insulted.
Who has insulted me? Tara has insulted me.
To arms, to arms Connaught to arms.
To arms but if you have not any
Take a table leg or a candle stick
A boot, or a stool or any old thing
Who has betrayed me? Tara has betrayed me.
To arms, to arms, Connaught to arms

goes out singing. Music, perhaps
drum & concertina to suggest breaking of wood
Enter the King of Tara drunk

King of Tara

Where is that beastly drunken lea
That says that I have insulted him.

Congal enters with two table leggs

Congal

I say it

King of Tara

What insult?

Congal

You don't ask me that

[NLI 8770 (2), 1r; IV. 1–12]

1

Act II
Scene ~~1~~ 2
A banquetting hall. Enter Congal alone, shouting, drunk
Congal
1 To arms, to arms, Connaught to arms,
2 Insulted & betrayed, betrayed & insulted.
3 Who has insulted me? Tara has insulted ~~me~~.
4 To arms, to arms Connaught to arms.
5 To arms but if you have not any
6 Take a table leg or a candle stick
or a stool
7 A boot, ~~of a shoe~~ or any odd thing
^ me
8 Who has betrayed^? Tara has betrayed ~~me~~
9 To arms, to arms, Connaught to arms

Goes out right. Music, perhaps
drum & concertina to suggest breaking of wood
Enter the King of Tara ~~slightly struck~~ drunk
King of Tara
10 Where is that beastly drunken lier.
11 That says that I have insulted him.
Congal enters with two table leggs
Congal
I say it
Ting of Tara
12 What insult!
Congal
How you
~~You~~ dare ask me that

Blue-black ink, except page number in upper right corner in pencil.

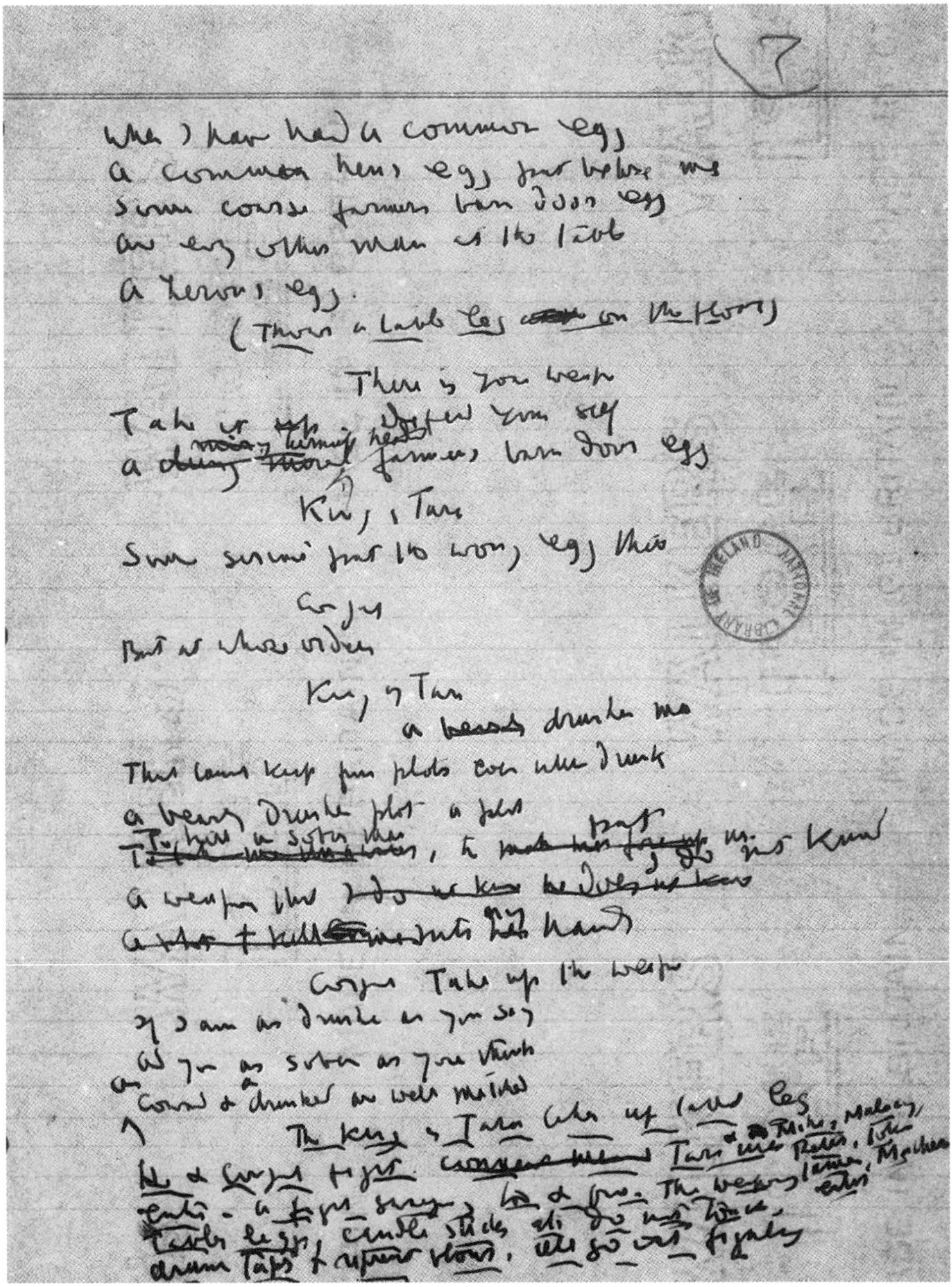

7

When I have had a common egg
A common hen's egg put before me
Some coarse farmer's barn door egg
An egg other men at the table
A heron's egg.

(Throws a table leg on the floor)

There is your weapon
Take it up. Defend your self
A ~~dung~~ ~~[illegible]~~ farmer's barn door egg

King of Tara

Some servant put the wrong egg there

Congal

But at whose orders

King of Tara

A ~~beastly~~ drunken man
That cannot keep from plots even when drunk
A very drunken plot a plot
~~To make me [illegible]~~, to ~~make me~~ ~~[illegible]~~ I do not know
A weapon that ~~I do not know he does not know~~
~~A [illegible] & kill~~ into his hand

Congal Take up the weapon
If I am as drunk as you say
And you as sober as you think
A coward & drunkard are well matched

The King of Tara takes up table leg
He & Congal fight ~~[illegible]~~ Tara men & Mike, Malachi, [illegible] enter — a fight scene, [illegible]. The weapons [illegible] table legs, candle sticks, etc. [illegible], drum taps & repeated blows, etc. [illegible]

2

1 When I have had a common egg
2 A common hens egg put before me
3 Some coarse farmers barn door egg
4 And evry other man at the table
5 A herons egg.

(Throws a table leg ~~at the~~ on the floor)

There is your weapn

6 Take it up. Defend your self

~~miry~~ turnip headed

7 A ~~dung mired~~ ^ farmers barn door egg

King of Tara

8 Some servant put the wrong egg there

Congal

9 But at whose orders

King of Tara

A ~~beastly~~ drunken man

10 That cannot keep from plots even when drunk
11 A beastly drunken plot a plot
12 To kill a sober man put

~~To take me unawares~~, to ~~make men force upon~~ us.

I do not know

13 A weapon that ~~I do not know~~ ~~he does nt know~~

my

14 ~~A plot to kill~~ ~~Congal~~ Into ~~his~~ hands

Congal Take up the weapon

15 If I am as drunken as you say
16 And you as sober as you think

A a

17 ^ coward & drunkerd are well matched

The King of Tara takes up table leg

& ~~M~~ Mike, Malacy,

He & Congal fight. ~~Connaught men &~~ Tara men Peter, John
enter — A fight sways, too & fro. The weapons James Mathias
table leggs, candle sticks etc do not touch, enter
drum taps to represent blows. All go out fighting

Blue-black ink, except page number in upper right corner in pencil.

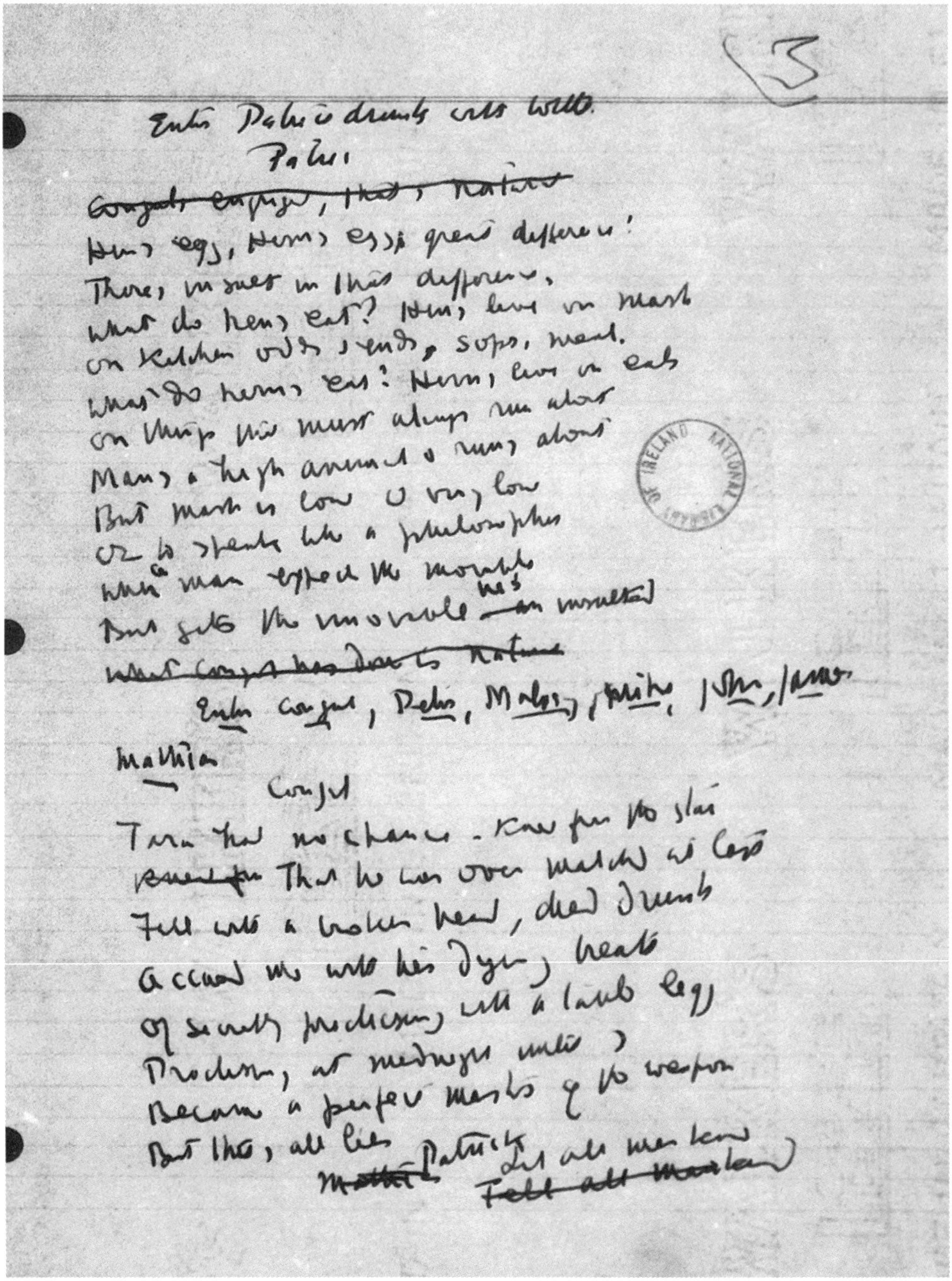

3

Enter Patrick drunk with bottle.

Patrick

~~Congal, Corney, that, Nature~~

Hens' eggs, Herne's eggs, great difference!
There's no sense in that difference,
What do hens eat? Hens live on mash
On kitchen odds & ends, sops, meal.
What do hernes eat? Hernes live on eels
On things that must always run about
Man's a high animal & runs about
But mash is low O very low
Or to speak like a philosopher
When a man expects the moveable
But gets the unmoveable his ~~an immortal~~
~~What Congal has done to Nature~~

Enter Congal, Peter, Malachi, Mike, John, James

Mathias

Congal

Tara knew no chance – knew from the start
~~knew from~~ That he was over matched at least
Fell into a broken head, died drunk
Accused me with his dying breath
Of secretly practising with a lamb's legs
Practising at midnight until
Became a perfect master of the weapon
But that's all lies

~~Mathias~~ Patrick Let all mankind ~~Tell all mankind~~

[NLI 8770 (2), 3^{r}; IV. 30–48]

3

Enter Patrick drunk with bottle

Patric

~~Congal engraged, that is natural~~
Hens egg, Herns egg; great difference!
Theres insult in that difference.
What do hens eat? Hens live on mash
On kitchen odds & ends, sops, meal.
What do herns eat? Herns live on eels
On things that must always run about
Mans a high animal & runs about
But mash is low O very low
Or to speak like a philosopher
a
When man expects the movable
he's
But gets the imovable — ~~an~~ insulted
~~What Congal has done is natural~~

Enter Congal, Peter, Malacy, Mike, John, James Mathias

Congal

Tara had no chance — knew from the star
~~Knew from~~ That he was over matchd at last
Fell with a broken head, died drunk
Accused me with his dying breath
Of secretly practicsing with a table legg
Practising at midnight until I
Became a perfect master of the weapon
But that s all lies

Patrick

~~Mathias~~ Let all men know
~~Tell all mankind~~

Blue-black ink, except stage directions at top and ll. 11/12, along with revisions to ll. 10–11, in a darker ink. Page number in upper right corner is in pencil.

[NLI 8770 (2), 4r; IV. 49–61]

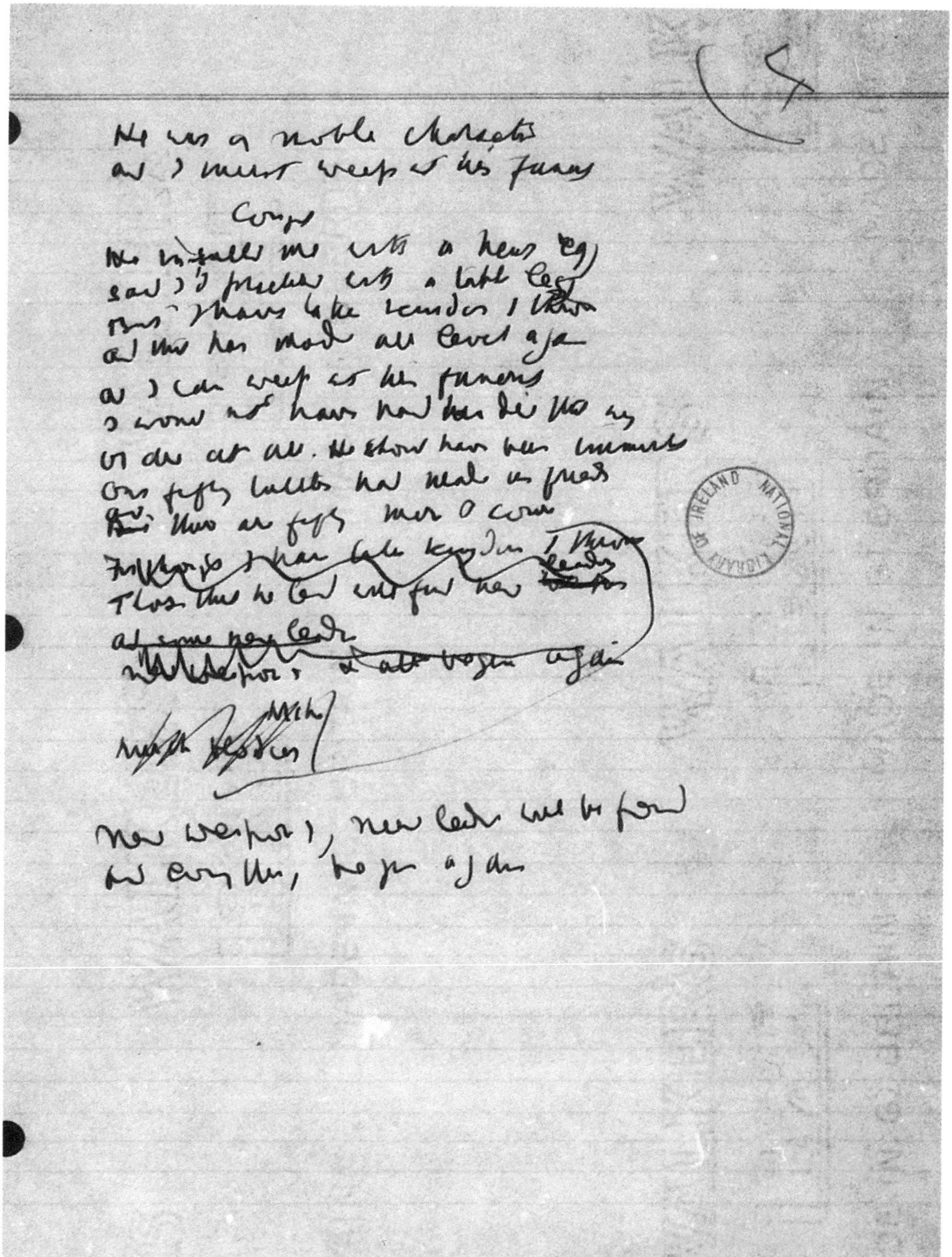
He was a noble character
and I must weep at his funeral

Chorus

He insulted me with a [illegible] egg
said I'd preached with a table leg
But I have taken vengeance I think
and this has made all level again
and I can weep at his funeral
I would not have had him die that way
or die at all. He should have been imprisoned
Our fifty bullets had made us friends
And there are fifty more O come
[illegible] I have taken vengeance I think
Those that we lead will find new leaders
and some new leader
[illegible] weapons & all begin again

[illegible]

new weapons, new leaders will be found
and everything begin again

[NLI 8770 (2), 4^{r}; IV. 49–61]

4

He was a noble character
And I must weep at his funeral
Congal
He insulted me with a hens egg
Said I'd practised with a table leg,
But I have taken Kindom & throne
And that has made all level again
And I can weep at his funeral
I would not have had him die that way
Or die at all. He shoud have been immortal
Our fifty battles had made us frieds
And
~~But~~ there are fifty more to come
For though I have taken Kingdom & throne
leaders
Those that he led will find new ~~weapons~~
~~And some new leader~~
~~New weapons & all begin again~~
~~Mike~~
~~Much blodier~~

New weapons, new leaders will be found
And evrything begin again

Blue-black ink, except for page number in upper right corner in pencil. "Much blodier" above l. 13 intended for insertion between ll. 11–12.

[NLI 8770 (2), 5r; IV. 49–50, 53, 56–58, 60–68]

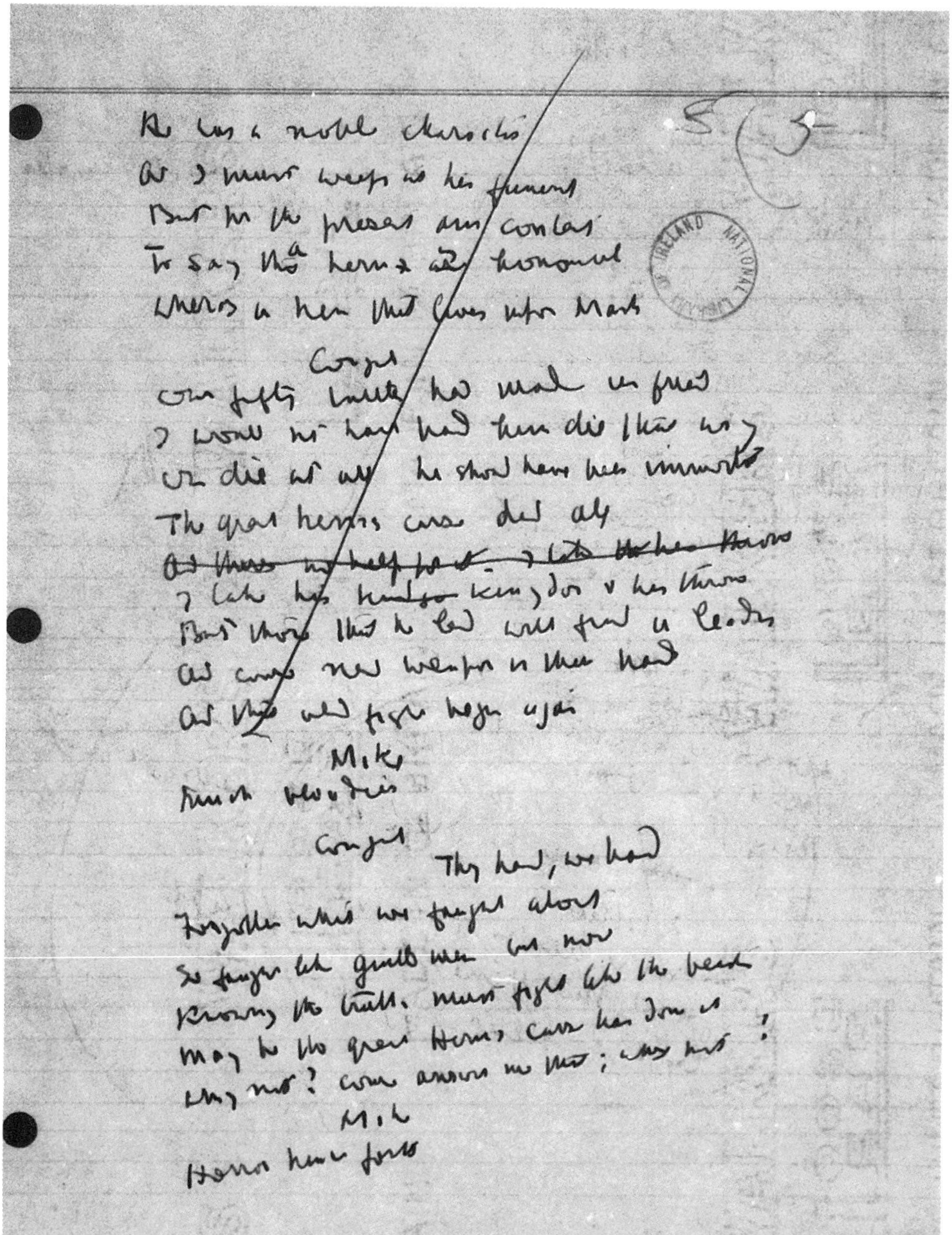

5 5

He was a noble character
And I must weep at his funeral
But for the present am content
                    a   is
To say that hern ~~s are~~ honourble
Wheras a hen that lives upon Mash
            Congal
Our fifty battles had made us friend
I would not have had him die that way
Or die at all he shoud have been immortal
The great herns curse did all
~~And theres no help for it. I take the his throne~~
I take his ~~Kindgom~~ Kingdom & his throne
But those that he led will find a leader
And come new weapons in their hands
And this old fight begin again
            Mike
Much bloodier
            Congal
                        They had, we had
Forgotten what we fought about
So fought like gentle men but now
Knowing the truth, must fight like the beasts
May be the great Herns curse has done it
Why not? Come answer me that; why not?
            Mike
Horror hence forth

Blue-black ink, except page numbers in upper right corner in pencil.

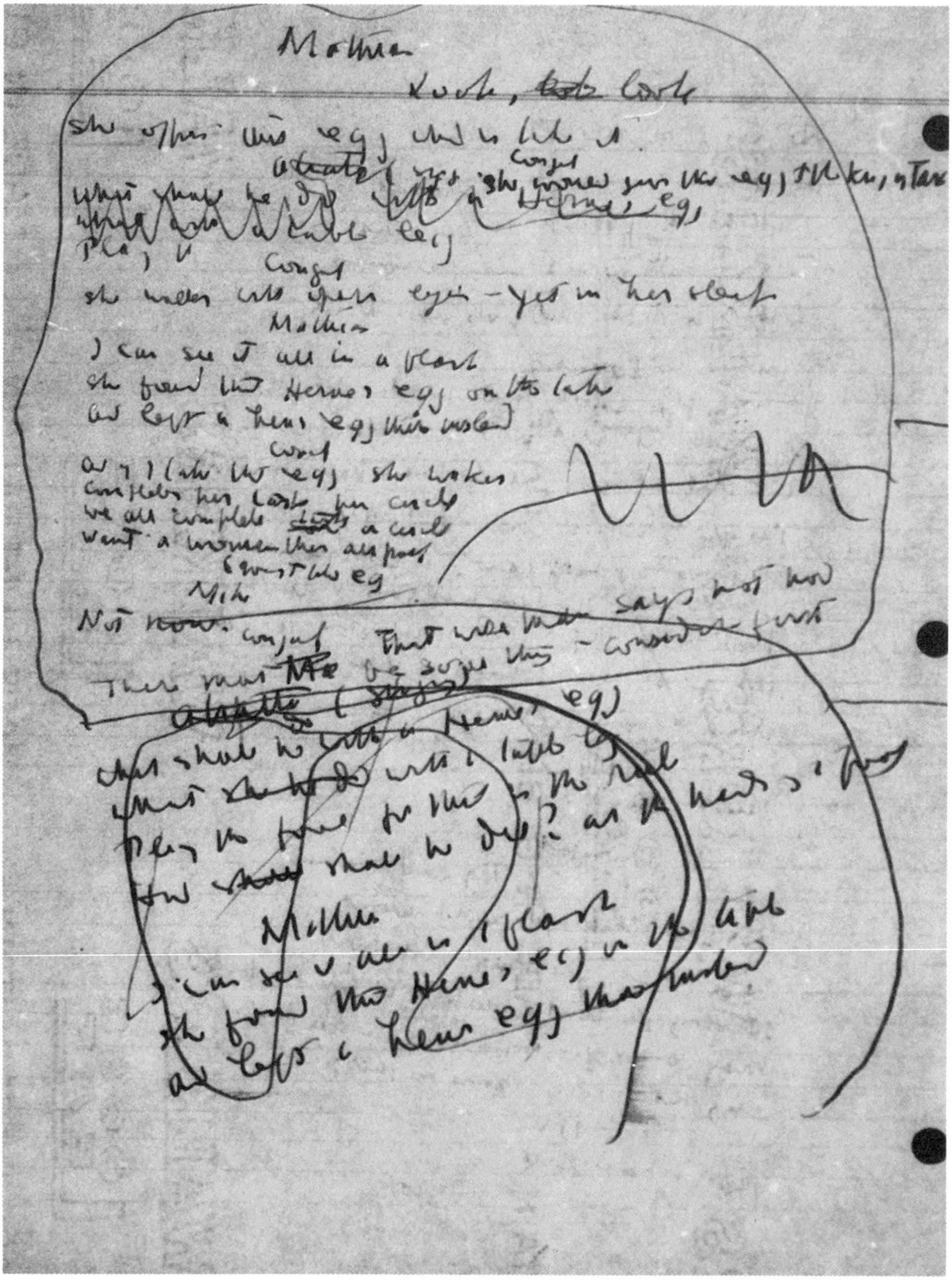

Mathias
Look, ~~lok~~ look
She offers this egg who is take it
Congal
~~Atrata~~ (sings She would give this egg to the King of Tara
What shall he do with a Hernes egg
What with a table leg
Play it
Congal
She walks with open eyes — Yet in her sleep
Mathias
I can see it all in a flash
She found that Herne s egg on the table
And left a hen s egg there instead
Congal
And if I take that egg she wakes
Completes her task her circle
task
We all complete ~~some~~ or circle
Want a woman then all puff
(goes to take eg
Mike
Not now.
Congal That wise man says not now
There must ~~Ma~~ be some thing to consider first
Atratta (Singing)
do
What shall he with a Hernes egg
What ~~sha he do~~ with a table leg
Play the fool for that is the rule
How ~~shall~~ shall he die? at the hands of a fool
Mathis
I can see it all in a flash
She found that Hernes egg on the table
And left a hens egg there insted

Lines 1–12 in light red ink and encircled in dark red. Lines 13–19 in blue-black, with general deletion and insertion of "do" in dark red. Arrow leading from "take eg" is in blue-black, deleted in blue-black. Lines 13–19 and then ll. 1–12 written to replace text between ll. 3–4 on 6r.

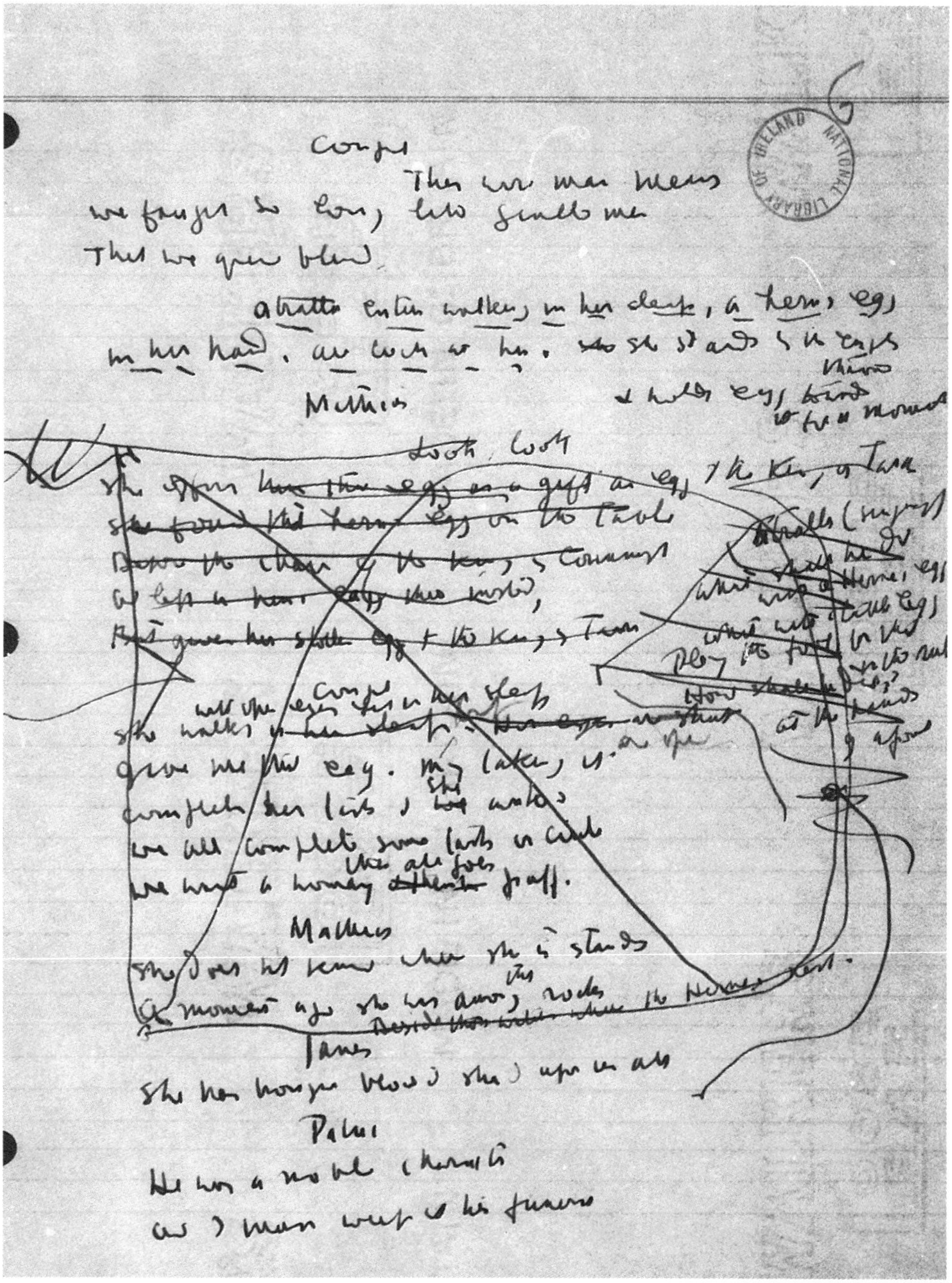

6

Congal

1 This wise man means
2 We fought so long like gentlemen
3 That we grew blind.

Atratta enters walking in her sleep, a herns egg In her hand. All look at her. ~~She~~ She stands by the empty throne & holds egg towards it for a moment

Mathias

4 Look, look
5 She offers him ~~the egg as a gift~~ an egg to ~~the King of Tara~~
6 ~~She found that herns egg on the table~~
7 ~~Before the chair of the King of Con~~naught
8 And ~~left a hens egg there insted,~~
9 ~~But gives her stollen egg to the King of Tara~~

Atratta (Singing)

10 What shall he do with a Herne s egg
11 what with a table legg
12 Play the fool for that is the rule
13 How shall he die?
14 At the hands of afool

Congal

with open eyes yet in her sleep

15 She walks ~~in her sleep. Her eyes are shut~~ ^ *but* *are open*
16 Give me that egg. My taking it
17 Completes her task & ~~we~~ she wakes
18 We all complete some task or circle
19 We want a woman ~~& then b~~ then all goes puff.

Mathias

20 She does nt know where she is standing
21 A moment ago she was among the rocks
22 Beside those waters where the Hernes nest.

James

23 She has brought blood shed upon us all

Patric

24 He was a noble character
25 And I must weep at his funeral

Blue-black ink. Addition to stage directions "She stands . . . moment" and large "X" deletion of ll. 4–9 and 15–22 are in dark red; l. 15 is deleted and revised in dark red, except "are shut" deleted in pencil, and "but" and "are open" added in pencil. Page number is in pencil. Line 22 is in greenish-black ink.

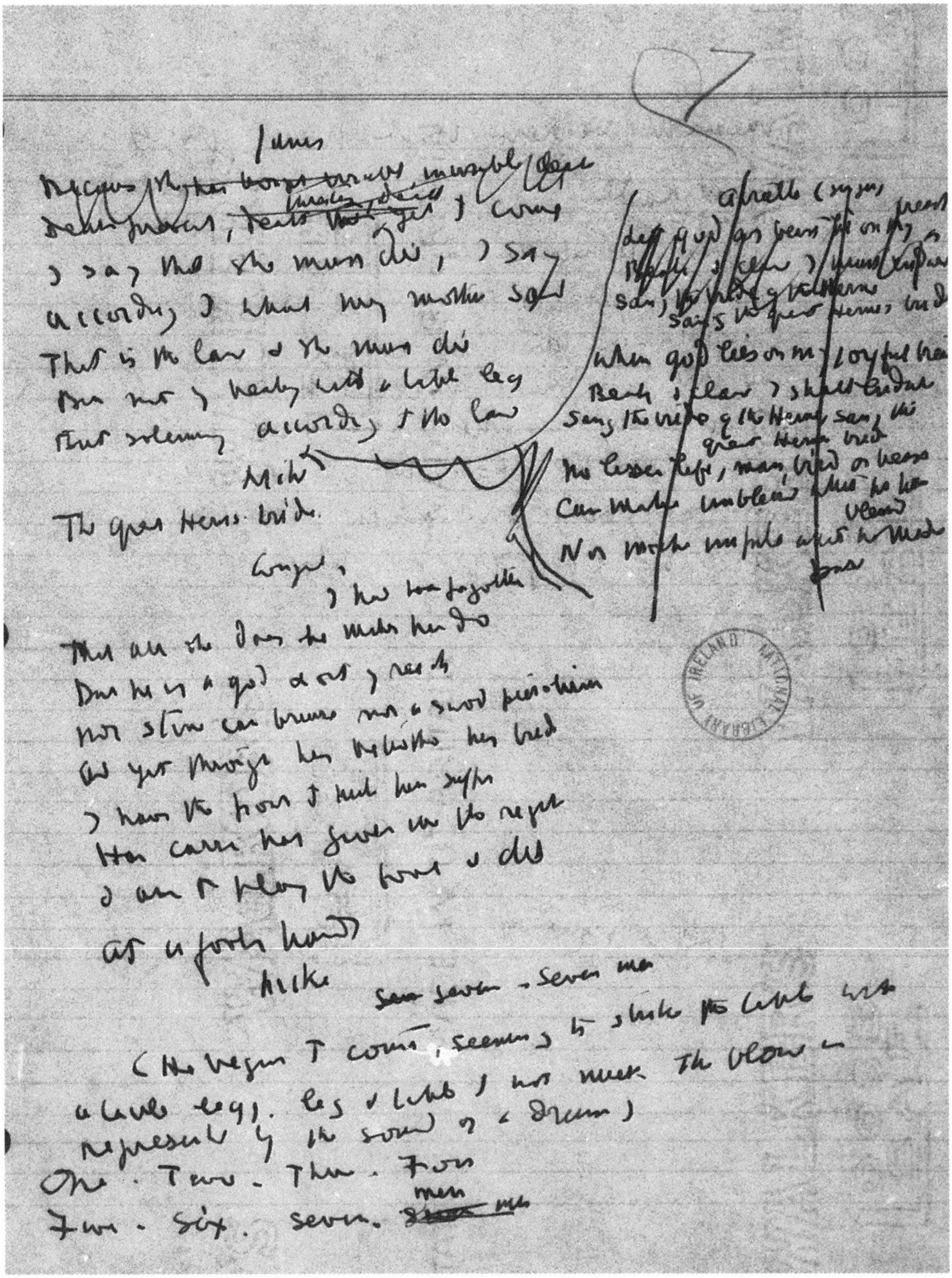

James

I say that she must die, I say
according to what my mother said
That is the law & she must die
But not by beating with a little leg
But solemnly according to the law

Mike

The great Herons bride.

Congal,

I had too forgotten

That all the days he makes her do

But stone can bruise nor a sword
…

I am to play the fool & did

As a fools …

Mike

Seven seven – seven men

(The vegar to come, seeming to strike the table with
a table leg. … The blow is
represented by the sound of a drum)

One . Two . Three . Four
Five . Six . seven . men

[NLI 8770 (2), 7[r]; IV. 88–107, 158–163]

7

James

Because ~~she has brought~~ visable invisable death
threatens, Death
Death present, ~~death that yet~~ to come

I say that she must die, I say
According to what my mother said
That is the law & she must die
But not by beating with a table leg
But solemly according to the law

Atratta (singing)

breast
Let god as beast lie on my ^
Beak & claw I must endure
Sang the bride of the Herne
Sang the great Herne s bride
When god lies on my joyful breast
Beak & claw I shall endure
Sang the bride of the Herne, sang the great Hernes bride
No lesser life, man, bird or beast
Can make unblessed what he has blessed
Nor make impure what he made pure

Mike

The great Herns bride

Congal,

I had ~~ha~~ forgotten
That all she does he makes her do
But he is a god & out of reach
Nor stone can bruise nor a sword pierce him
A yet through his betrothed his brid
I have the powr to make him suffer
His curse has given me the right
I am to play the fool & die
At a fools hand

Mike

~~Seve~~ Seven — Seven men

(He begins to count, seeming to strike the table with a table legg. leg & table do not meet. The blow is represented by the sound of a drum)

One. Two. Three. Four
men
Five. Six. Seven. ~~Seven men~~

Blue-black ink except deletions and additions, ll. 1–2, in dark red. Page number in upper right corner is in pencil.

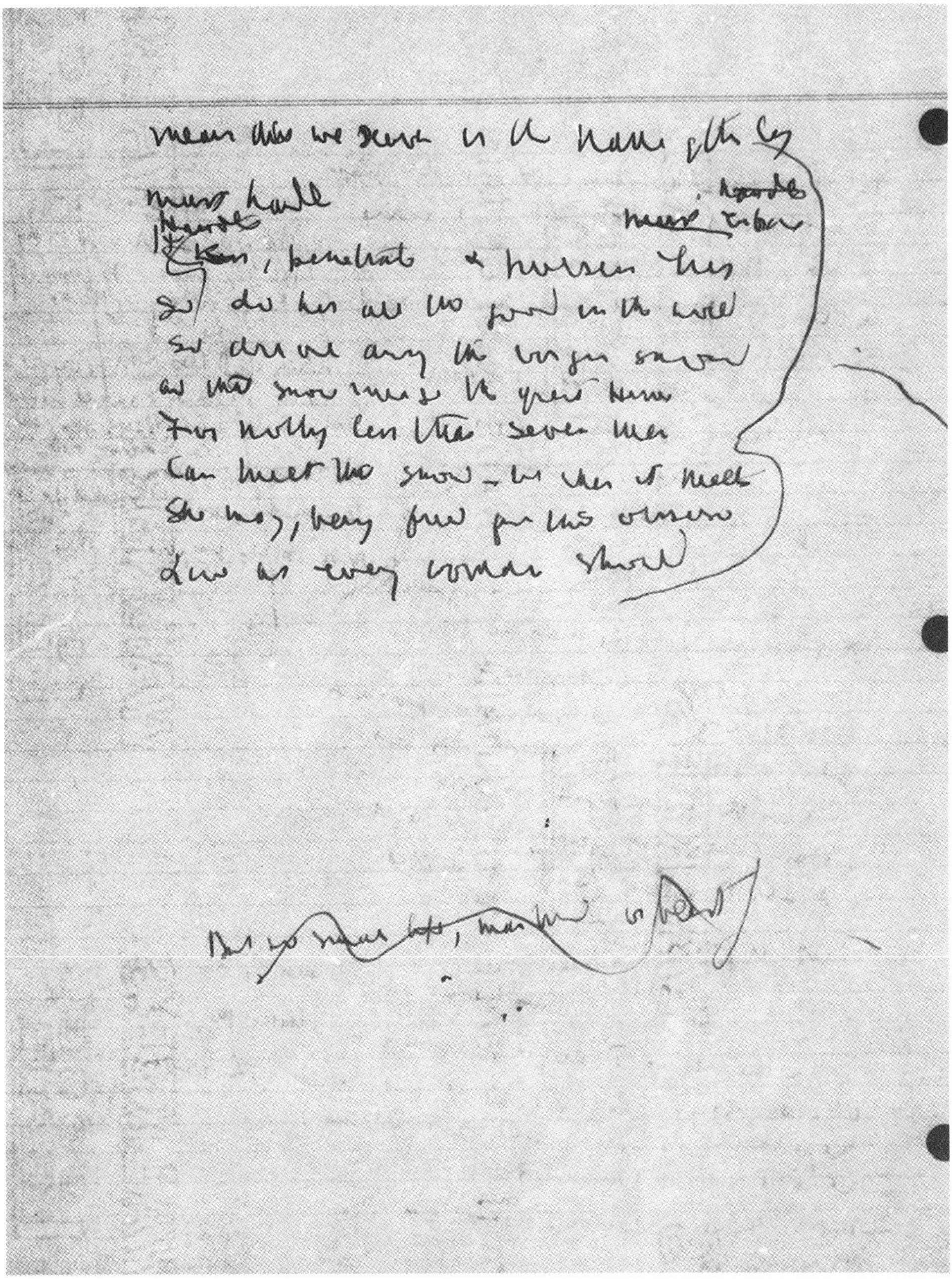
So do her all the good in the world
For nothing less than seven men
Can meet the snow
Live as every woman should

[NLI 8770 (2), 7v; IV. 111–19, 161]

Means that we seven in the name ofthe law

Must handle ~~handle~~
~~Handle~~ ~~must~~ embrace
~~It Kiss~~, penetrate & possess her
So do her all the good in the world
So drive away the virgin snow
And that snow image the great Herne
For nothing less than seven men
Can melt that snow — but when it melts
She may, being freed from this obsession
Live as every woman should

~~But no smal life, man bird or beast~~

Dark red ink, except l. 1 and "must handle" (above l. 2) in blue-black. Lines 1–9 replace ll. 5–20 on 8r.

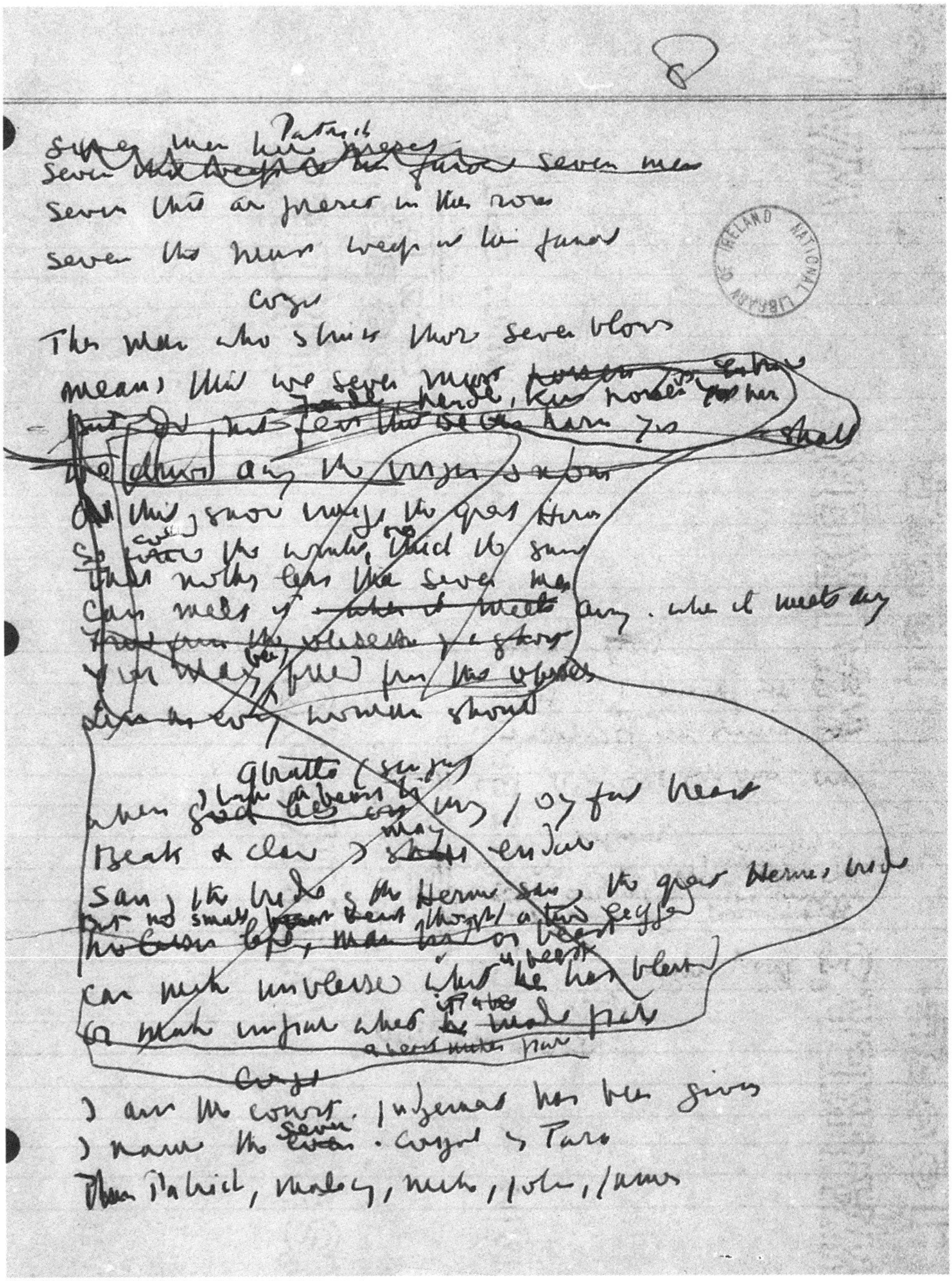
8

[illegible]
Seven that are present in the room
Seven that must weep at his funeral
Congal
This man who strikes those seven blows
Means that we seven must [illegible]
[illegible]
[illegible]
[illegible]
[illegible]
[illegible]
[illegible]
[illegible]
[illegible]
[illegible]
Attracta (sings)
[illegible]
[illegible]
[illegible]
[illegible]
[illegible]
[illegible]
[illegible]
Congal
I am the court. Judgement has been given
I name the seven. Congal of Tara
Then Patrick, Malachi, Mike, John, James

[NLI 8770 (2), 8^r; IV. 108–19, 158–63, 120–22]

8

Patrick
Seven men here present
Seven that ~~weep at his funeral seven men~~
Seven that are present in this room
Seven that must weep at his funeral
Congal
This man who struck those seven blows
Means that we seven must ~~possess, embrace~~
s
Fondle, handle, Kiss posses ~~you~~ her
But do not fear that we can harm you shall
We drive away the virgin snow
And that snow image the Great Hern
cold so
So ~~fierce~~ the winter, thick the snow
That nothing less than seven men
Can melt it ~~& when it melts~~ away. when it melts away
Freed from the obsessions of a ghost
bee
You may ^ freed from that obssesn
Live as evry woman should
Atratta (Singing
I take a beast to
When ~~god lies on~~ my j oyful breast
may
Beak & claw I ~~shall~~ endure
Sang the bride of the Herne sang the great Hernes bride
But no small ~~beest~~ beast though a two legged
~~No lesser life, man bird or~~ beast
a beast
Can make unblessed what ~~he~~ has blessed
~~it a bea~~
Or make impure what ~~he made pure~~
a beast makes pure
Congal
I am the court. Judgement has been given
Seven
I name the ~~even~~. Congal of Tara
~~Then~~ Patrick, Malacy, Mike, John, James

In blue-black except "her", above l. 5, horizontal deletion above l. 1, and deletion lines through center section in dark red; arrow from 7^v in dark red; and "a beast makes pure" and "a bea", below and above l. 20, added in red. Page number in upper right corner in pencil.

[NLI 8770 (2), 8v; IV. 169, 133–38]

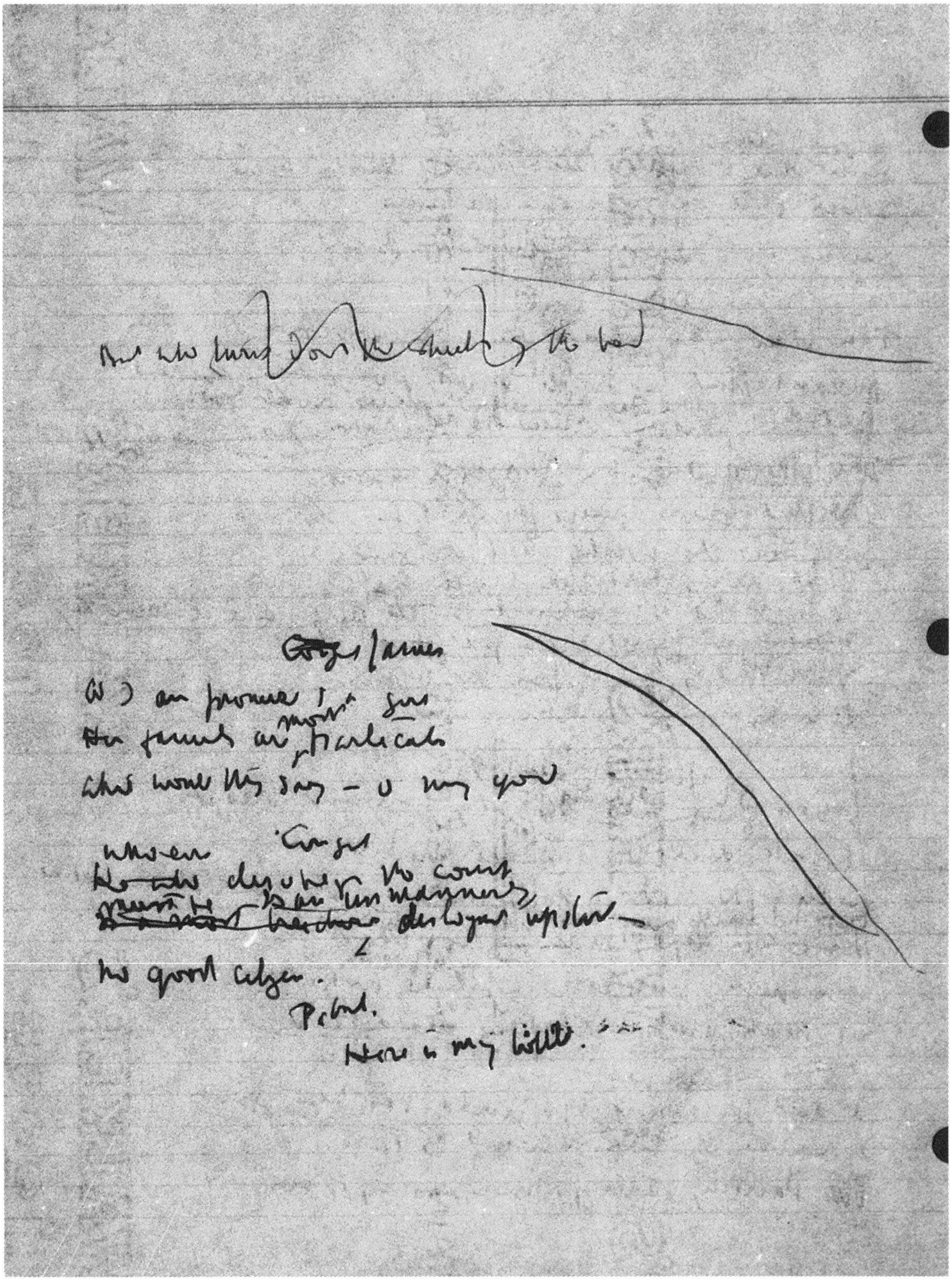

[NLI 8770 (2), 8^{v}; IV. 169, 133–38]

~~But who turns down the sheets of the bed~~

~~Congal~~ James
And I am promised to a girl
most
Her family are ^ particular
What would they say — O my god

Congal
Whoever
~~He who~~ disobeys the court
~~must~~ be Is an unmannerly,
~~Is a most treacherous~~ ^ disloyal upstart —
No good citizen.

Patrik.
Here is my bottle.

Blue-black ink, except l. 1 and top arrow leading to 9^{r} in dark red. Arrow from ll. 2–7 interpolates them at l. 17 on 9^{r}.

[NLI 8770 (2), 9r; IV. 123, 164–9, 124–31, 136–9]

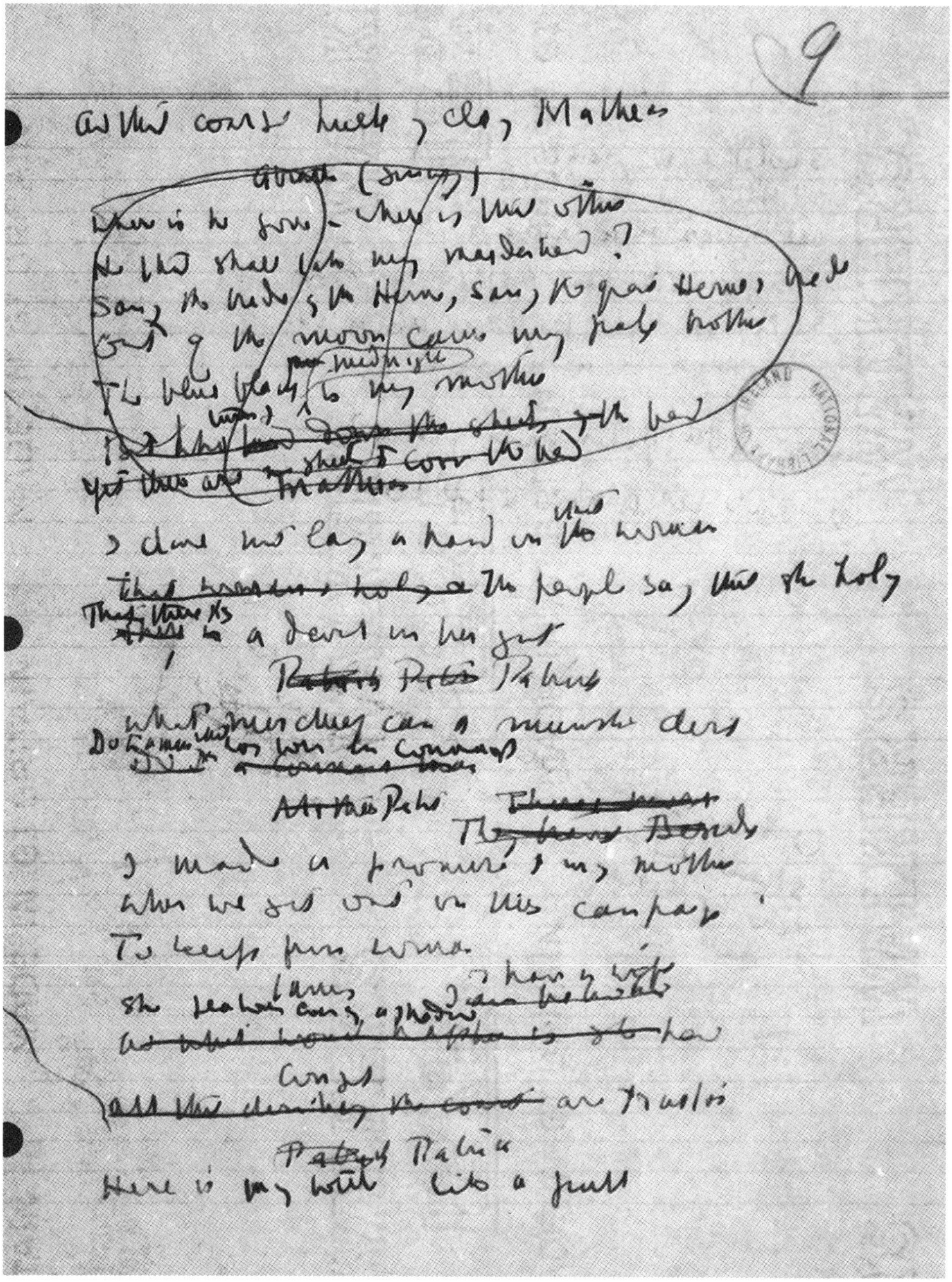

9

1 And that coarse hulk of clay Mathias

Atratta (Singing)
2 Where is he gone — where is that other
3 He that shall take my maidenhead?
4 Sang the bride of the Herne, Sang the great Herne s bride
5 Out of the moon came my pale brother
~~min~~ midnight
6 The blue black^ is my mother
turns
~~But who turnd down the sheets of the~~ bed
7 ~~Yet there are no sheets to cover~~ the bed
Mathias
that
8 I dare not lay a hand on ~~the~~ woman
T
~~That womans holy &~~ t}he people say that she holy
That there is
9 ~~There is~~ a devil in her gut
~~Patrick~~ ~~Peter~~ Patrick
10 What mischief can a Munster devil
that
11 Do to a man^was born in Connagt
~~Do to a Connact man~~
~~Mathes~~ Peter ~~Theres munst~~
~~They have Besides~~
12 I made a promise to my mother
13 When we set out on this campaign
14 To keep from woman
James I have a wife
~~I am betrothed~~
15 She jealous even of a shadow
16 ~~And what would happen if she herd~~
Congal
17 ~~All that disobey the court~~ are traitors
~~Patrick~~ Patrick
18 Here is my bottle take a pull

Blue-black ink, except deletions ll. 2–7 in red ink; "midnight", l. 6, added in greenish-black ink; l. 7 deleted in red ink; arrow from top of 8v in red ink; page number in upper right corner in pencil.

[NLI 8770 (2), 9ᵛ; IV. 151–56]

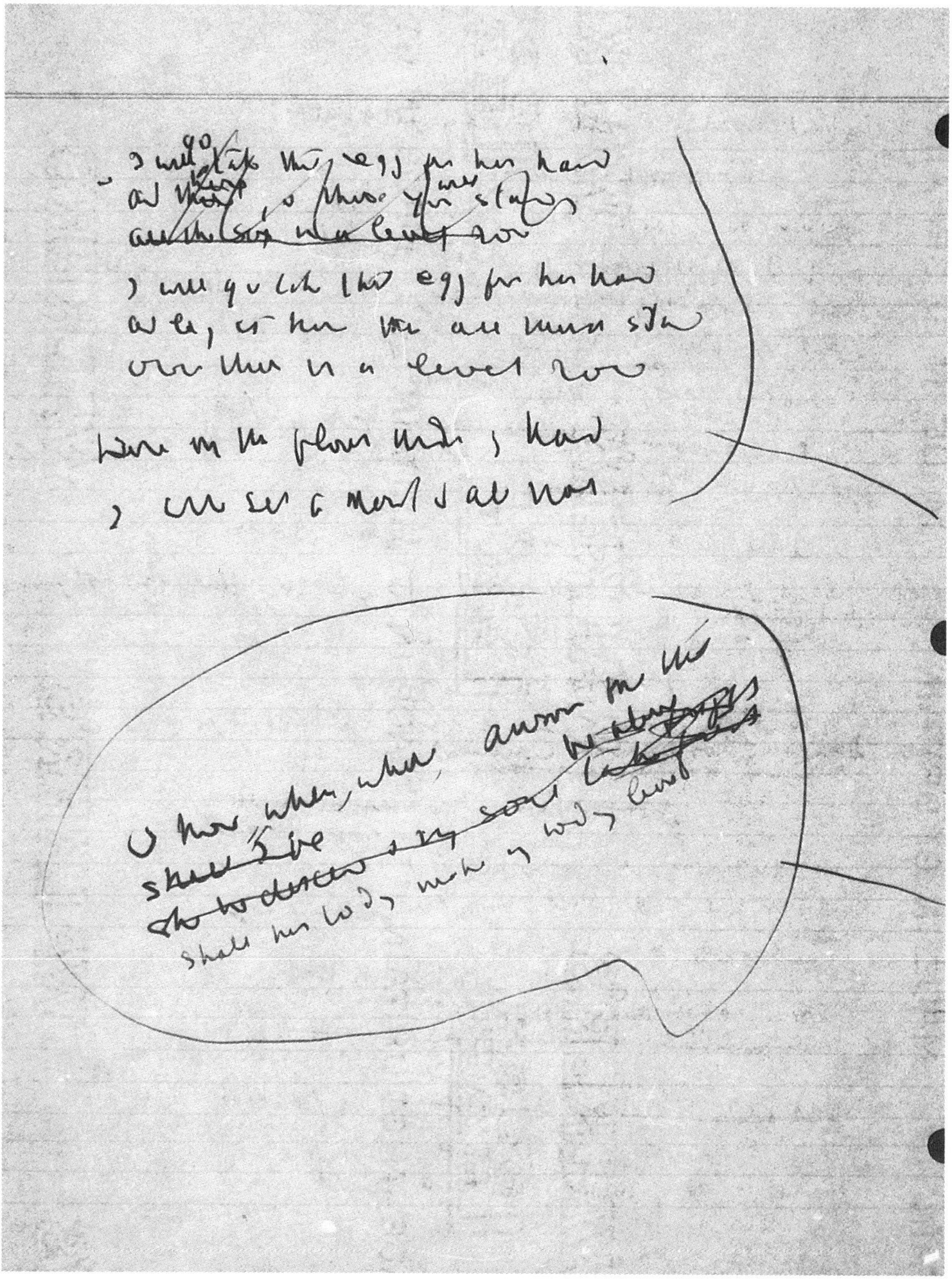

[NLI 8770 (2), 9^{v}; IV. 151–56]

go
I will ^ take that egg from her hand
~~here~~ will
And ~~there,~~ & there you stand
~~All the six in a level row~~

1 I will go take that egg from her hand
2 And lay it here then all must stand
3 Over there in a level row

4 Here on the floor under my hand
5 I will set a mark & all [?throw]

6 O how, when, where answer but this
~~Shall I be~~ ~~be alive~~
~~fright~~
7 ~~Sh he descend & my soul take fright~~
8 Shall his body make my body live

Lines 1–3 in dark red ink, as are deleted lines at top of page; arrow to page 10^{r} in red; ll. 4–7 in blue-black; l. 7 deleted and l. 8 added in red. Line circling ll. 6–8 and leading to 10^{r} is in dark blue-black. Lines 1–5 replace ll. 11–13 on 10^{r}; ll. 6–8 replace ll. 17–23 on10^{r}.

[NLI 8770 (2), 10r; IV. 139–55, 158–75]

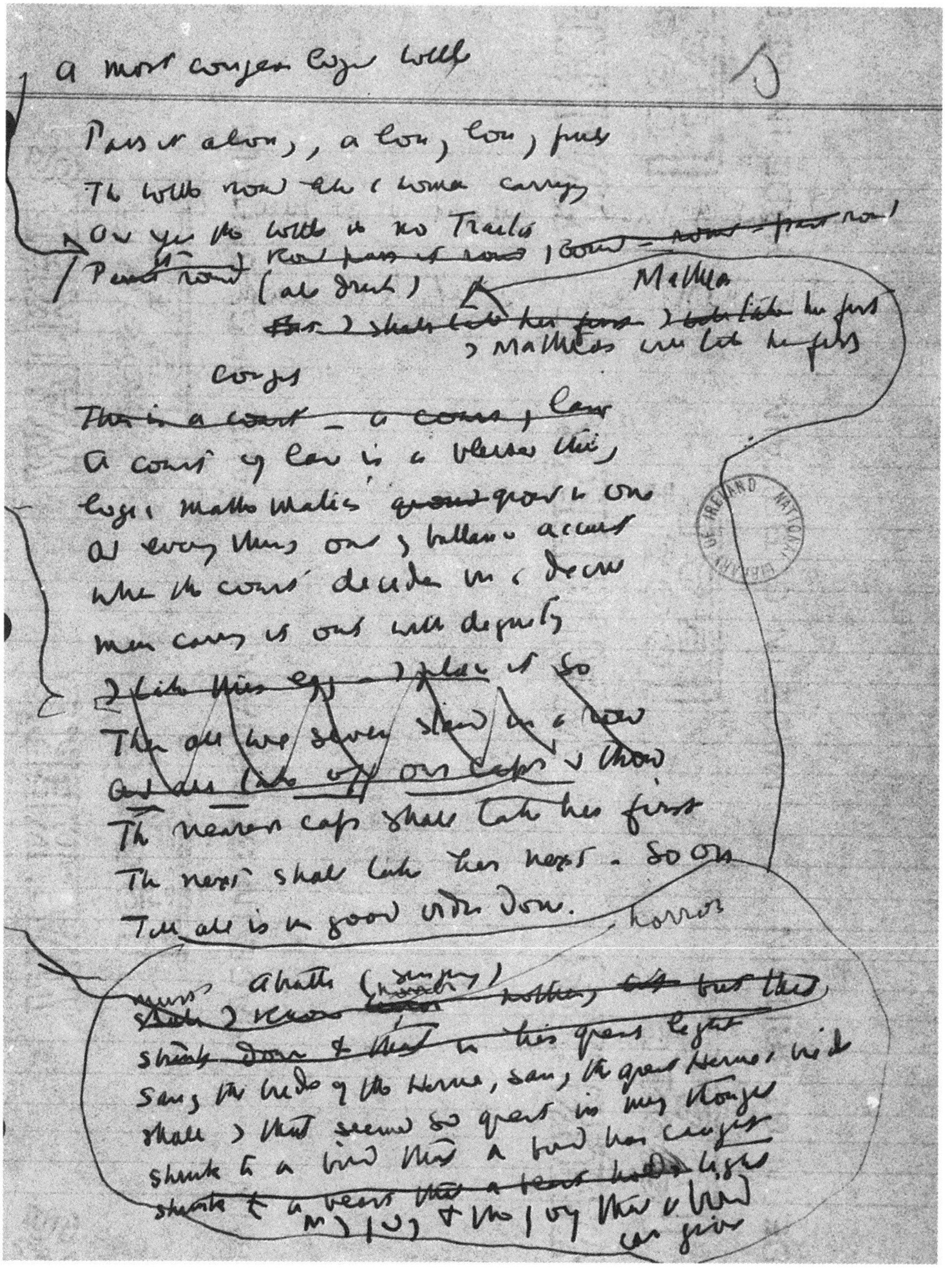

10

1 A most congen loyal bottle

2 Pass it along, a long long pull
3 The bottle round like a woman carrying
4 And yet the bottle is no Traitor
it ~~Round pass it round~~ ~~Round — round — pass round~~
~~Passes round~~
(all drink) Mathias
5 ~~But I shall take her first~~ ~~I will take her first~~
I Mathias will take her first

Congal
~~This is a court — a court of law~~
6 A court of law is a blessed thing
7 logi c mathe matics ~~ground~~ grow in one
8 And every thing out of ballance accurst
9 When the court decides on a decree
10 Men carry it out with dignity
11 ~~I take this egg — I place~~ it so
12 ~~Then all we seven stand in a row~~
13 ~~And all take off our caps~~ & throw
14 The nearest cap shall take her first
15 The next shall take her next — so on
16 Till all is in good order done.
horror
Atratta (Singing)
Must ~~horror~~
17 ~~Shall I know terror nothing but but that~~
18 ~~Struck down to that in his great light~~
19 Sang the bride of the Herne, sang the great Herne s bride
20 Shall I that seemed so great in my thought
21 Shrink to a bird that a bird has caught
22 ~~Shrink to a beast that a beast holds~~ tight
23 My joy to the joy that a bird
can give

Blue-black ink except ll. 5 and 11–13 deleted in red. Page number in upper right corner is in pencil; "horror", above l. 17, and "Must", at the beginning of the line, added in pale ink. Lines 17–23 (Attracta's song) meant to be transposed above l. 5, as indicated by Yeats's encircling and arrow.

[NLI 8770 (2), 11r; IV. 156–69]

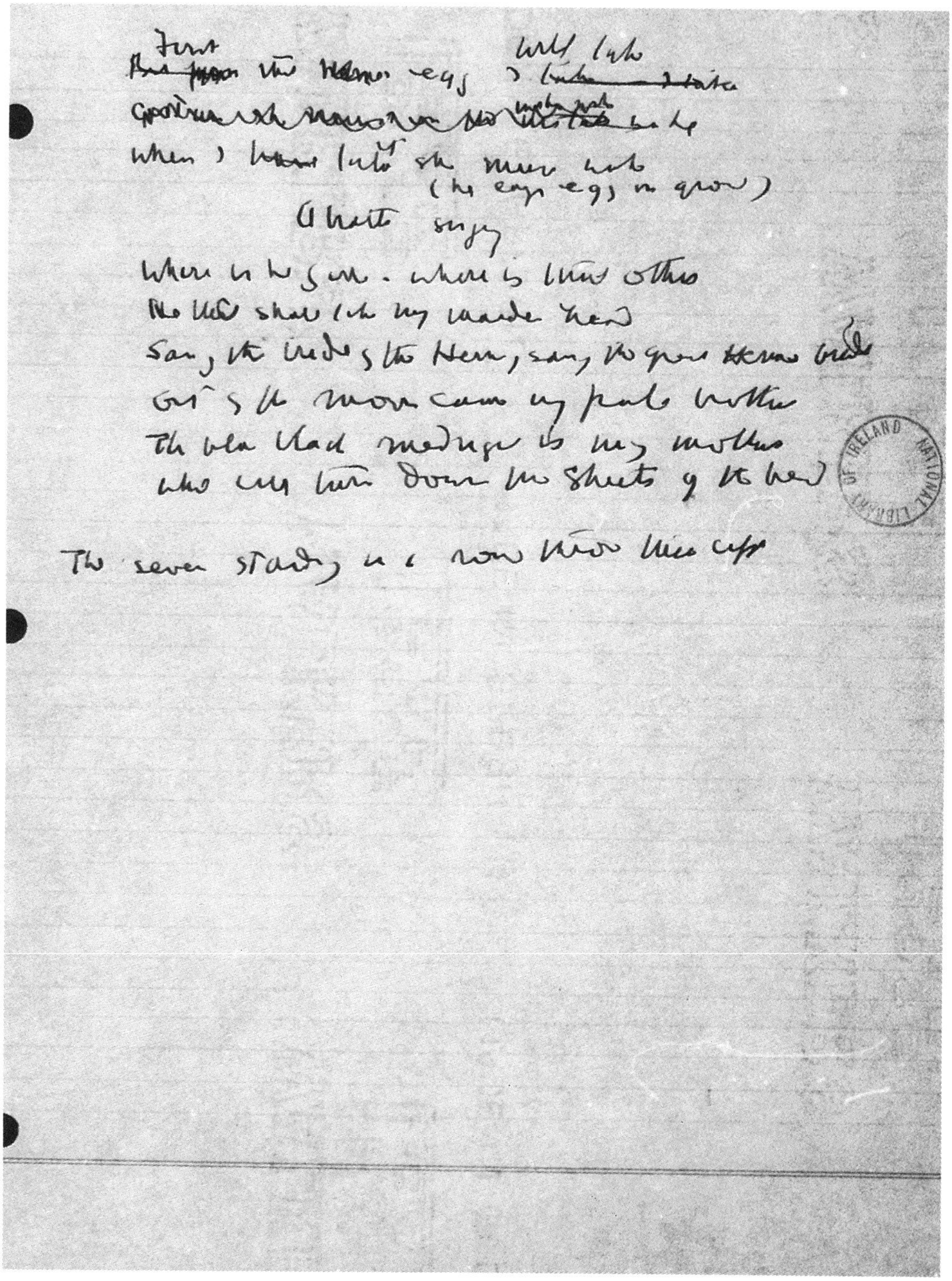
First [illegible] the Heron's egg I [illegible]
[illegible]
When I [illegible] into the [illegible]
(the eggs eggs [illegible])
[illegible] singing
Where is the [illegible] – where is that other
The [illegible] shall [illegible] my maiden head
Say, the bride of the Heron, say, the great Heron bride
Out of the moon came my pale brother
The blue black midnight is my mother
Who will turn down the sheets of the bed
The seven standing in a row [illegible] like cups

[NLI 8770 (2), 11^{r}; IV. 156–69]

First   will take
1 ~~But now~~ this ~~Hernes~~ egg I ~~take — I take~~
make wake
And to us she must come then her take wake
it
2 When I ~~have~~ take she must wake
(he lays egg on ground)
Atratta singing
3 Where is he gone — where is that other
4 He that shall take my maiden head
5 Sang the bride of the Hern, sang the great Herns bride
6 Out of the moon came my pale brother
7 The blue black midnight is my mother
8 Who will turn down the sheets of the bed

9 The seven standing in a row throw their caps

On the verso of 10^{v}, facing, Yeats wrote in blue-black ink:
I need a need a mark & so must tak
The herns egg & let her wake
which revises l. 1, above.

Red ink.

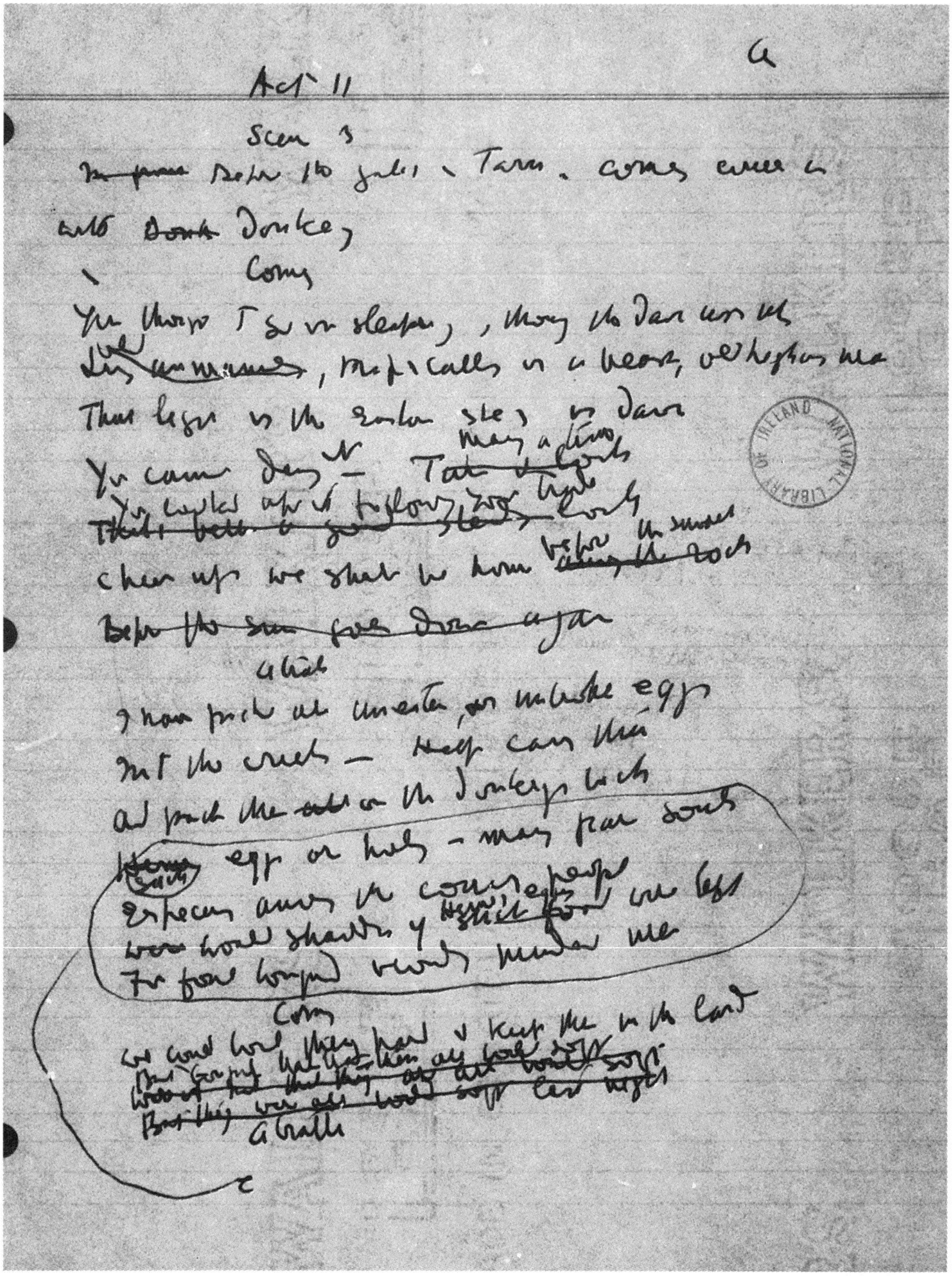

[NLI 8770 (2), 12r; V. 1–15]

a

Act II

Scene 3

~~In front~~ Before the gates of Tara. Corney comes in
with ~~Donk~~ donkey

Corny

1 You thought to go on sleeping, though the dawn was up
~~old~~
2 Lazy ~~unmanely~~, Rapscalln of a beast, old highway ma
3 That light in the Eastern sky is dawn
it Many a time
4 You cannot deny — ~~Turn & look~~
5 You lookd upon it following your trade
~~Thats better a good steady~~ look
before the sunset
6 Cheer up we shall be home ~~among the rock~~
~~Before the sun goes down again~~

Atrata

7 I have packed all uneaten or unbroke eggs
8 Into the creels — Help cary them
9 And pack them ~~all~~ on the donkeys back
10 ~~Herne~~ eggs are holy — many pure souls
Such
11 Especaly among the couny people
Herne s eggs
12 ~~Were~~ Would shudder if ~~such food~~ were left
13 For foul tongued bloody minded men

Corny.

14 We could boil them hard & keep them in the lardr
15 But Congal has had them all boild soft
~~Were it not that they are all boild soft~~
~~But they were all boild soft last night~~

Atratta

Blue-black ink. Lines 10–13 are transposed to bottom of page.

[NLI 8770 (2), 12^v; V. 19, 21–2]

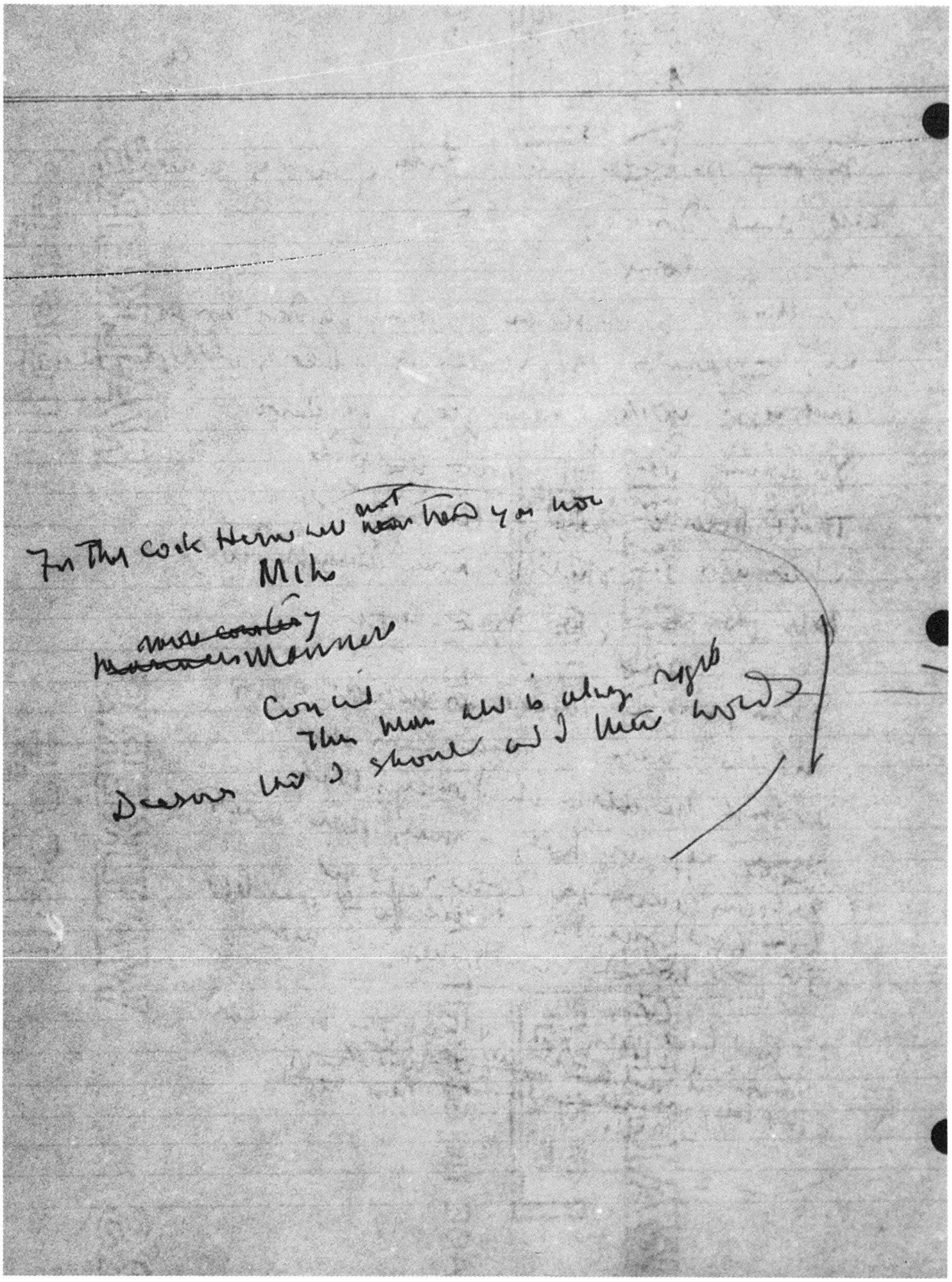

[NLI 8770 (2), 12^{v}; V. 19, 21–2]

not
1 For That cock Herne will ~~never~~ tread you now
Mike
~~more courtesy~~
2 ~~Manners~~ Manners

Congal
This man who is always right
3 Desires that I should add these words

Blue-black ink, except l. 1 in dark red, and second "Manners" in l. 2 in mixed red-black. Arrow interpolates these lines between ll. 6–7 on 13^{r}.

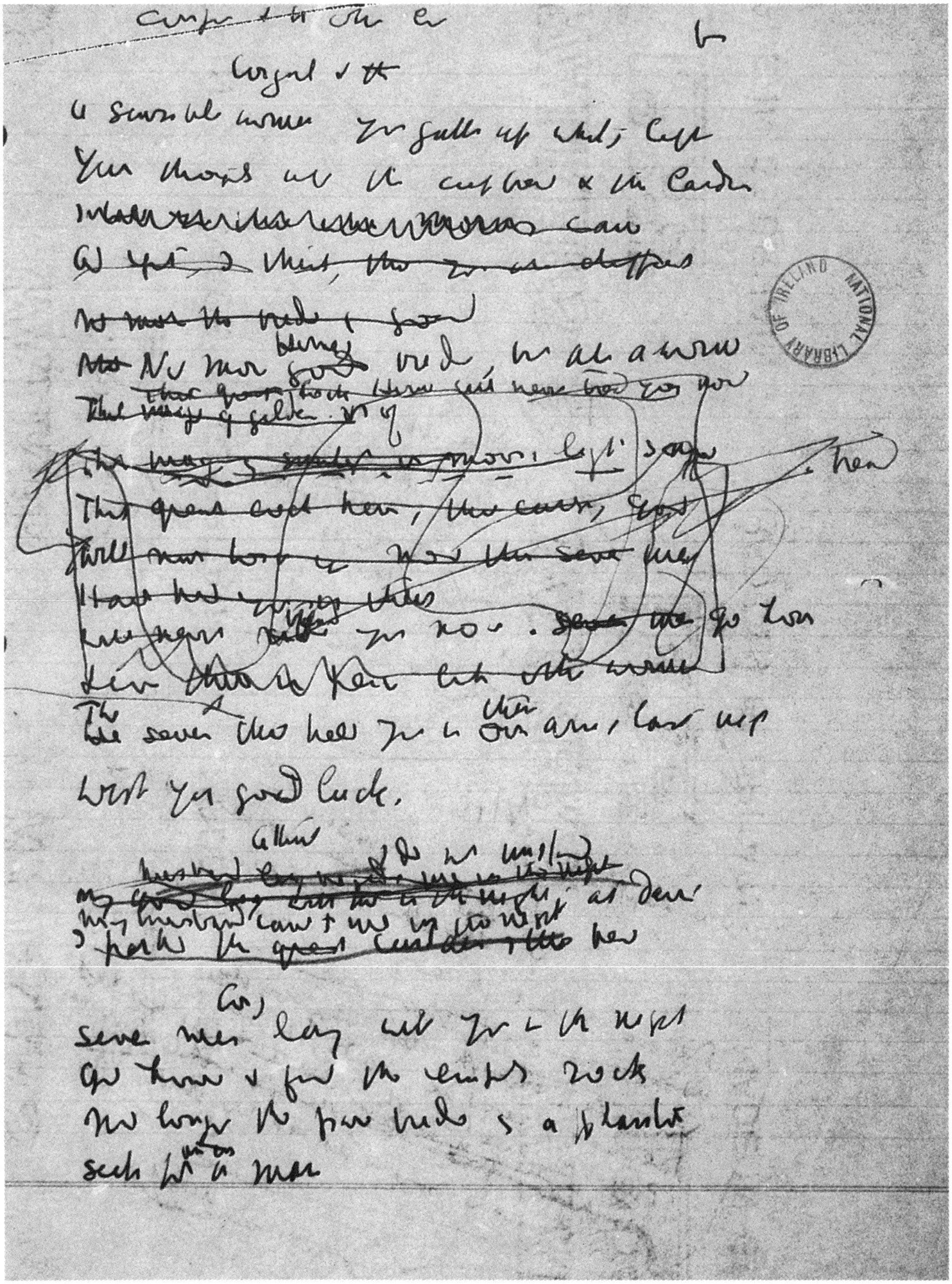

[NLI 8770 (2), 13^{r}; V. 16–28]

Congal & the othrs enr   b

Congal & the

1 A sensible woman   You gather up whats left
2 Your thoughts upon the cupboard & the larder
~~I told you that when morning came~~
~~And Yet, I think, that you are different~~
~~No more the bride of god~~

Hernes

3 ~~Mo~~ No more ~~gods~~ bride, but all a wom
~~That great cock Herne will nevr tred you now~~
~~That image of golden or of~~
~~This image of sunlight or moon~~ light snow
4 ~~That great cock hern, that cursing god~~   tread
~~Will never love y now that seven men~~
~~Have had you in their~~
~~tread~~
5 Will never ~~ride~~ you now. ~~Seven men~~ Go hom
6 Live there in peace lik othr women
The   there
7 ~~We~~ seven that held you in our arms last nigh
8 Wish you good luck.

Attract

I do not understand
~~husband lay beside me in the night~~
~~My god lay with me in the night~~   at dawn
9 My husband came to me in the night
~~I parted the great curtain of his bed~~

Cong

10 Seven men lay with you in the night
11 Go home & find the empty rocks
12 No longer the pure bride of a phantom
~~an un~~
13 Seek for a man

Blue-black ink, except line added below l. 3 and general deletion of ll. 3–6 in red; variants of l. 9 deleted in pencil.

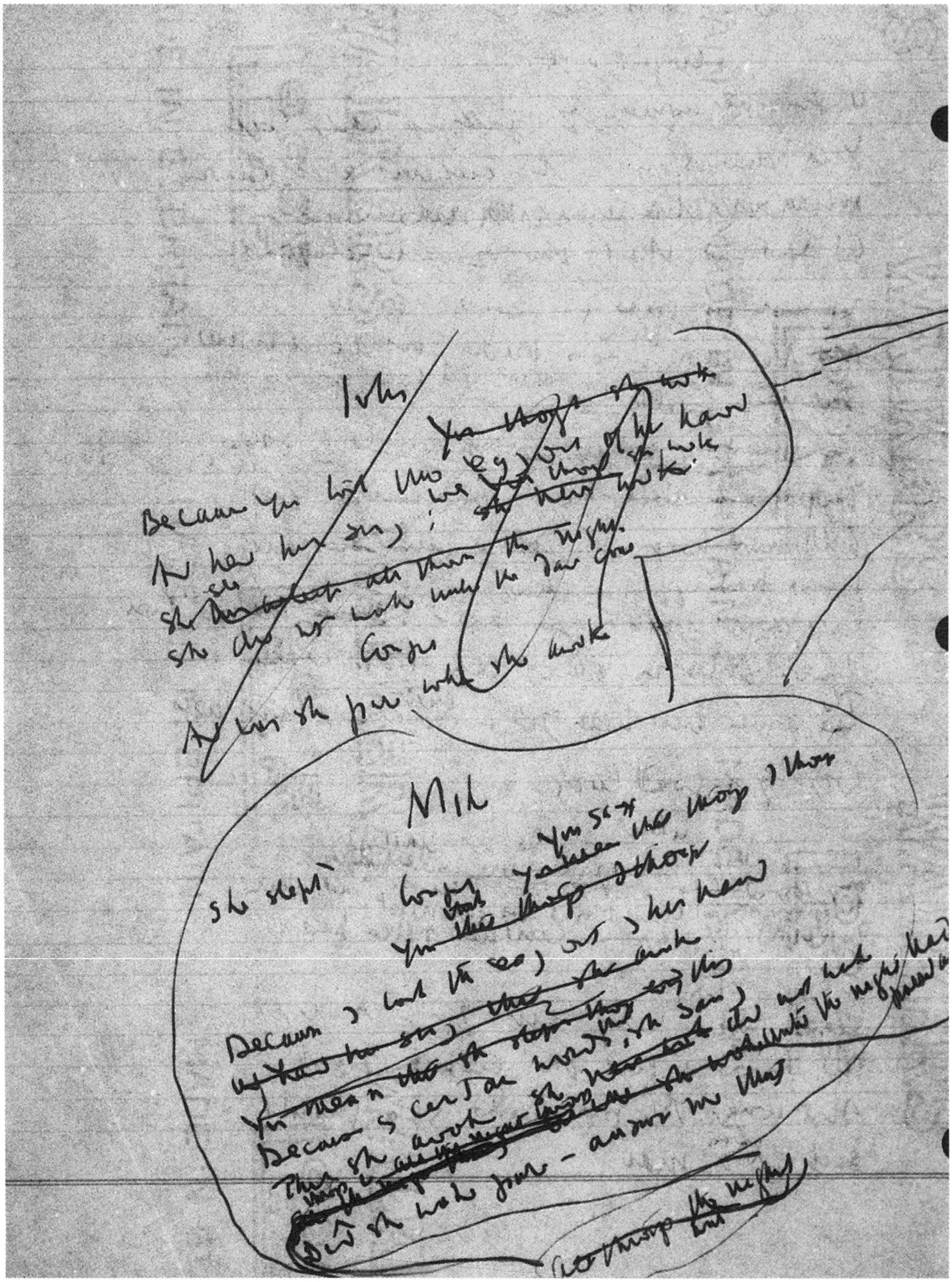

[NLI 8770 (2), 13^{v}; V. 31–6]

John
~~You thought she woke~~
1 Because you took that egg out of her hand
we ~~You~~ thought she woke
2 And herd her song; ~~she nevr woke~~
she
~~She was asleep all thruh the night.~~
3 She did not wake until the dawn came
Congal
4 And was she pure when she awoke

Mike
5 She slept
Congal You say
~~think~~ ~~You mean~~ that though I thoug
~~You that though I thought~~
6 Because I took the egg out of her hand
~~And herd her sing that she awoke~~
~~You mean that sh slept throug evry~~ thing
that
7 Because of certain words, she sang
8 That she awoke — she ~~nevr woke~~ did not wake
through ~~All the night~~ through
~~All ^ the night through but once she woke~~ Until the night had
passed away
9 Did she wake pure — answer me that

~~All through the night~~
~~that~~

Blue-black ink. Lines 1–4 interpolated between ll. 2–3 on 14^{r}, repositioned between ll. 3–4, then deleted and replaced by ll. 5–9.

[NLI 8770 (2), 14r; V. 28–30, 37–46]

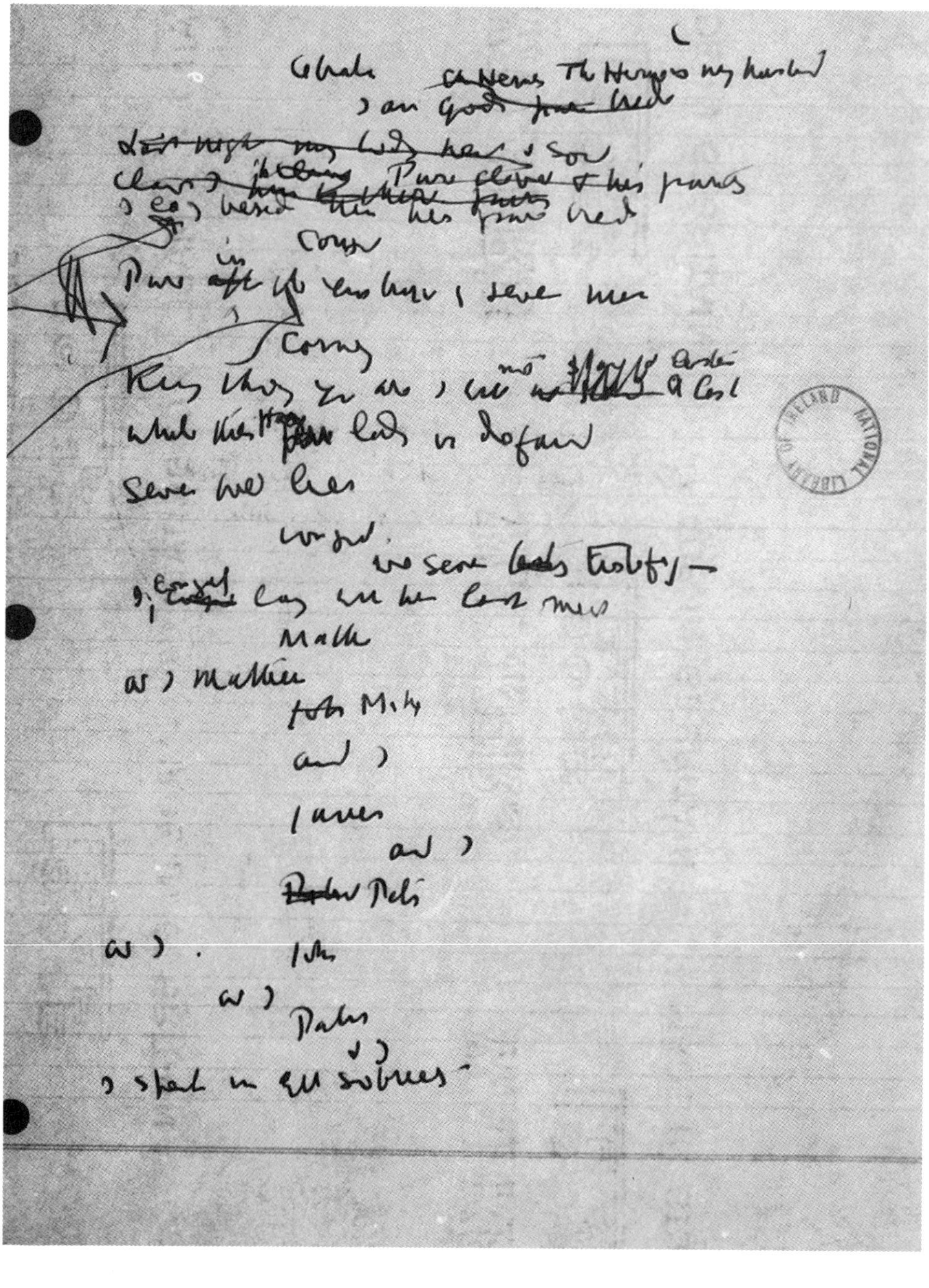

[NLI 8770 (2), 14^{r}; V. 28–30, 37–46]

c

Atrata

1 ~~the Hernes~~ The Herne is my husband

~~I am Gods pure bride~~

~~Last night my body heart & soul~~

~~I clung~~ ~~Pure clove to his purity~~

~~Clove to him in there purity~~

2 I lay beside him his pure bride

Congal

in

3 Pure ~~after~~ the embraces of seven men

Corney

not ~~stand &~~ listen

4 King thog you are I will ~~nt stand~~ & list

~~pure~~

5 While this ~~pure~~ lady is defamd

6 Seven told lies

Congal

We seven ~~testy~~ testify —

Congal

7 I ^ ~~Congal~~ lay with her last *night*

Mathi

8 And I Mathias

~~Joh~~ Mike

And I

James

And I

~~Peter~~ Petr

9 And I.

John

And I

Patrc

& I

10 I speak in all sobriety

Blue-black ink, except deletions of three lines between ll. 1 and 2 beginning "Last night . . ." and (2d half) "Pure . . ." and "Clove to him . . ." in red-black ink, as are l. 2 and revision of l. 3.

[NLI 8770 (2), 14v; V. 60–64, 49–50]

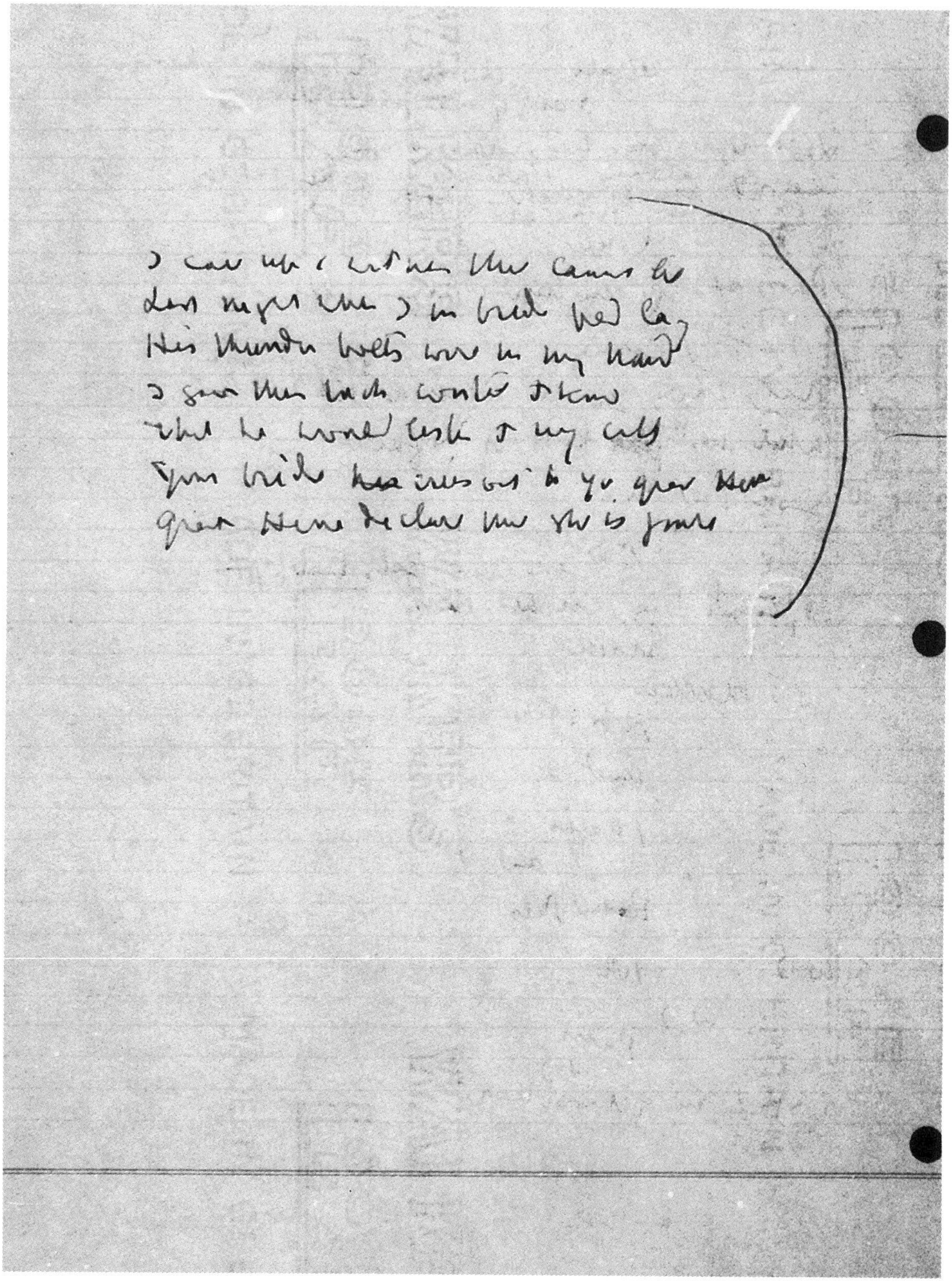

[NLI 8770 (2), 14^{v}; V. 60–64, 49–50]

I call up a witness that cannot lie
Last night when I in bride bed lay
His thunder bolts were in my hand
I gave them back content to know
That he would listn to my call
Your bride ~~has~~ cries out to you great Hern
Great Herne declare that she is pure

Dark red ink. These lines replace ll. 2–11 on 15^{r}.

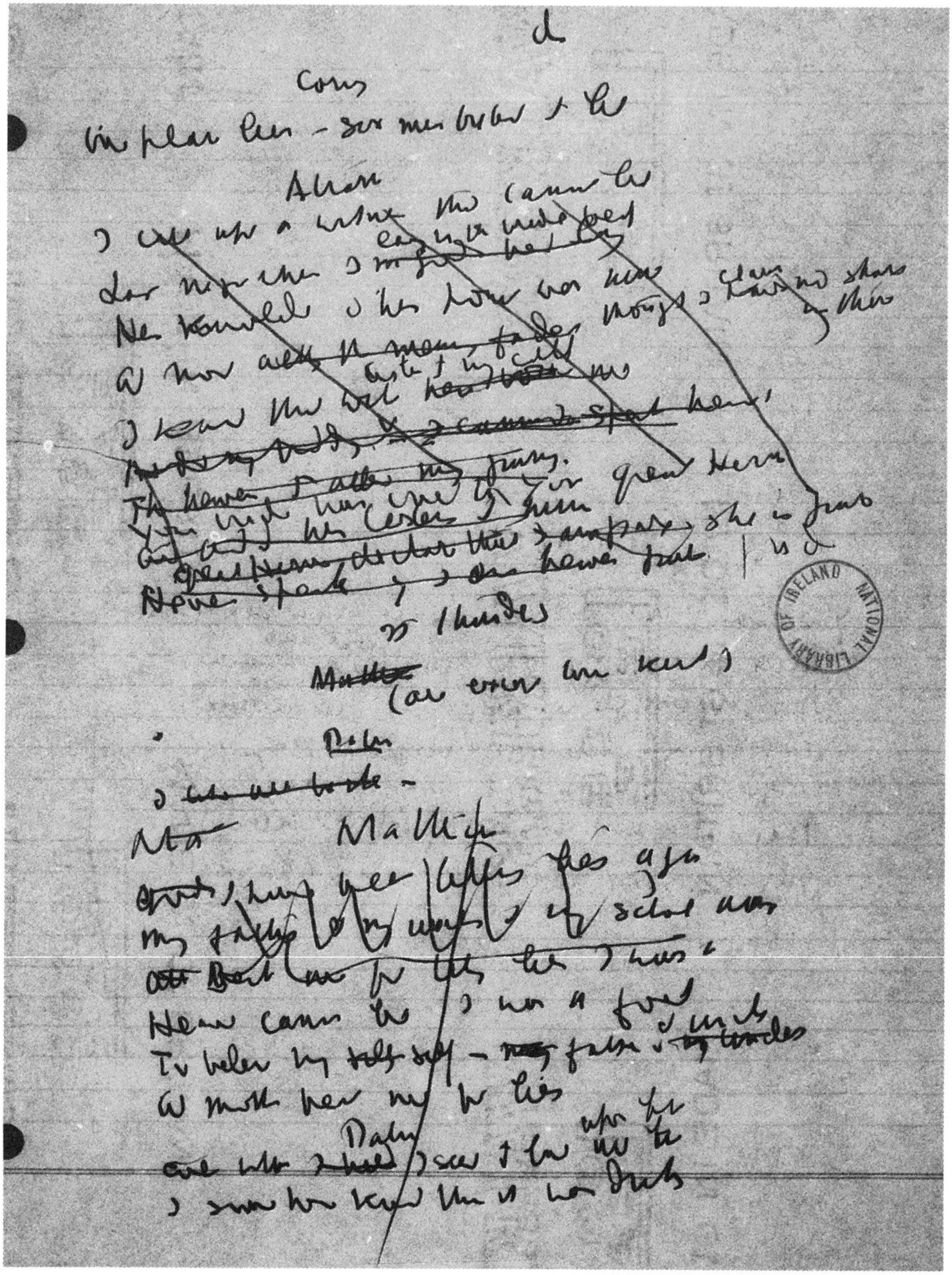

d
Corny
1 One plain lier — Six men bribed to lie
Atract
2 I call upon a witnes that cannot lie
lay in the bride bed
3 Last night when I ~~in gods bed lay~~
4 His knowlede & his powr wer mine
claim
5 And now ~~althog the memry fades~~ though I ~~have~~ no share
listen to my call   in these
6 I know that will ~~hear both me~~
7 ~~And do my bidding — I command speak heavens~~
8 ~~The heaven to attest my puriy~~.
9 ~~Your bride has cried to you.~~ Great Hern
10 ~~And And I will listen to him~~
11 ~~Great Herne declare that I am pure~~ she is pure
~~Heven speak if I am hernes~~ pure brid   [?]
It thunders
~~Mathias~~
(all except Con Kneel)
~~Peter~~
~~I take all back~~ —
~~Ma~~ Mathias
~~God~~ I have been telling lies again
12 My father & my uncles & my schol mas
~~All Beat me for teling lies I was a~~
13 Heave cannt lie I was a fool
& uncle
14 To beleve my ~~self~~ self — ~~my~~ father ~~& my uncles~~
15 And mothr beat me for lies
Patri   upon her
16 even when ~~I held~~ I seemd to lie on her
17 I some how knew tha it was drink

Blue-black ink, except for deletion of ll. 2–11, all of l. 9, revision of l. 11, and arrow from 14v, all in dark red.

[NLI 8770 (2), 15v; V. 60–9]

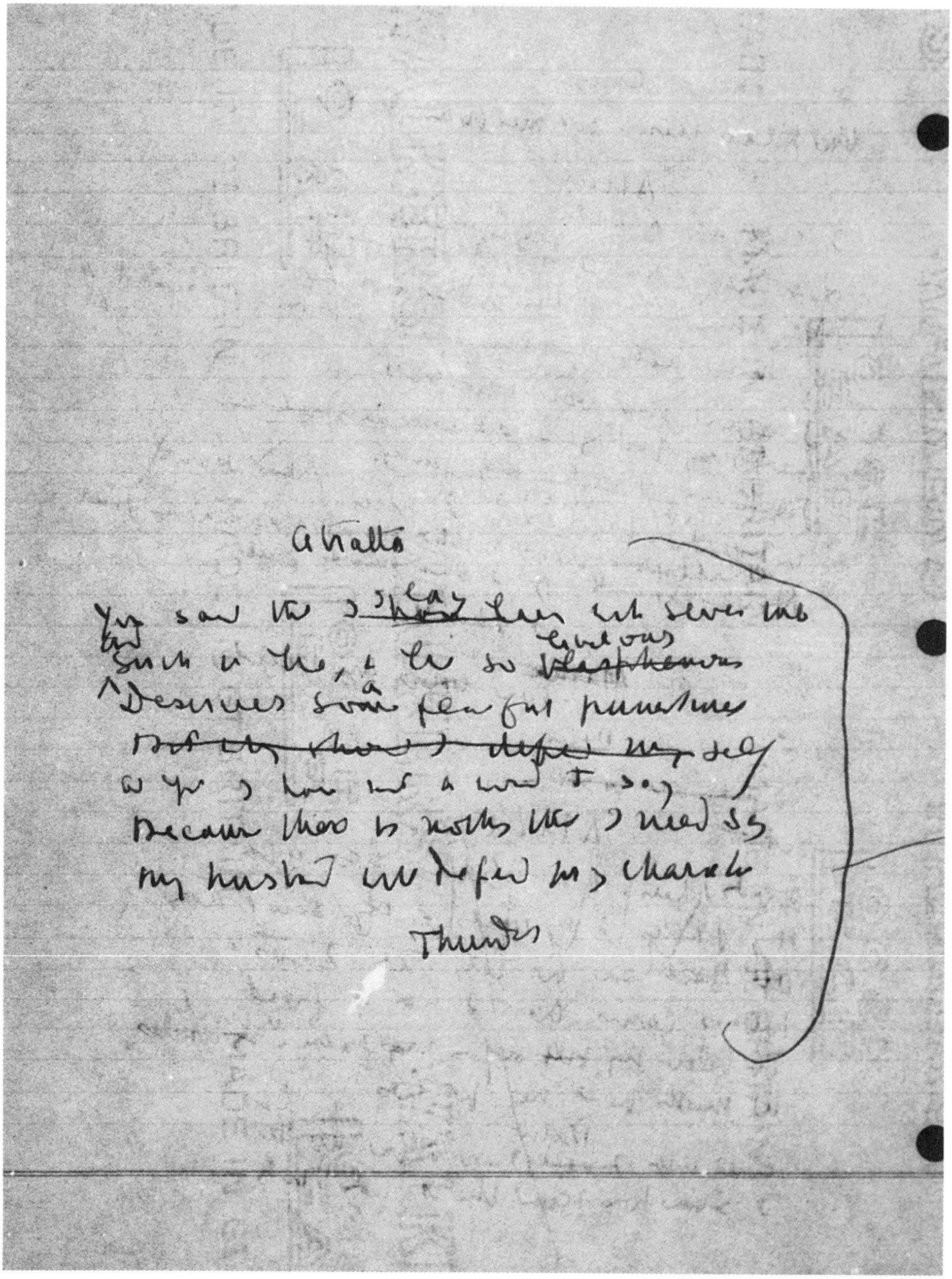

Attracta

You saw the s clay [illegible] with seven men
Such a lie, a lie so libelous blasphemous
Deserves some a fearful punishment
But why should I defend my self
As for I have not a word to say
Because there is nothing that I need say
My husband will defend my character

Thunder

[NLI 8770 (2), 15^{v}; V. 60–9]

Atratta

I lay
You said that ~~I have lain~~ with seven men
And libelous
^ Such a lie, a lie so ~~blasphemous~~
a
Deserves ~~some~~ fearful punishment
~~But why shoud I defend myself~~
And yet I have not a word to say
Because there is nothing that I need say
My husband will defend my character
Thunder

Dark red ink, except "Atratta" in light red. These lines replace ll. 7–17 on 16^{r}.

[NLI 8770 (2), 16^{r}; V. 54–69]

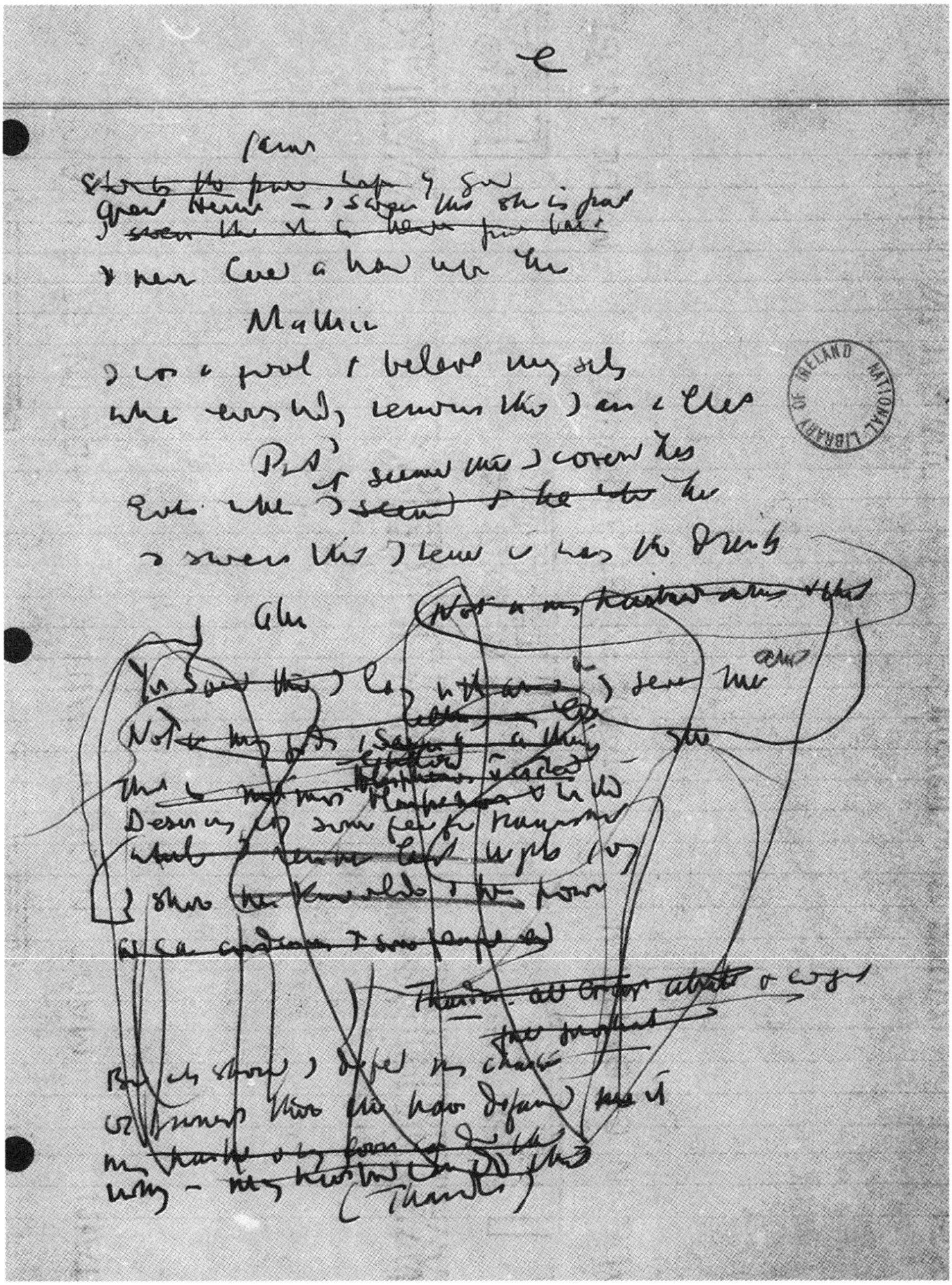

[NLI 8770 (2), 16^{r}; V. 54–69]

e

James
~~She is the pure wife~~ of god
Great Herne — I swear that she is pure
1 I ~~swear that she is heavens pure bride~~
2 I never laid a hand upon her
Mathias
3 I was a fool to believe my self
4 When everybody knows that I am a lier
Pat
it seemed that I covered her
5 Even when ~~I seemed to lie upon~~ her
6 I swear that I knew it was the drink
Attr ~~Not in my husbands arms & that~~
a *arms*
7 ~~You said that I~~ lay in ~~the arms~~ of seven men
telling a lie
8 ~~Not in my gods~~, ~~Saying a thing~~ She
libellous —
9 ~~That is mt most blasphemous & wickd~~
~~blasphemous~~ & wickd
10 Deserving of some fearful punishment
11 ~~While I rem ber last nights~~ joy
12 ~~I share his knowelde & his powr~~
13 ~~And can condemn to some fearful end~~
~~Thunder. All except Atratt~~ & Congal
~~fall prostrate~~
14 But why shoud I defend my chastity
15 Or punish those that have defamed ~~me~~ it
16 ~~My husband & my lover can do that~~
17 Why — ~~my husband can do that~~
(Thunder)

Blue-black ink, except revisions in ll. 6–17 in darker ink, and deletion strokes across ll. 7–17 in dark and light red; "the arms", l. 7, and ll. 11–12 deleted in pencil.

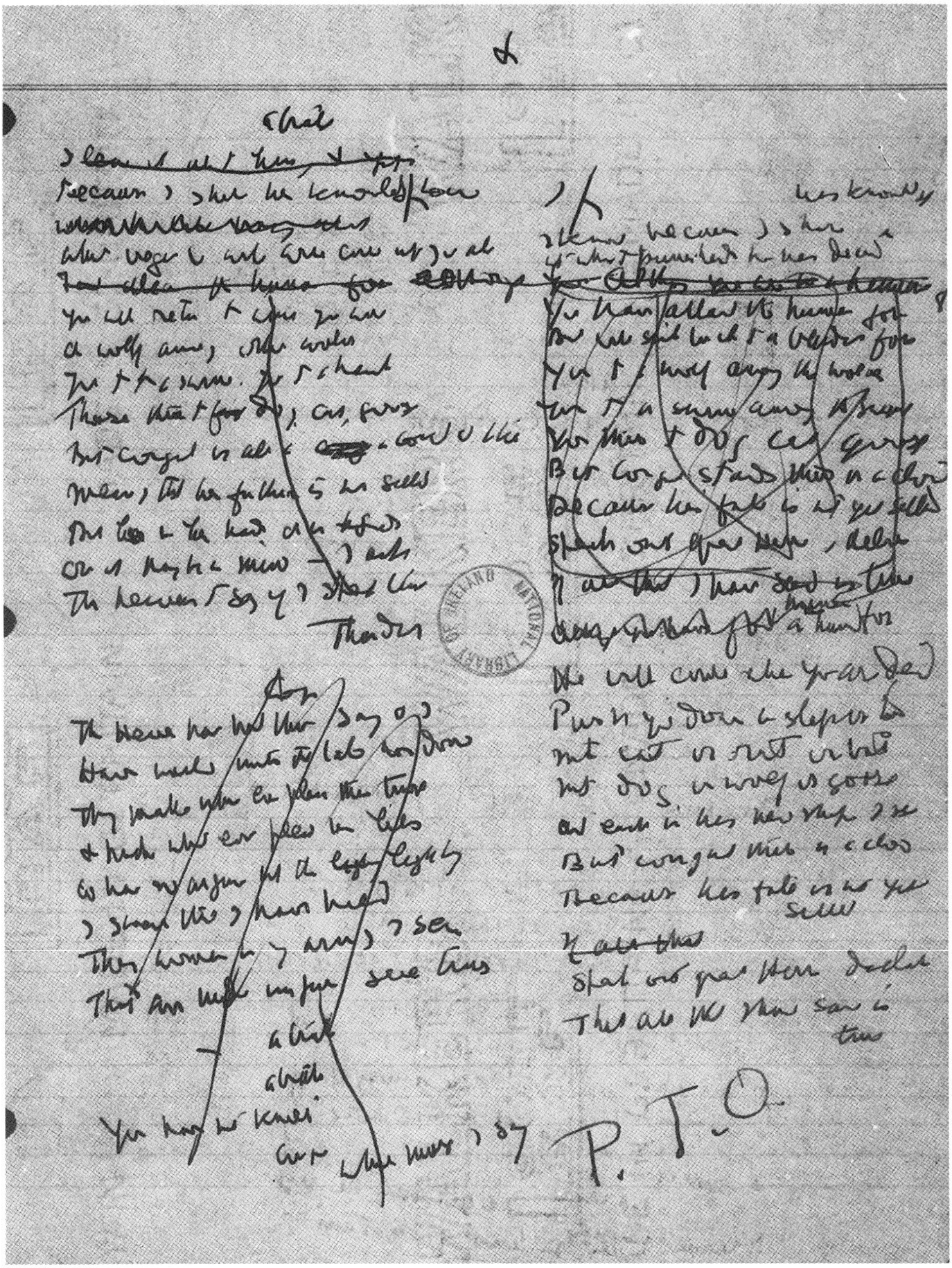

[NLI 8770 (2), 17r; V. 70–80, 82–7]

Atratt
I ~~leave it all to him, & yet~~
1 Because I share his knowledg ^know
~~what he will bring about~~
2 What began & what will come upon you all
~~For altho the human form~~ ~~Although~~
3 You will return to what you were
4 A wolf among other wolves
5 You to be a swine. You to a hawk
6 These three to ~~fox~~ dog, cat, goose
7 But Congal is all a ~~Cong~~ a coud & that
8 Means that his future is not setled
9 But lies in his hands or in ~~th~~gods
10 Or it may be in mine — I ask
11 The heavens to say if I speak true
Thunder

Cong
12 The Heave hav had their say & I
13 Have waited until the tale was done
14 They make what ever please them truth
15 & make what ever please us lies
16 And have no argum but the ~~ligh~~ lighting
17 I swear that I have held
18 This woman in my arms & seven
19 That hav made impur seve times
Atrat
Atrata
20 You have not knelt
Congal
What must I say

f

I ^ his knowledg
I know because I share ^ *1*
and what punishment he has decreed *2*
You Although you are in a human f *3*
You have attand the human form *4*
But will sink back to a beasts form *5*
You to a wolf among the wolves *6*
You to a swine among the swine *7*
You three to dog cat goose *8*
But Congal stands there in a cloud *9*
Because his fate is not yet settled *10*
Speak out Great Herne, delre *11*
If all that I have said is true *12*
human for
Although you have found a hundred *13*
He will come when you are ded *14*
Push you down a stepor two *15*
Into cat or rat or bat *16*
Into dog or wolf or goose *17*
And each in his new shape I see *18*
But Congal there is a cloud *19*
Because his fate is not yet *20*
settld
~~If all that~~
Spek out great Hern declare *21*
That all I have said is *22*
true

P. T. O.

Left column in blue-black ink. Right column ll. *1–2*, *13–22* in light red; ll. *3–12* in blue-black, deleted in dark red; "P.T.O.", at bottom, and "I" and caret, at top of right column, in blue-black.

[NLI 8770 (2), 17v; V. 81–7, 93–100, 16–7]

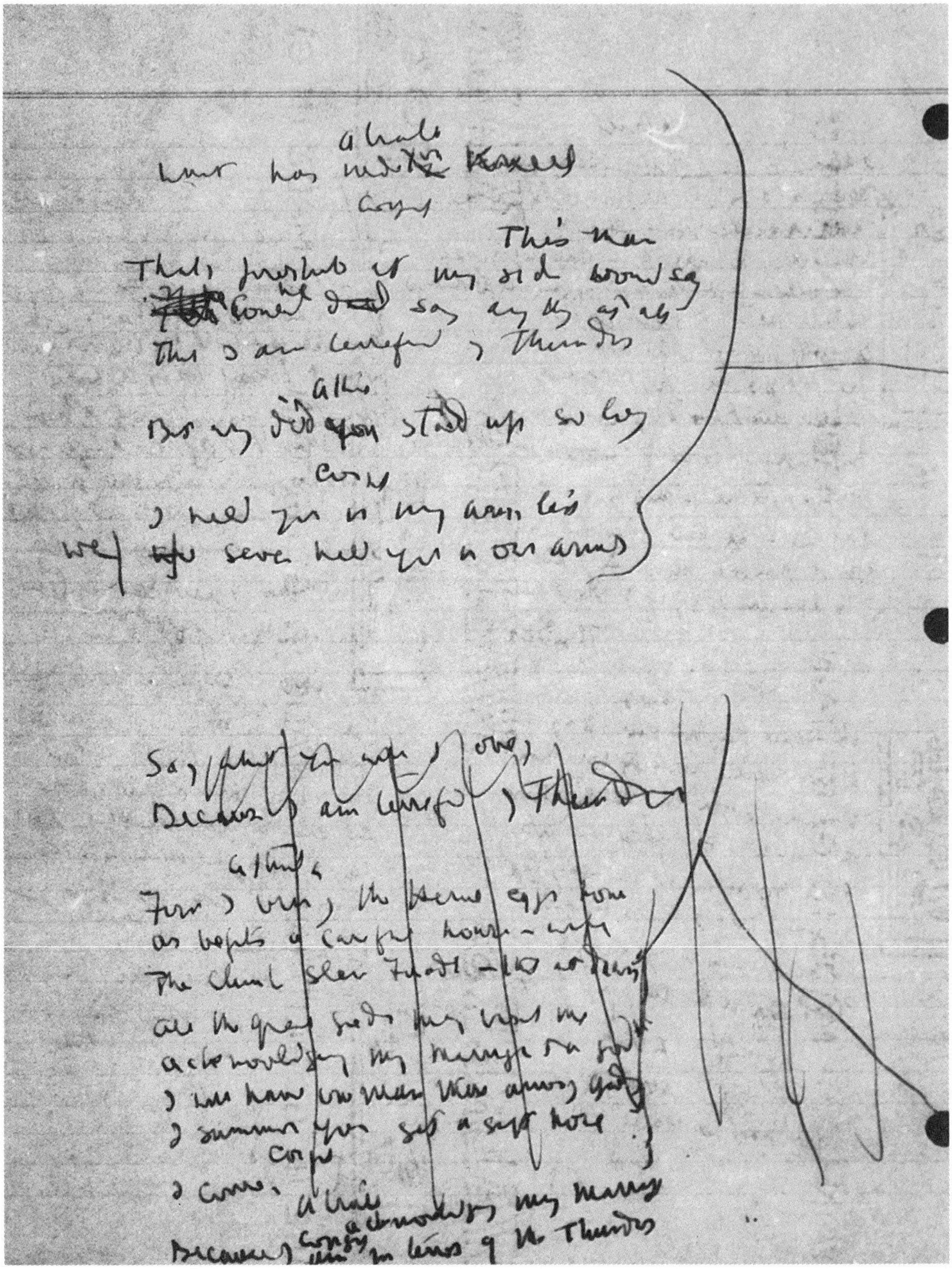

[NLI 8770 (2), 17v; V. 81–7, 93–100, 16–7]

Atrata

you
1 What has made ~~yu~~ kneel

Congal

2 This man
3 Thats prostrate at my side woud say

~~If he~~ {C he
4 ~~If he~~ {could ~~dared~~ say any thing at all
5 That I am terrified of thunder

Attra

{y
6 But why did{you stand up so long

Congal

7 I held you in my arms last
8 We/ ~~We~~ Seven held you in our arms

9 Say what you will I obey
10 Because I am terrifid of Thunder

Attrata

11 First I bring the Herne eggs home
12 As befits a careful house-wife
13 Then Climb Slev Fuadh — that at dawn
14 All the Great gods may visit me
15 Acknowledging my marrige to a god
16 I will have one man there among Gods
17 I summon you get a swift hors

Congal

18 I come.

Atratt

acknowledging my marrage

Congal

19 Because I am in terror of the Thunder

Lines 1–5 in blue-black ink; ll. 6–19 in dark red. Arrows to 18r in red; addition to l. 4 with corresponding deletion in red. Vertical deletion of ll. 9–18 in blue-black. Final "d" in both "did" and "stand", and correction to "you", l. 6, in blue-black.

[NLI 8770 (2), 18r; V. 88–100]

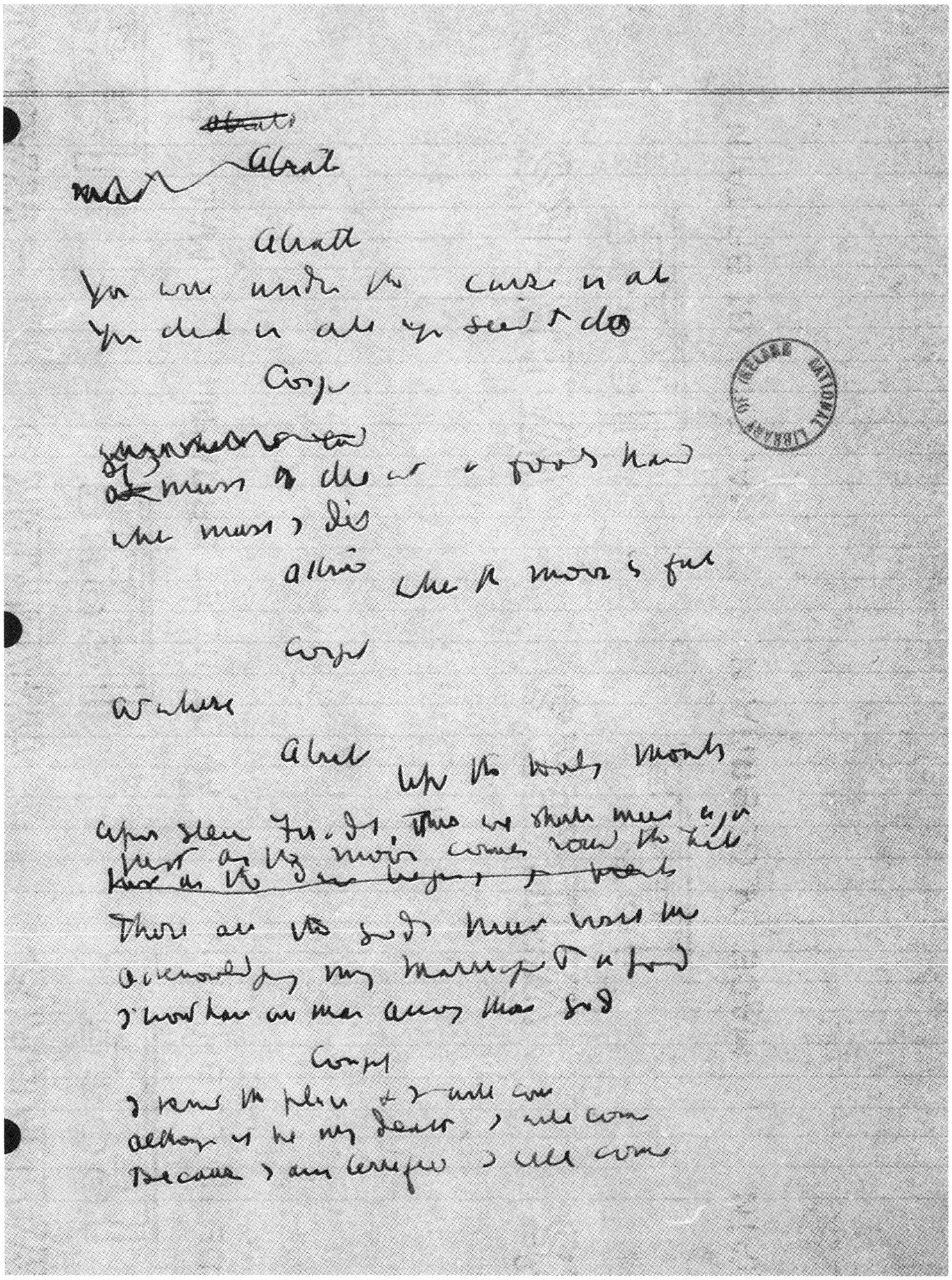

[NLI 8770 (2), 18r; V. 88–100]

~~Atrata~~
~~Atrata~~
~~Meet~~

Atratta
You were under the curse in all
You did in all you seemed to do
Congal
~~When shall it end~~
If I
~~And~~ must I die at a fools hand
When must I die
Attrat
When the moon is ful
Congal
And where
Atrata
Upon the Holy Montn
Upon Sleiv Fuadh. There we shall meet aga
Just as the moon comes round the hill
~~Just as the dawn begins to break~~
There all the gods must visit me
Acknowledging my marriage to a god
I would have one man among those gods
Congal
I know the place & I will come
Although it be my death I will come
Because I am terrified I will come

Blue-black ink, except "Atrata" in first line written in red and then deleted in blue-black. This page is apparently a fair copy of earlier work: arrows leading from 17v are not continued here. From this point onward pages are unnumbered, and no red ink appears.

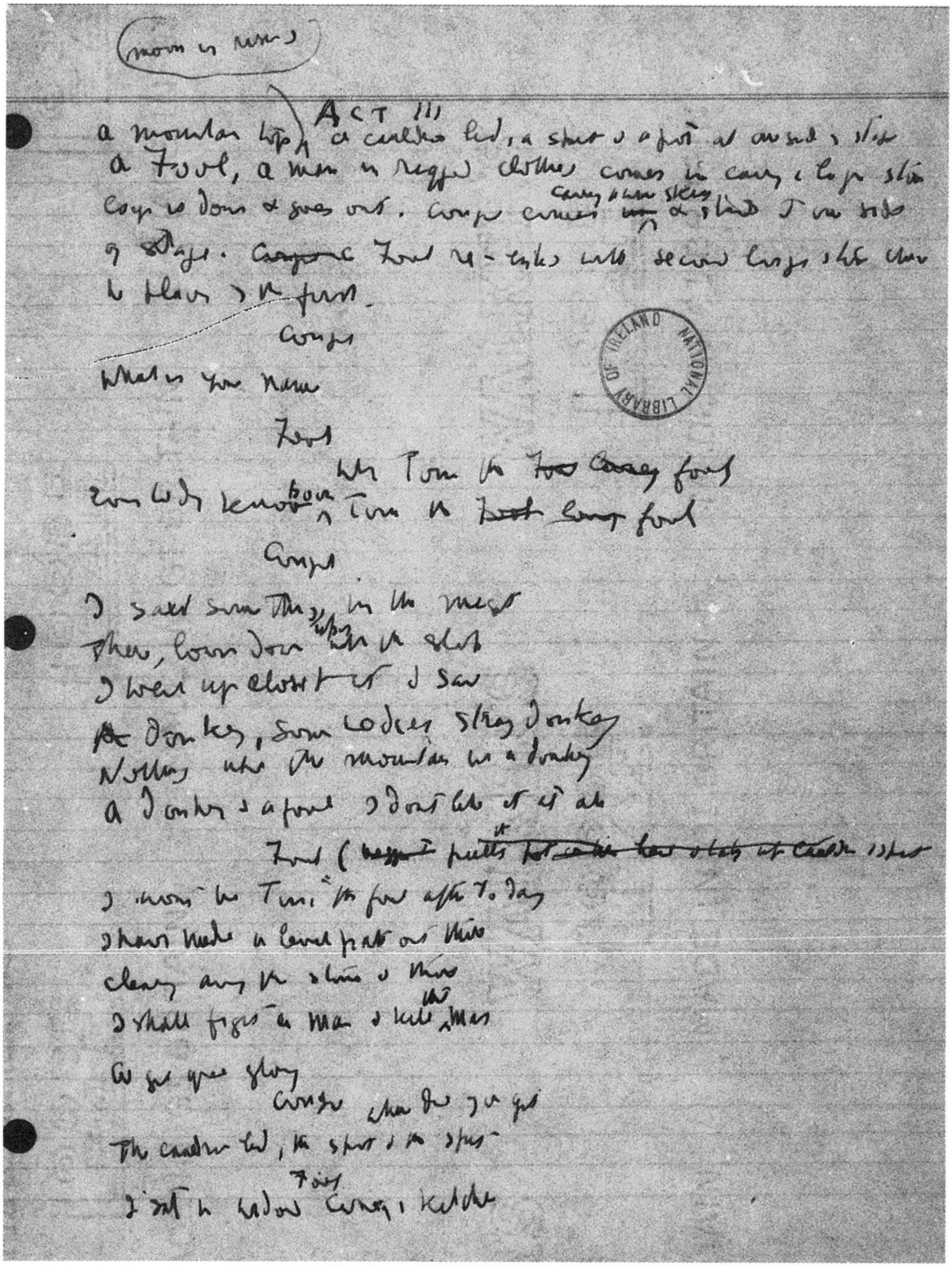

(moon is rising)

ACT III

a mountain top, a cauldron lid, a spit & a pot at one side of stage a Fool, a man in ragged clothes comes in carrying a large stone lays it down & goes out. Congal comes in carrying a few sticks & stands at one side of stage. Fool re-enters with second large stone & lays it close to place of the first.

Congal

What is your name

Fool

Why Tom the ~~Fool~~ Crazy fool

Every body knows ~~know~~ Tom the ~~[illegible]~~ Crazy fool

Congal

I saw something in the night

There, coming down upon the slope

I went up closer & I saw

~~A~~ A donkey, some widow's stray donkey

Nothing upon the mountain but a donkey

A donkey is a fool I don't like it at all

Fool (~~[illegible]~~ puts it ~~[illegible] & takes up cauldron & spit~~

I mean to be Tom the fool after to-day

I have made a level path over there

clearing away the stones & there

I shall fight a man & kill the man

& get great glory

Congal what did you get

The cauldron lid, the spit & the spit

I got the widow[?] Fair[?] Congal's kitchen

[NLI 8770 (2), 19^{r}; VI. 1–14]

moon is rising

Act III

A mountain top^ a cauldron lid, a spit & a pot at one side of stage
A Fool, a man in ragged clothes comes carry a large stone
carry a wine skin
lays it down & goes out. Congal comes ~~in~~ ^ & stands to one side
of stage. ~~Congal &~~ Fool re-enters with second large stone which
he places by the first.

Congal

1 What is your name

Fool

Why Tom the ~~Fool~~ ~~looney~~ fool
poor
2 Everybody knows ^ Tom the ~~Fool~~ ~~looney~~ fool

Congal

3 I saw something in the mist
upon
4 There, lower down upn the slop
5 I went up close to it & saw
6 A donkey, some bodies stray donkey
7 Nothing upon the mountain but a donky
8 A donky & a fool I don't like it at all
it

Fool (~~beggins to~~ putts ~~pot on his head & taks up cauldrn~~ & spit

9 I wont be Tom "the fool after to day
10 I have made a level patch out there
11 Clearing away the stone & there
that
12 I shall fight a man & kill ^ man
13 And get grea glory

Congal

Where did you get
14 The cauldrn lid, the spot & the spit

Fool

15 I sat in widow Cooneys kitchen

Blue-black ink.

[NLI 8770 (2), 20r; VI. 15–27, 29–33]

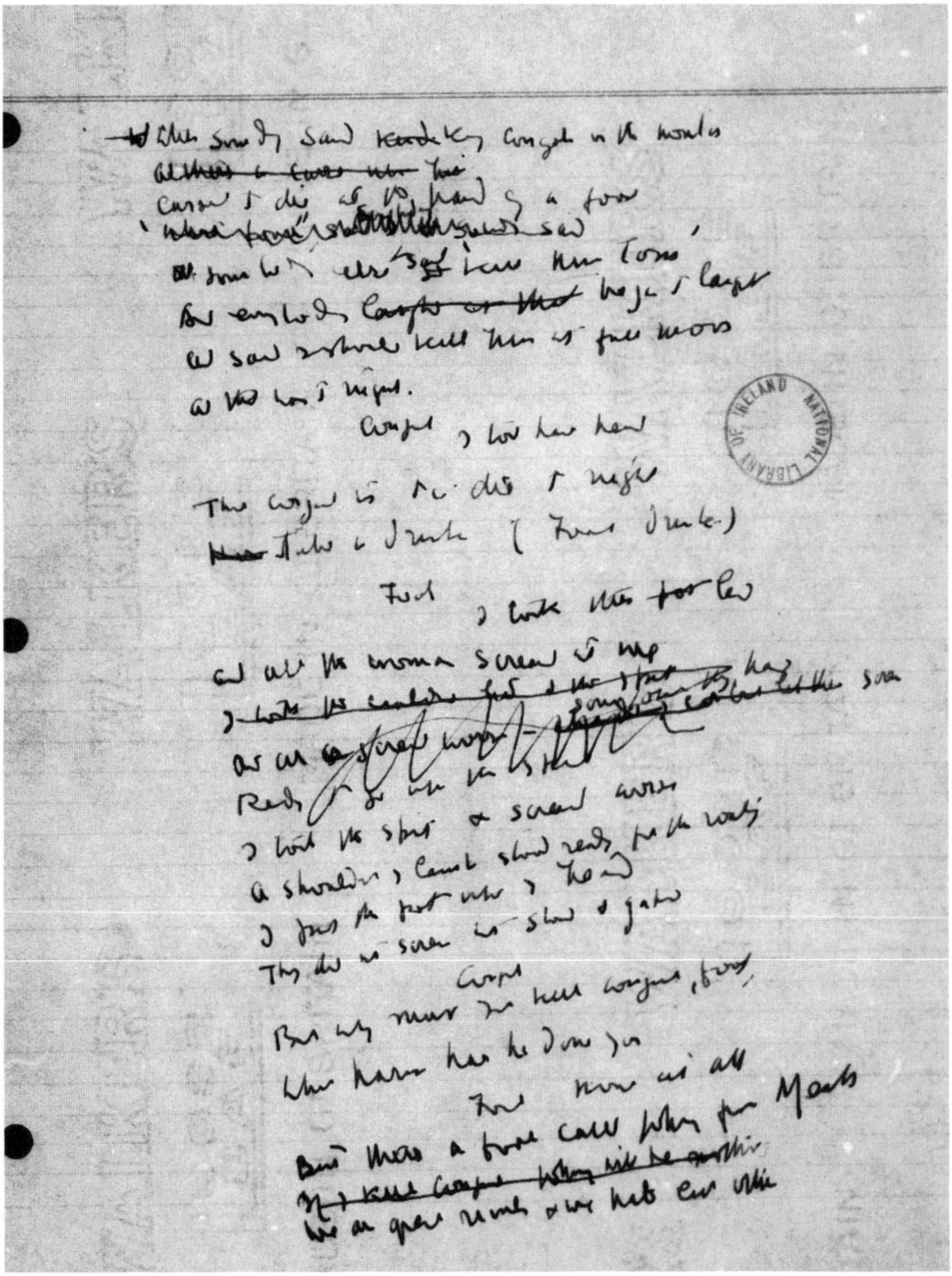

[NLI 8770 (2), 20^{r}; VI. 15–27, 29–33]

1 ~~W~~ When somebody said ~~Kind~~ King Congals on the moutin
~~And thers a curse upon his~~
2 Cursed to die at the hand of a fool
somebody
~~'What fool'', said I — sombdy said~~
said
3 A Somebody else ~~go~~ 'Kill him Tom'
4 But evrybody ~~laughd at that~~ began to laugh
5 And said I should Kill him at full moon
6 And that was to night.
Congal
I too have herd
7 That Congal is to die to night
T
8 ~~Here~~ {take a drink (Fool drinks)
Fool
I took this ~~pot~~ lid
9 And all the women screamd at me
~~I took the cauldrn lid & the spit~~
some joint they had
And all ~~er~~ scremd worse — ~~chiding [?or] but let them~~ screm
Redy to go upon the spit
10 I took the spit & scremd worse
11 A shoulder of lamb stood ready for the roasting
12 I put the pot upon my head
13 They did nt screm but stood & gaped
Congal
14 But why must you kill Congal, fool,
15 What harm has he done you
Fool None at all
16 But thers a fool called Johny from Meath
~~If I kill Congal Johny will be nothin~~
17 We are great rivals & we hate each other

Blue-black ink.

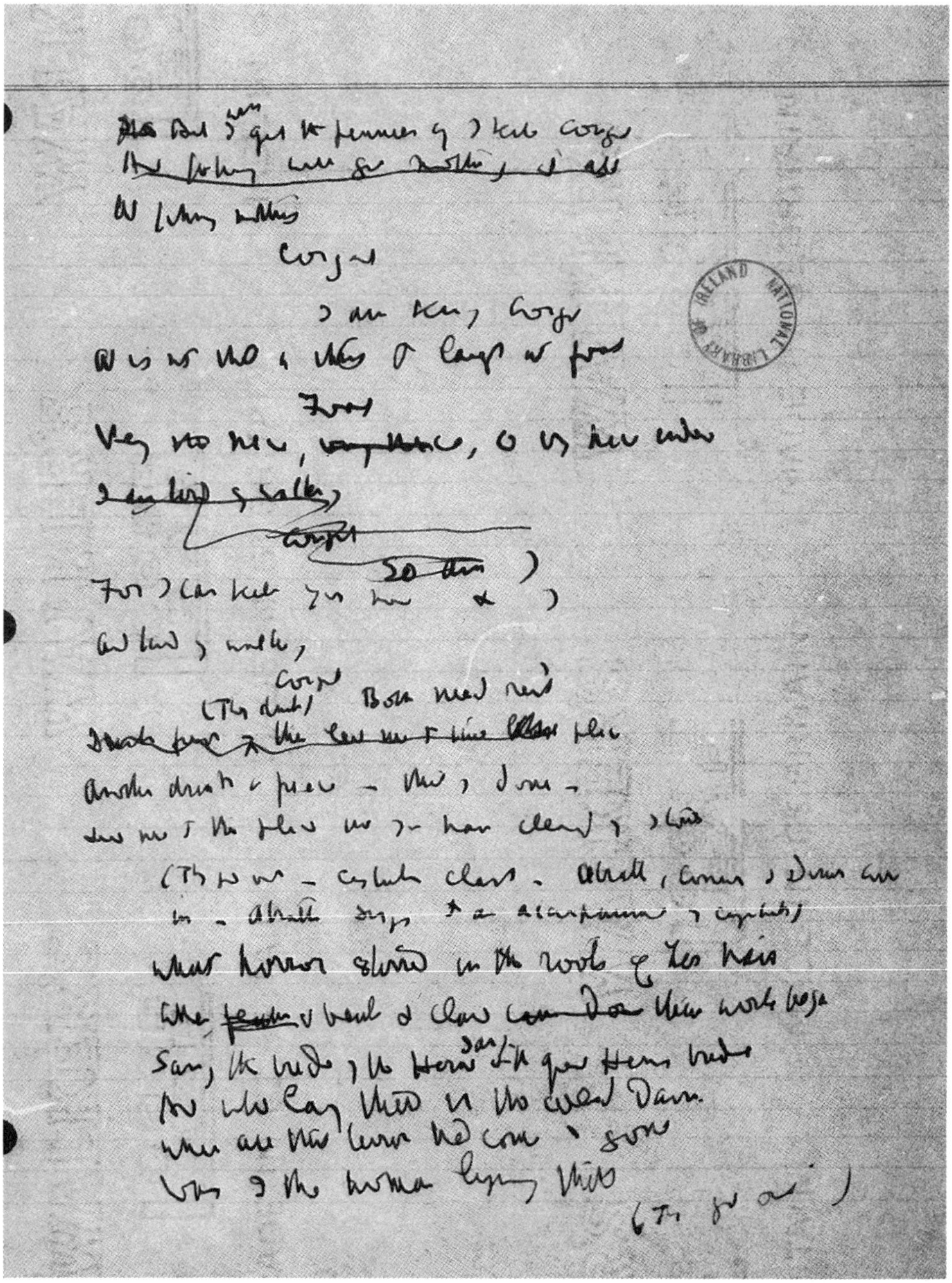

[NLI 8770 (2), 21^{r}; VI. 33–40, 44–50]

will
1 ~~I c~~ But I get the pennies if I kill Congal
~~And Johny will get nothing at all~~
2 And Johny nothing

Congal

I am King Congal
3 And is not that a thing to laugh at fool

Fool

4 Very ~~ni~~ nice, ~~very nice,~~ O vry nice inded
~~I am tired of walking~~

~~Congal~~

~~So am I~~
5 For I can kill you now & I
6 Am tired of walking

Congal

(They drink) Both need rest
~~Drink first~~ — ^ ~~then lead me to this house~~ place
7 Another drink a piece — that is done —
8 Lead me to the place that you have cleard of stones

(They go out — cymbals clash. Atratt, Corney & Doney come in — Atratta sings to an accompaniment of cymbals)

9 What horror stirred in the roots of her hair
10 When ~~feather~~ & beak & claw ~~came down~~ their work began
Sang
11 Sang the bride of the Herne ~~&~~ the great Herns bride
12 And who lay there in the cold dawn
13 When all that terror had come & gone
14 Was I the woman lying there

(they go out)

Blue-black ink.

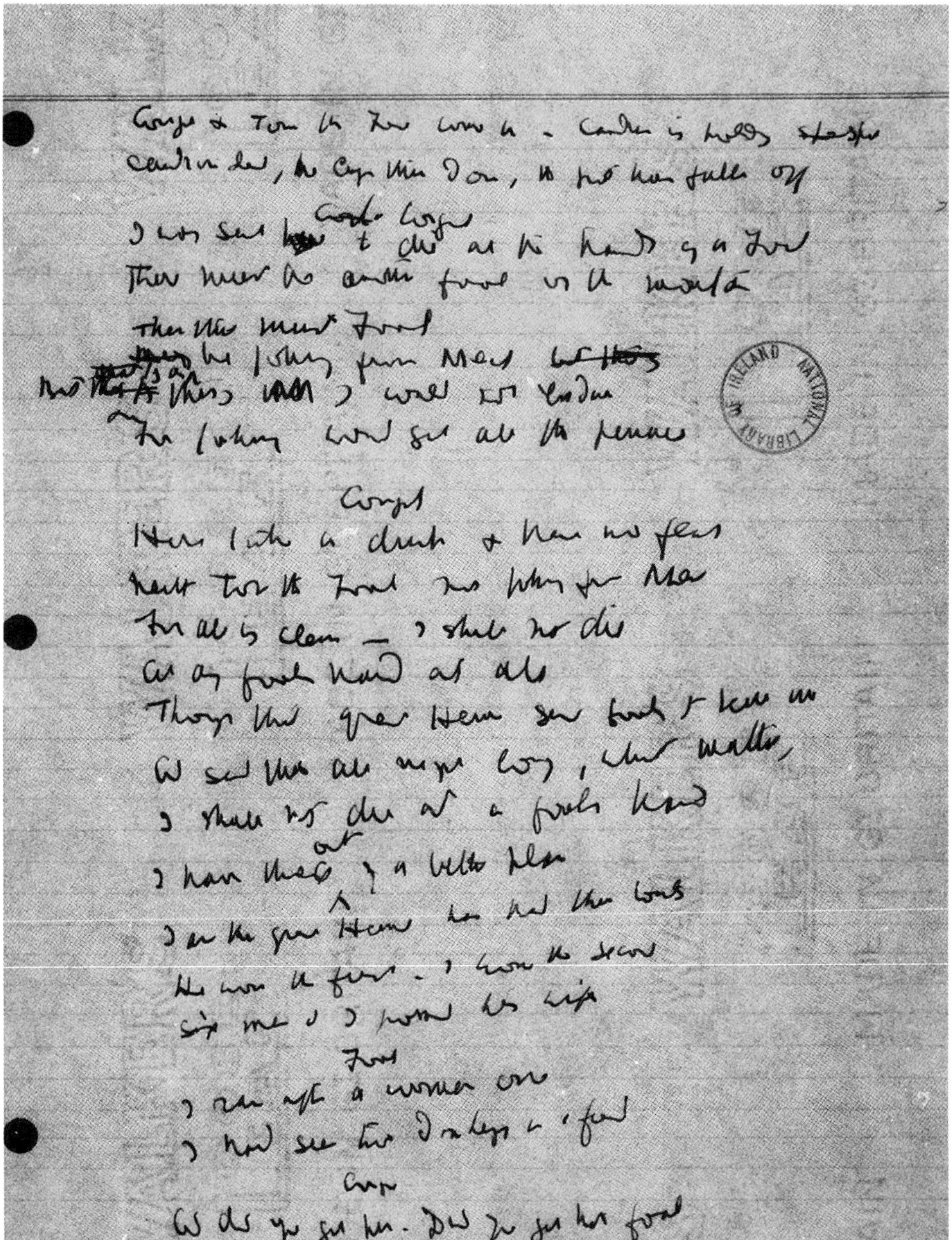
Congal & Tom the Fool come in – Candle in holly [illegible]
candle in hand, the Cup [illegible], he had have fallen off
I was sent Congal to die at the hands of a Fool
There must be another fool in the world
Than this mere Fool
may be Johnny from Mear
But that is a thing that I would not endure
For Johnny would get all the pennies
Congal
Here I with a drink & have no fear
Neither Tom the Fool nor Johnny from Mear
For all is clear – I shall not die
At any fool's hand at all
Though the great Herne seem fool & kill me
He said that all might say, what matter,
I shall not die at a fool's hand
I have thought of a better plan
I and the great Herne have had three bouts
He won the first – I won the second
Six men & I possessed his wife
Fool
I ran after a woman once
I had seen two donkeys in a field
Congal
And did you get her. Did you get her fool

[NLI 8770 (2), 22r; VI. 50–65]

Congal & Tom the Fool come in — Cauldren is holding ~~sp~~ spit
Cauldron lid, he lays them down, the pot has falln off

~~Conl~~ Congal

1 I was sent ~~here~~ to die at the hands of a Fool
2 There must be another fool on the mountain

Fool

Then this must
3 ~~May~~ be Johny from Meat ~~but that is~~
that is a ^
4 But ~~that~~ A thing ~~we~~ I could not endure
5 For Johny would get all the pennies

Congal

6 Here take a drink & have no fear
7 Neith Tom the Fool nor Johny from Meat
8 For all is clear — I shall not die
9 At any fools hand at all
10 Though that great Hern send fools to kill me
11 And send them all night long, what matter,
12 I shall not die at a fools hand
out
13 I have thought ^ of a better plan
14 I and the great Herne hav had thre bouts
15 He won the first. I won the second
16 Six men & I possed his wife

Fool

17 I ran after a woman once
18 I had seen two donkeys in a field

Congal

19 And did you get her. Did you get her fool

Blue-black ink, with ll. 3–4 corrected in a darker shade.

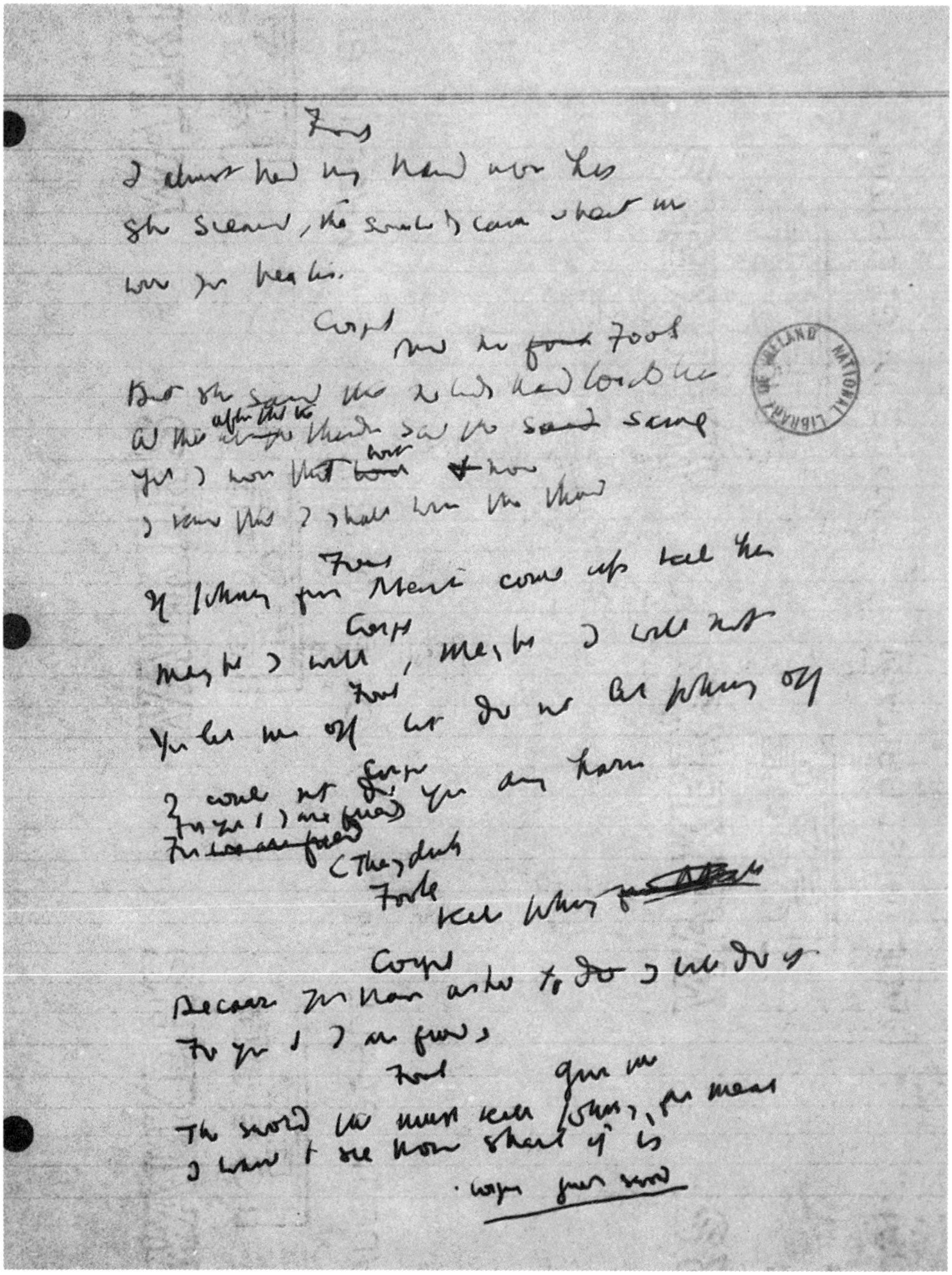

Fool
I almost had my hand upon her
She screamed, the soldiers came & beat me
were [illegible] beating.

Congal
And now you fancy Fool
But she screamed that [illegible] had [illegible]
At this ~~[illegible]~~ after that he [illegible] saw the ~~sacred~~ scene
Yet I won that ~~[illegible]~~ won & now
I know that I shall win the [illegible]

Fool
If Johnny from Meath come up kill him

Congal
Maybe I will, maybe I will not

Fool
You let me off but do not let Johnny off

Congal
I would not do you any harm
For you & I are friends
~~For we are friends~~
(They drink)

Fool
Kill Johnny ~~[illegible]~~

Congal
Because the Heron asked to do I will do it
For you & I are friends

Fool
Give me
The sword we must kill Johnny from Meath
I want to see how sharp it is
· Congal gives sword

[NLI 8770 (2), 23^{r}; VI. 66–81]

Fool
I almost had my hand upon her
She screamed, then somebody came & beat me
Were you beaten.
Congal
No no ~~fool~~ Fool
But she said that nobody had touched her
after that the
And then ~~all the~~ thunder said the ~~said~~ same
bout
Yet I won that ~~bout~~ & now
I know that I shall win the third
Fool
If Johny from Meath come up kill him
Congal
May be I will, may be I will not
Fool
You let me off but do not let Johny off
Congal
I could not do you any harm
For you & I are friends
~~For we are friend~~
(They drink
Foole
Kill Johny ~~from Meath~~
Congal
Because you have asked to ~~do~~ I will do it
For you & I are friends
Fool
Give me
The sword that must kill Johny from Meat
I want to see how sharp it is
Congal gives sword

Lines 1–7 in blue-black ink, remainder in a darker shade, along with revisions to ll. 5 and 6.

[NLI 8770 (2), 23^{v}; VI. 86–7]

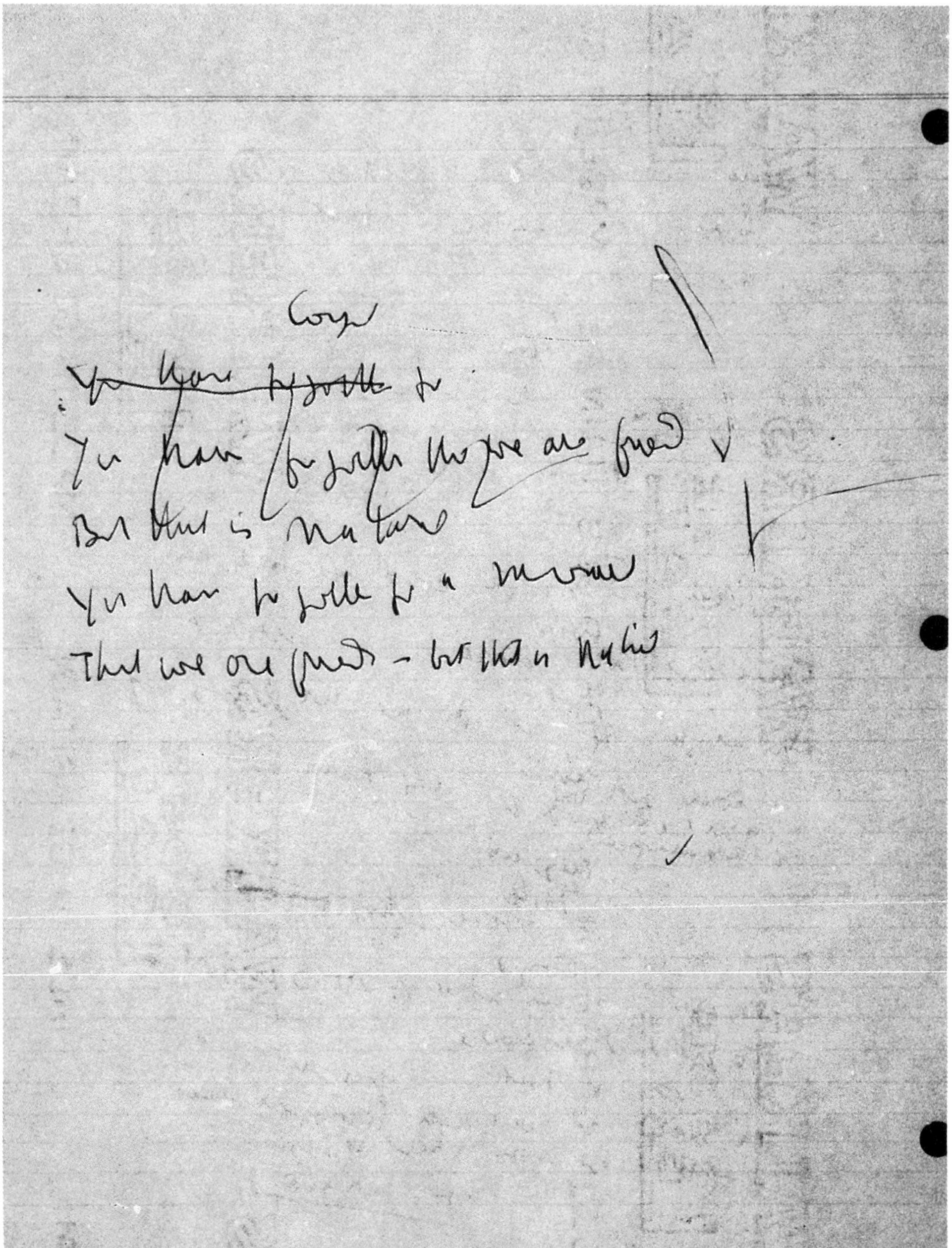

[NLI 8770 (2), 23^{v}; VI. 86–7]

Congal

~~You have forgottn~~ fr
You have forgottn that we are friend
But that is natural
You have for gotten for a moment
That we are friends — but that is Natrel

Blue-black ink. Arrow interpolates lines above l. 3 on 24^{r}.

[NLI 8770 (2), 24r; VI. 84–102]

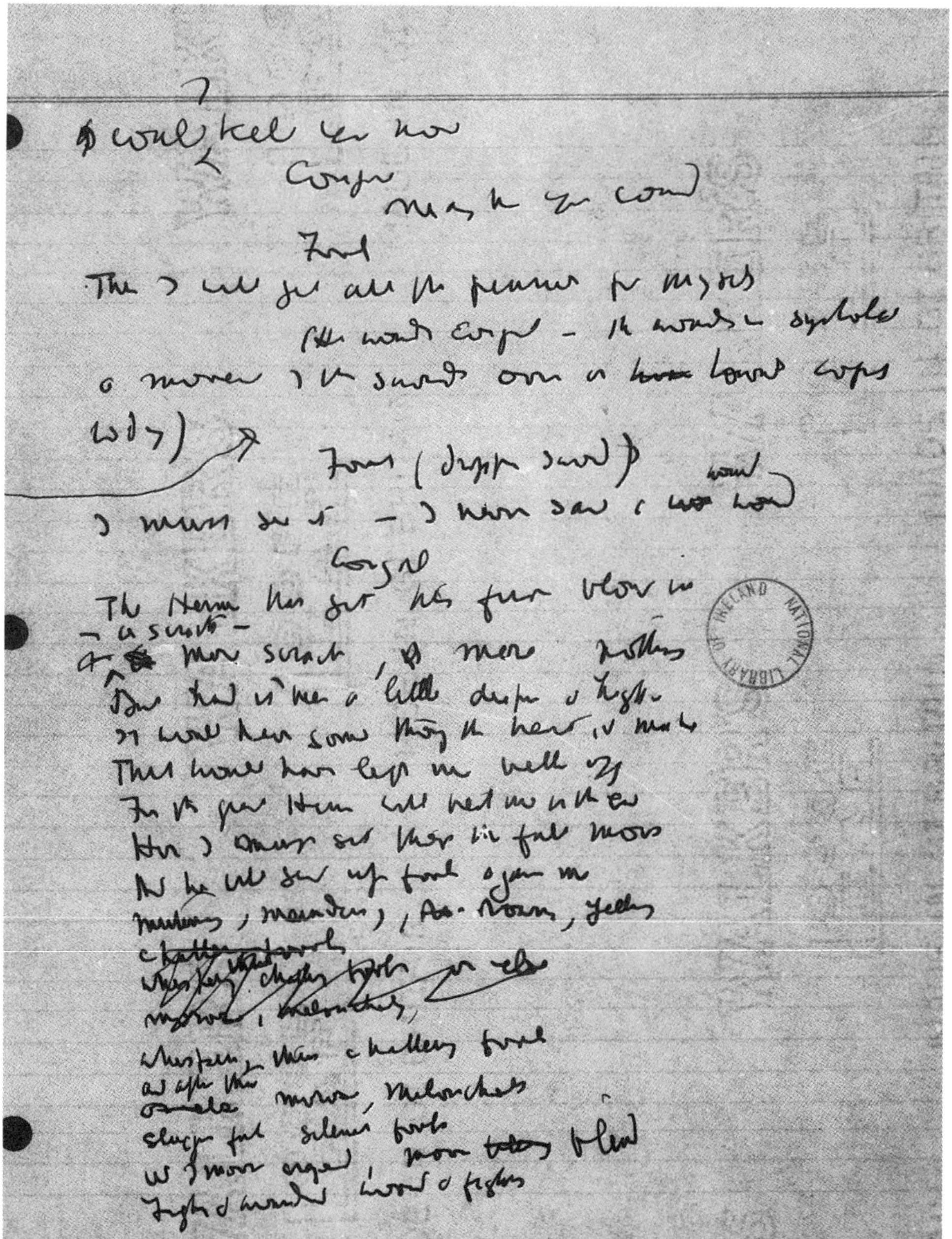

I
1 I could^ Kill you now
Congal
may be you could
Fool
2 Then I will get all the pennies for myself
(He wounds Congal — the wound is symbolic
a movement of the sword over or ~~near~~ towards Congals
body)
Fool (dropping sword) I
wound
3 I must see it — I never saw a ~~wo~~ wound
Congal
4 The Herne has got his first blow in
— a scratch —
5 A ^ ~~A~~ mere scrach, a mere nothing
6 But had it been a little deeper & higher
7 It would have gone through the heart, & ma be
8 That would have left me bettr off
9 For the great Hern will beat me in the end
10 Here I must sit thrg the full moon
11 And he will send up fools agans me
12 Muterring, meandering, ~~ro~~ roaring, yelling
~~Chattering fools~~
[?Men]
Whispering chatter fools or else
morose, melancholy,
13 Whispering then chattering fools
And after them
14 ~~Or else~~ morose, melancholy
15 Sluggis fat silent fools
16 And I moon crazed, moon ~~bling~~ blind
17 Fighting & wounded wound & fighting

Black or blue-black ink.

[NLI 8770 (2), 25r; VI. 103–121]

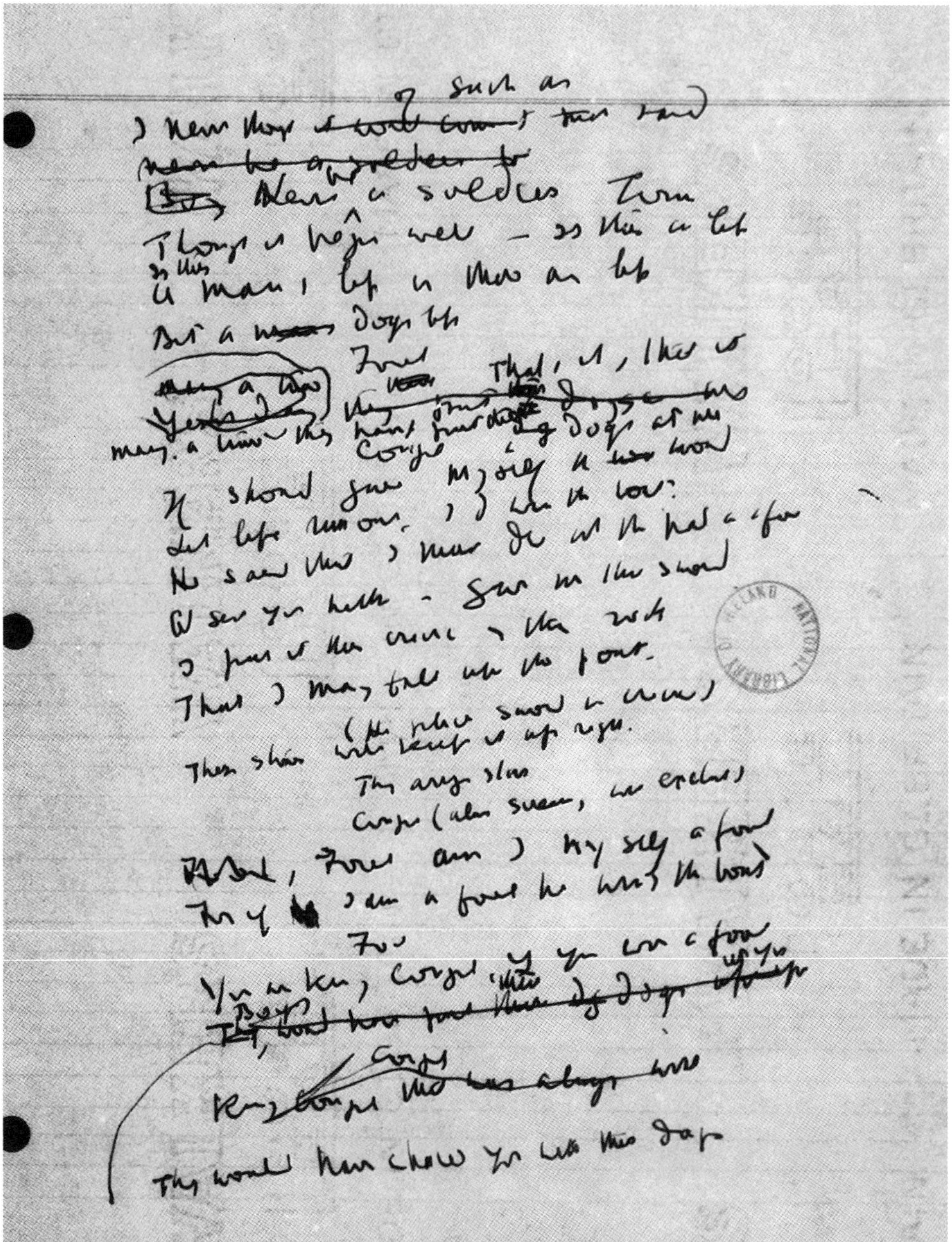

of such an
1 I never thougt ~~it would come to such~~ an end
~~Never be a soldier to~~
{N be
2 ~~But~~ {nevr^ a soldier Tom
3 Though it begin well — is this a life
Is this
4 A man s life is there any life
5 But a ~~mans~~ dogs life
Fool
6 That s it, that it
~~Many a time have~~
~~Yester day they put their dogs at me~~
7 many a time they have put ~~dogs th~~
~~d g~~ dogs at me
Congal
8 If shoud give my self a ~~wo~~ wound
9 Let life run out, I d win the bout.
10 He said that I must die at the hand of a foo
11 And sent you hithr — Give me that sword
12 I put it this crevic of the rock
13 That I may fall upon the pont.
(He place sword in crevice)
14 These stones wil keep it up right.
They arrge stons
Congal (almos screaming with exctmt)
15 ~~Fo ol,~~ Fool am I my self a fool
16 For if ~~we~~ I am a fool he wins the bout
Fool
17 You are King Congal. If you were a fool
~~Boys~~ their upon you
18 ~~They, would have put there dg dogs upon you~~
Congal
19 ~~King Congal that was always wise~~
20 They would have chaced you with ther dogs

Black or blue-black ink. Line 20 replaces l. 18.

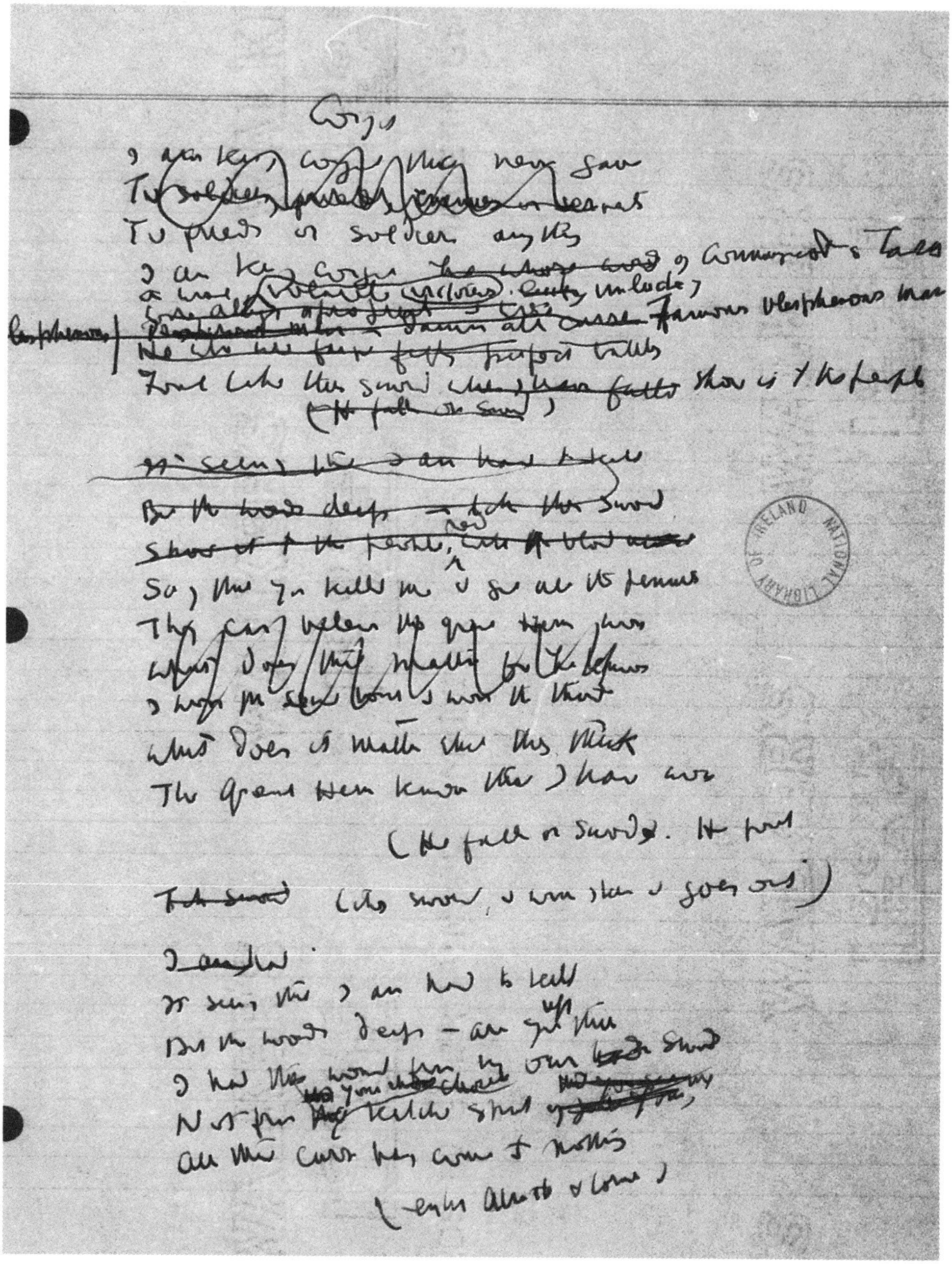

[NLI 8770 (2), 26^{r}; VI. 120–30]

Congal

1 I am King Congal that nevr gave
~~To soldiers, friends, enemies or servants~~
2 To friends or soldiers any thing
3 I am King Congal ~~he whose word~~ of Connaught & Tara
4 A wise voluble victorius. ~~lucky~~ unlucky
~~Whose always a frnd great & wise~~
~~Blasphemous /~~ ~~blasphemous man~~ — ~~damn all curses~~ Famous blasphemous man
5 He ~~who has fought fifty perfect battles~~
6 Fool take this sword ~~when I have fallen~~ show it to the people
(~~He falls on sword~~)
7 ~~It seems that I am hard to kill~~
8 ~~But the wounds deep — take this sword~~
red
9 ~~Show it to the people ^ with the blood upon it~~
10 Say that you killd me & get all the pennies
11 They can beleive the great Hern won
12 What does that matter for he knows
13 I won the second bout I won the third
14 What does it matter what they think
15 The Great Hern knows that I hav won
(He falls on sword~~).~~ Here fool
~~Tak sword~~ takes sword & wine skin & goes out)
~~I am hard~~
16 It seems that I am hard to kill
up
17 But the wounds deep — are you there
18 I had this wound from my own ~~hand~~ sword
~~tht~~ your ~~chose~~ chosen ~~that you gave me~~
19 Not from ~~that~~ kitchen spit ~~of your Fools~~
20 All that curse has come to nothing
(enter Atratta & Corne)

Blue-black ink, with revisions to ll. 3–6 in darker ink.

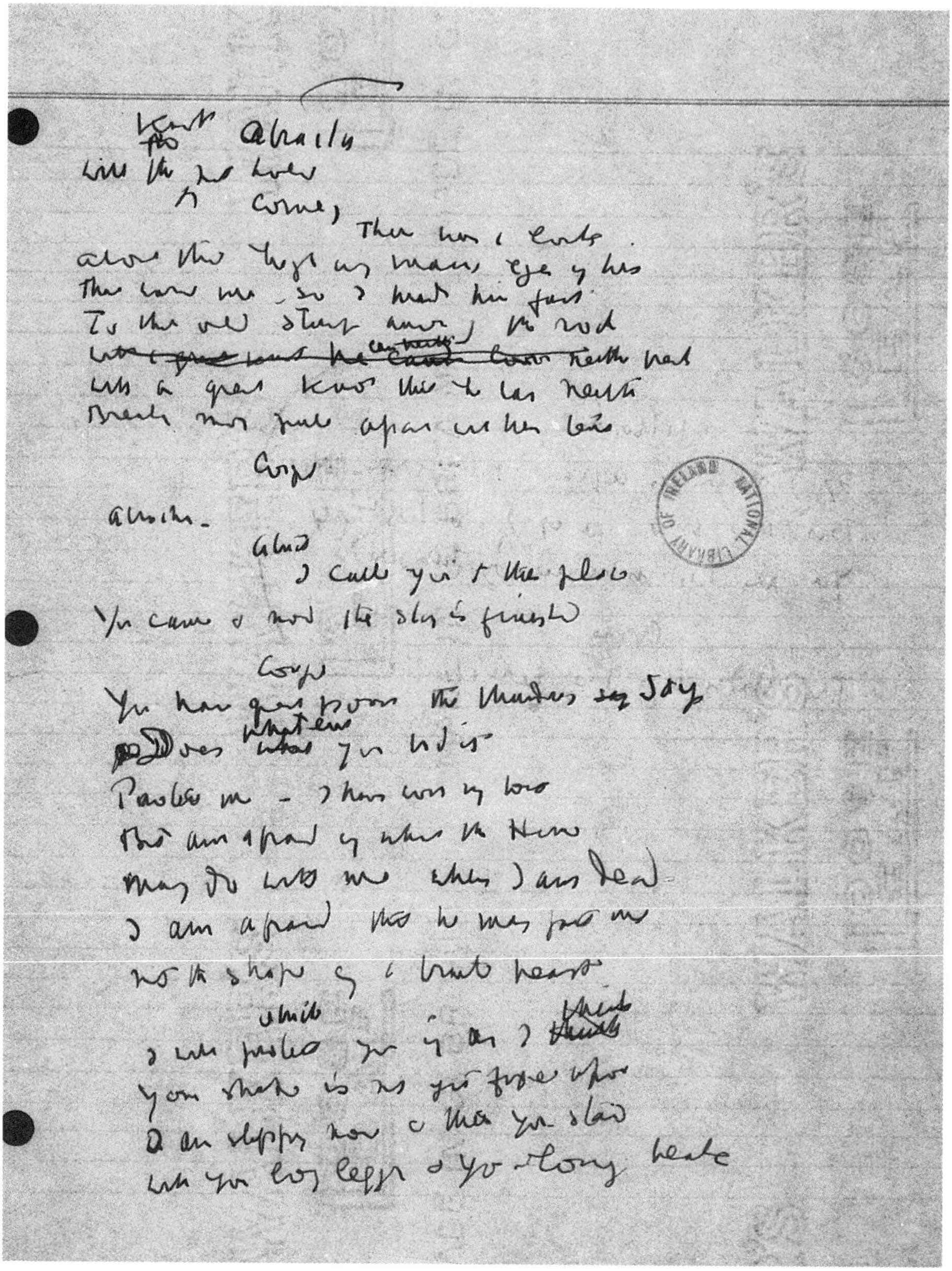
Attracta
Will the [illegible]
to Congal,
Then [illegible]
above the [illegible] man's eye of his
Then [illegible] me – so I [illegible] him fast
To the old stump among the rocks
With a great [illegible] that he has [illegible]
Break my [illegible] apart with her [illegible]
Cong
Attracta –
Attrac
I call you to this place
You came & now the story is finished
Cong
You have great power the Watchers say Joy
Does whatever you bid it
Protect me – I have lost my love
But am afraid of what the Herne
May do with me when I am dead
I am afraid that he may put me
into the shape of a brute beast
I will protect you if as I think
Your shade is not yet fixed upon
I am sleeping now & then you slide
with your long legs & your long beak

[NLI 8770 (2), 27^{r}; VI. 131–49]

Knot   Atracta
~~no~~
Will the ^ not hold
Corney
There was a look
Abou that high wy mans eye of his
That warned me, so I made him fast
To that old stump among the rock
can ~~neithr~~
~~With a great knot he cann loosen~~ neithr break
With a great Knot that he can neith
Break nor pull apar wit his teeth
Congal
Atracta —
Atract
I calld you to this place
You came & now the story is finished
Congal
You have great powers the thundres ~~say~~ Says
{D   what evr
~~&~~ {does ~~what~~ you bid it
Protect me — I have won my bout
But am afraid of what the Herne
May do with me when I am dead
I am afraid that he may put me
Into the shape of a brute beast
Atratta
think
I will protect you if as I ~~think~~
Your shape is not yet fixed upon
I am slipping now & there you stand
With your long leggs & yo rlong beak

Blue-black ink, except "Atracta" at top and at ll. 15/16 and revisions to l. 5 ("can") and ll. 9–10 in darker ink.

[NLI 8770 (2), 27ᵛ; VI. 156–59]

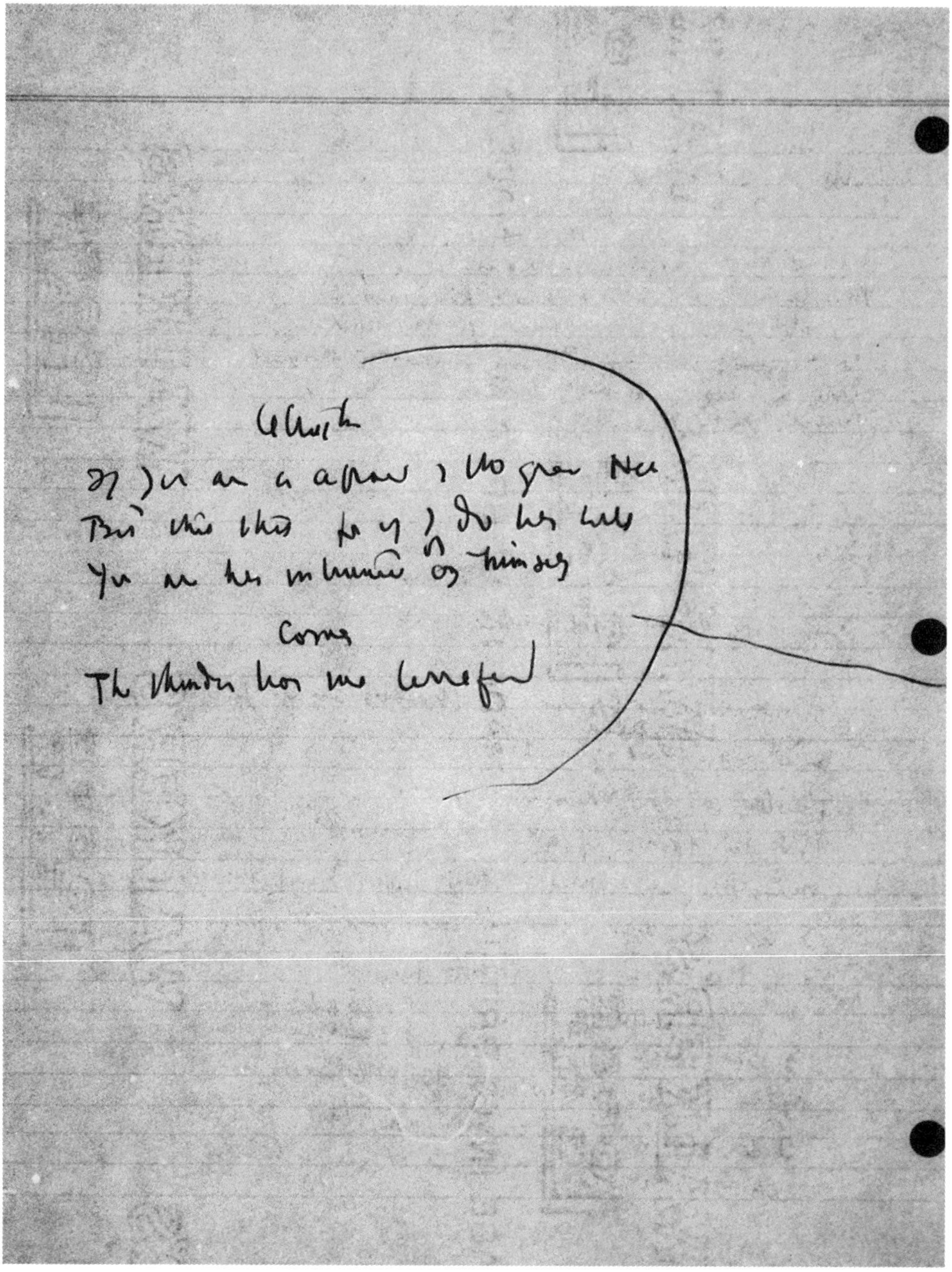

[NLI 8770 (2), 27^{v}; VI. 156–59]

Atracta
If you are a afraid of the grea Hern
But this that for if I do his will
or
You are his in trument or himself
Corney
The thunder has me terrefied

Black or blue-black ink. Arrow interpolates these lines at l. 7 on 28^{r}.

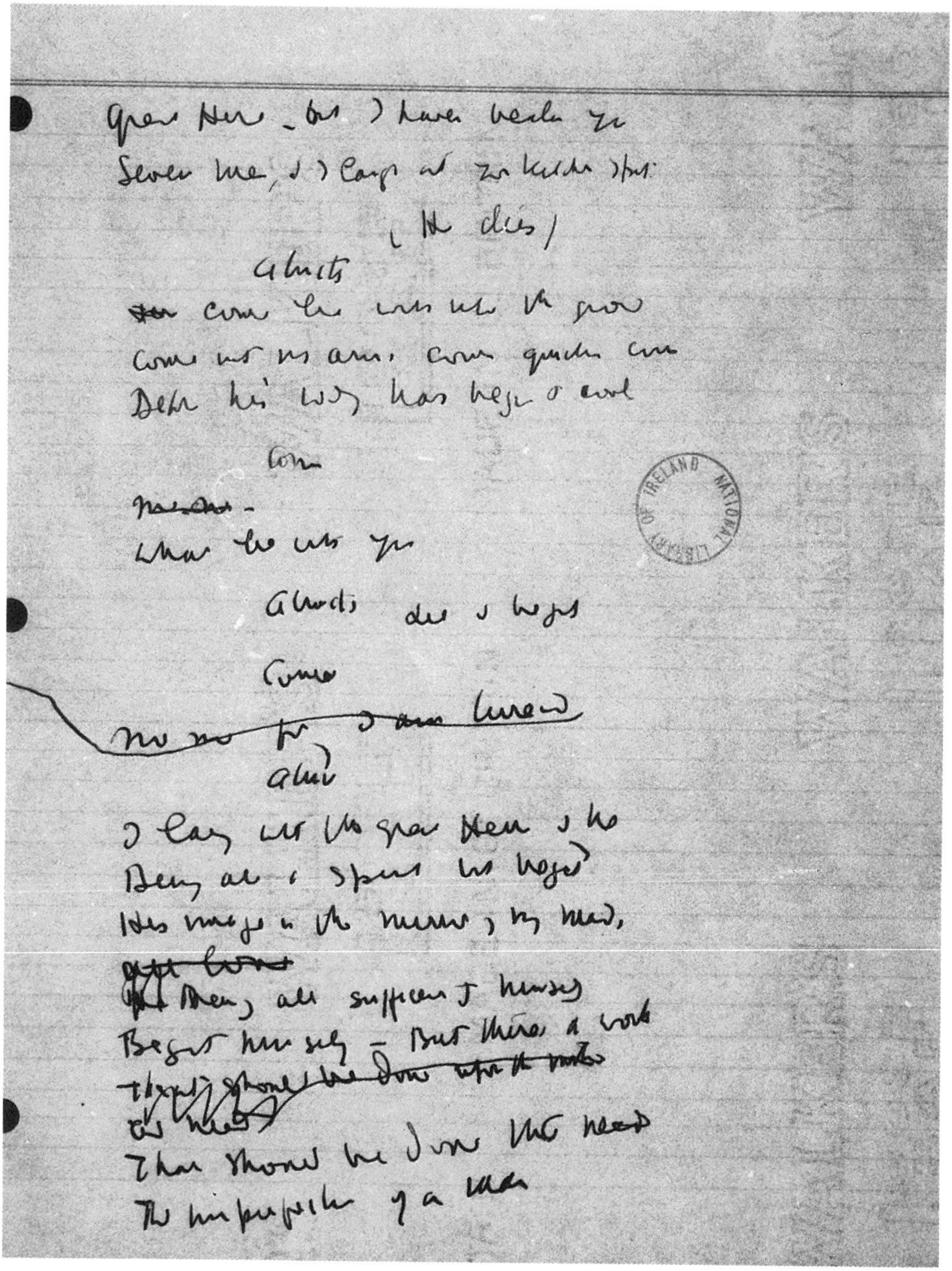

[NLI 8770 (2), 28r; VI. 150–65, 167]

1 Great Herne — but I have beaten you
2 Seven me, & I laugh at your kitchn spit
(He dies)

Atracta

3 ~~For~~ Come lie with upon the ground
4 Come into my arms come quick come
5 Before his body has begun to cool

Corne

~~No, no~~ —
6 What lie with you

Atracta

Lie & beget

Corne

7 ~~No no for I am terrefied~~

Atract

8 I lay with the great Hern & he
9 Being all a spirit but begot
10 His image in the mirror of my mind,
~~All lone~~
{B
11 ~~He~~ {being all sufficen To himself
12 Begot himself — But theres a work
[That should be done upon the montain
[And needs
13 That should be done that needs
14 The imperfectn of a man

Lines 1–5 in blue-black ink, remainder in darker ink.

[NLI 8770 (2), 29r; VI. 167–78]

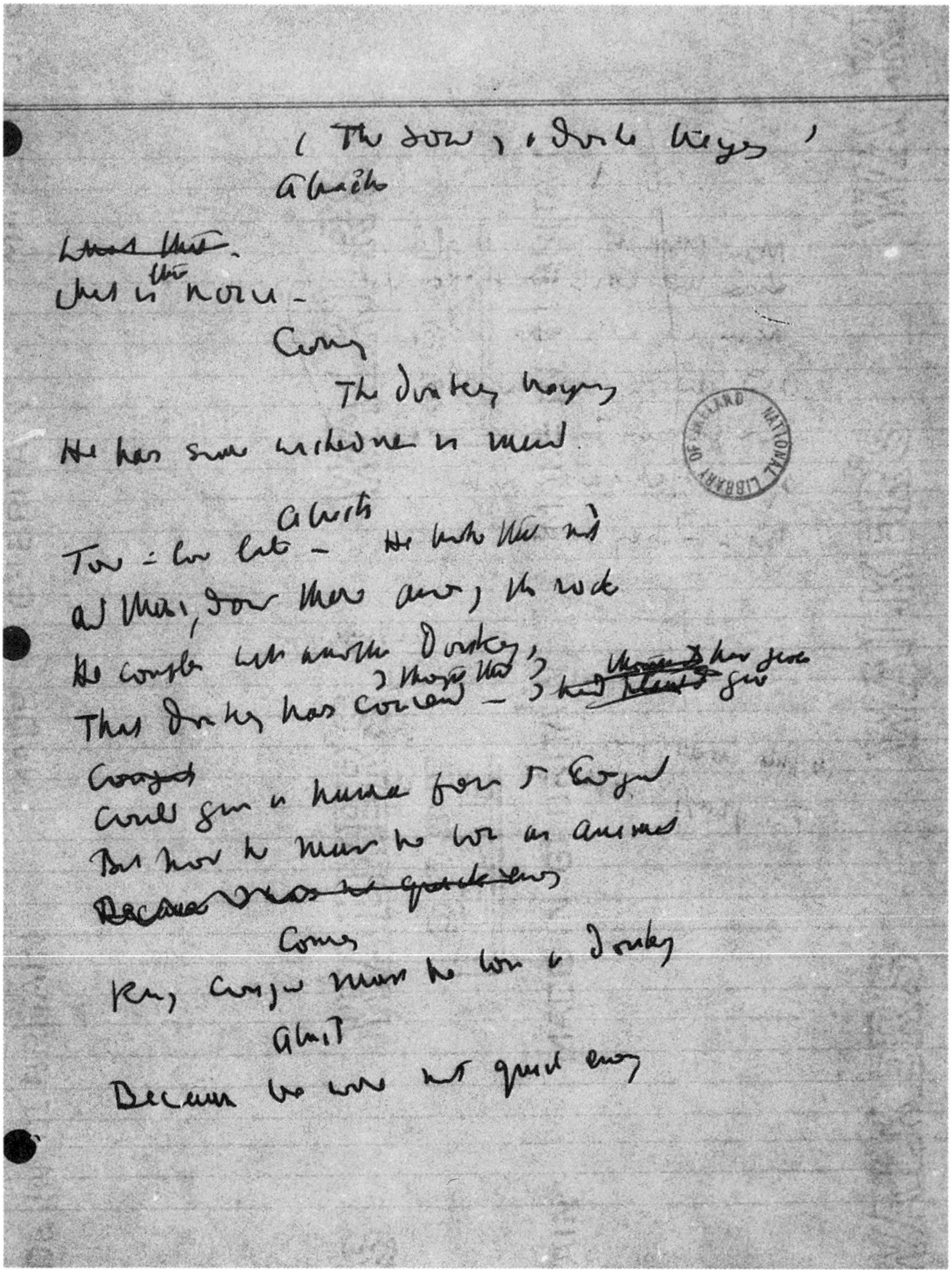

(The sound of a donke braying)

Atracta

~~What that~~

this

1 What is noise —

Corny

The donky braying

2 He has some wickednes in mind

Atracta

3 Too — too late — He broke that not

4 And there, down there among the rocks

5 He couples with another donkey,

I thought that I ~~thought to~~ hav given

6 That donkey has conceived — I ~~had pland to~~ give

~~Congal~~ {C

7 Could give a human form to {congal

8 But now he must be born an animal

~~Because I was nt quick enog~~

Corney

9 King Congal must be born a donkey

Atract

10 Because we were not quick enoug

Black or blue-black ink.

The Texas Typescript

[Texas, p. 1]

THE HERNE'S EGG.

SCENE I.

(Mist and rocks, high up on back cloth; a rock, its base hidden in mist, on this rock stands a great herne. They should be suggested, not painted realistically. Many men fighting with swords and shields, but sword and swordm shield and sword, never meet. The men move rythmically as if in a dance; when swords approach one another cymbals clash; when swords and shields approach drums boom. The battle flows out at one side; two Kings are left fighting in the centre of the stage; the battle returns and flows out at the other side. The two Kings remain but are now face to face and motionless. They are Congal, King of Connacht, and Aedh, King of Tara.)

CONGAL
How many men have you lost ?
AEDH
Some five and twenty men.
CONGAL
No need to ask my losses.
AEDH
Your losses equal mine.
CONGAL
They always have and must.
AEDH
Skill, strength, arms matched.

No periods following scene numbers; no parentheses around stage directions. HE

Text preceded in HE by title page and list of PERSONS
CONGAL, King of Connaught
AEDH, King of Tara
CORNEY, Attracta's servant
MIKE, PAT, MALACHI, PETER, JOHN, Connaught soldiers
ATTRACTA, A Priestess
KATE, AGNES, MARY, Friends of Attracta
Soldiers of Tara
A FOOL

1 rocks; . . . backcloth a *HE*
2 mist; *HE*
3 They] All *HE*
5 sword, shield *HE*
11 remain, *HE*
12 Connaught *HE; so throughout*
2 five-and-twenty *HE*

NLI 30,485 directed: "correct descripn of scene. Move Herne Etc".

[Texas, p. 2]

- 2 -

CONGAL

Where is the wound this time?

AEDH

There, left shoulder-blade.

CONGAL

Here, right shoulder-blade.

AEDH

Yet we have fought all day.

CONGAL

This is our fiftieth battle.

AEDH

And all are perfect battles.

CONGAL

Come, sit upon this stone
Come and take breath awhile.

AEDH

From day-break until noon
hopping among these rocks,

CONGAL

Nothing to eat or drink.

AEDH

A story is running round
Concerning two rich fleas.

CONGAL

We hop like fleas, but war
Has taken all our riches.

---

12 are] were *HE*
13 stone. *HE*
15 noon, *HE*
16 Hopping . . . rocks. *HE*

Lines 18–19 supplied in NLI 30,485 with false start “g” crossed out before “running”.

[Texas, p. 3]

- 3 -

AEDH

Rich, and rich, so rich that they
Retired and bought a dog.

CONGAL

Finish the tale and say
What kind of dog they bought.

AEDH

Heaven knows.

CONGAL

You must have thought
What kind of dog they bought.

AEDH

Heaven knows.

CONGAL

Unless you say,
I'll up and fight all day.

AEDH

A fat, square, lazy dog,
No sort of scratching dog.

[Texas, p. 4]

- 4 -

SCENE II.

(The same place as in previous scene. Corney enters leading a donkey, a donkey on wheels like a child's toy, but life-size.)

CORNEY

A tough, rough mane, a tougher skin,
Strong legs though somewhat thin,
A strong body, a level line
Up to the neck along the spine,
Show a good donkey, and all are spoilt
By a Mayo highwayman's rapscallion eye !
What matter that before your present shape
You could slit purses and break hearts
Upon the rocky road to Dublin.
You are a donkey now, a chattel,
A taker of blows, not a giver of blows.
You would — no tricks, my beauty,
No, not one kick upon the shins.

(Congal, Pat, Mike, and others enter, in the dress and arms of the previous but without shields.)

CONGAL

I have learned of a great hernery
Among these rocks, and that a woman,
Prophetess or priestess named Attracta
Owns it — take this donkey and man,
Look for the creels, pack them with eggs.

MIKE

Manners.

CONGAL

This man is in the right.
I will ask Attracta for the eggs
If you will tell how to summon her.

Scene: . . . enters, leading . . . *HE*
4 spine. *HE*
5–6 All good points, and all are spoilt
By that rapscallion Clareman's eye! *HE*
7 What if before *HE*
8 hearts, *HE*
9 *omitted HE*
12 No tricks, you're not in County Clare, *HE*
13 shin. *HE*
13/14 . . . Mike, James, Mathias, Peter, John, enter, . . . previous scene but . . . *HE*
16 priestess, . . . Attracta, *HE*
19 Manners! *HE*

CORNEY

**A flute lies there upon the rock
Carved out of a herne's thigh.
Go pick it up and play the tune
My mother calls 'The Great Herne's Feather'.
If she has a mind to come, she will come.**

CONGAL

That's a queer way of summoning.

CORNEY

**This is a holy place and queer;
But if you do not know that tune
'The Great Herne's Feather', custom permits
That I can play it instead of you,
But you must cross my hands with silver.**

(Congal gives monwy and Corney plays flute)

CONGAL

Go pack the donkey creels with eggs.

(All go out except Congal and Mike. Attracta enters.)

ATTRACTA

**For a thousand or ten thousand years
For who can count so many years,
Some woman has lived among these rocks,
The great herne's bride, or, promised bride,
And when a visitor has played the flute
Has come or not. What would you ask?**

CONGAL

**Tara and I have made a peace;
Our fiftieth battle fought there is no need
Of preparations for the next;
He and all his principal men,
He and all his principal men,
I and all my principal men,**

30-31 Custom permits that I should play it, *HE*
32 hands] hand *HE*
32/33 money, . . . flute. *HE*
34 years,
37 Great Herne's . . . or promised *HE*
41 fought, *HE* no need] need *HE*
42 preparation *HE*
43/44 *omitted HE*

---

35 NLI 30,485 corrected "to" to "so".

[Texas, p. 6]

- 6 -

Take supper at his principal house
This night, in his principal city, Tara,
And we have set out minds upon
A certain or novelty

MIKE

Herne's eggs.

CONGAL

This man declares our need;
A donkey, both creels packed with eggs,
Somebody that knows the mind of a donkey
For donkey-boy.

ATTRACTA

Custom forbids:
Only the women of these rocks
Betrothed or married to the herne,
The god or ancestor of hernes,
Can eat, handle, or look upon these eggs.

CONGAL

Refused ! Must old campaigners lack
The one sole dish that takes their fancy,
My cooks that might have proved their skill,
Because a woman thinks that she
Is promised or married to a bird ?

MIKE

Mad.

CONGAL

Mad ! This man is right,
But you are not to blame for that.
Women thrown into despair
By the winter or their virginity
Take its abominable snow,
As boys take common snow and make
An image of god or bird
To feed their sensuality:

---

47 our *HE*
48 A certain novelty or relish. *HE*
53 rocks, *HE*
54 Herne, *HE*
56 these] those *HE*
59 that] what *HE*
62 Mad.] Mad! *HE*
65 or] of *HE*
67 snow, *HE*
68 or bird or beast *HE*

58–59 Inserted in NLI 30,485 to replace three lines, but with "what" for "that" in l. 59.

[Texas, p. 7]

- 7 -

70 **Ovid took all literally**
71 **And though he sang it neither knew**
72 **What lonely lust dragged down the gold**
73 **That crept on Danae's lap, nor knew**
74 **What rose against the moony feathers**
75 **When Leda lay upon the grass.**
ATTRACTA
76 **There is no reality but the great herne.**
MIKE
77 **The cure.**
CONGAL
Why that is easy said;
78 **An old campaigner is the cure**
79 **For everything that woman dreams,**
80 **Even I myself, had I but time.**
MIKE
81 **Seven men.**
CONGAL
This man of learning means
82 **That seven men packed into a day**
83 **Or dawdled out through seven years**
84 **And not a weather-stained, war-battered**
85 **Old campaigner such as I,**
86 **Are needed to melt away the snow**
87 **That's fallen among these wintry rocks.**
ATTRACTA
88 **There is no happiness but the great herne.**
CONGAL
89 **It may be that life is suffering**
90 **But youth that has not yet known pleasure**
91 **Has not the right to say so; pick,**
92 **Or be picked by seven men,**
93 **And we shall talk it out again.**

---

70 Ovid had a literal mind, *HE*
76 Great Herne. *HE*
77 Why, *HE*
79 dreams — *HE*
82 That *del to* But *Macmillan*
84–85 *moved to 81/82 with* And *del to* But *Macmillan*
86 away] down *HE*
88 Great Herne. *HE*
89 suffering, *HE*

---

72 In NLI 30,485 "dragged" was substituted for "dropped".
76 Revision in NLI 30,485, apparently for this line, reads "delete 'is'".

[Texas, p. 8]

- 8 -

ATTRACTA

Being betrothed to the great herne
I know what be known: I burn
Not in the flesh but in the mind;
Chosen out of all my kind
That I may lie in a blazing bed
And a bird take my maidenhead,
To the unbegotten I return,
All a womb and a funeral urn.

(Enter Corney, Pat, James, Mattias, with Donkey. A creel packed with eggs is painted upon the side of the donkey.)

CORNEY

Think of yourself; think of the songs:
Bride of the herne, and the great herne's bride,
Grow terrible: go into a trance.

ATTRACTA

Stop !

CORNEY

Bring the god out of your gut;
Stand there asleep until the rascals
wriggle up his beak like eels.

ATTRACTA

Stop !

CORNEY

The country calls them rascals,
I, sacrilegious rascals that have taken
Every new-laid egg in the hernery.

ATTRACTA

Stop ! When have I permitted you
To say what I may, or may not do ?
But you and your donkey must obey
All big men who can say their say.

---

94 Great Herne *HE*
95 be] may be *HE*
101/102 Mathias, etc., *HE (so spelled throughout)*
101/102 the Donkey. *HE*
103 Herne, . . . Great Herne's *HE*
107 Wriggle upon *HE*

102–105 Correction in NLI 30,485 reads
Think of yourself, think of the song
Bride of the Herne & the Great Herne's Bride
Grow terrible: go into a trance
Attracta
Stop

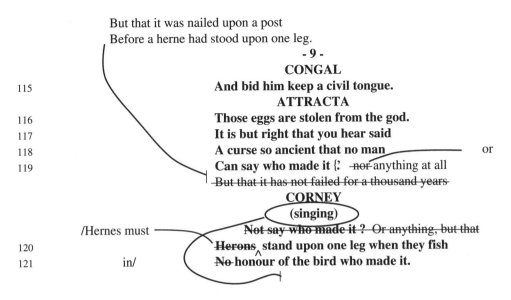

But that it was nailed upon a post
Before a herne had stood upon one leg.

- 9 -

CONGAL

115 **And bid him keep a civil tongue.**

ATTRACTA

116 **Those eggs are stolen from the god.**
117 **It is but right that you hear said**
118 **A curse so ancient that no man** or
119 **Can say who made it** {? ~~nor~~ anything at all
~~But that it has not failed for a thousand years~~

CORNEY

(singing)

~~**Not say who made it ?**~~ ~~Or anything, but that~~
/Hernes must
120 ~~**Herons**~~ ^ **stand upon one leg when they fish**
121 in/ ~~**No**~~ **honour of the bird who made it.**

---

119 Can say who made it, any thing at all
But that it was nailed upon a post
And has not failed these thousand years.
Maybe it was the Great Herne who made it. *HE; last line drafted in Harvard as* I think it was the Great Herne made it *del to reading of HE*

In ABY, or *inserted before* any *and comma del then restored after* post. And . . . made *del and replaced by:*

Before ~~or~~ ~~had~~
~~When~~ an herne ^ stood ~~upon~~ one leg
upon
Before a herne had stood on one
leg

120–121 *as revised but* In *HE*
121/122 (singing) *del Harvard; omitted HE*

The two lines at top of page, in an editor's hand, replace l.119, revised and then deleted by WBY. Other revisions are in the editor's hand.

This they nailed upon a post
That night my leg was lost
Said the old, old herne that had but one leg.

He that a herne's egg dare steal
Shall be changed into a fool
Said the old, old herne that had but one leg.
And to end his raving breath
At a fool's hand must meet death
Insert **Said the old, old herne that had but one leg.**

I think it was the Great Herne made it,
Pretending that he had but the one leg,
To fool them all; but the Great Herne or another
It has not failed these thousand years.

Insert here

CONGAL

That I shall live and die a fool,
And die upon some battlefield
At some fool's hand, is but natural,
And needs no curse to bring it.

MIKE.

Pickled !

CONGAL

He says that I am an old campaigner
Robber of sheepfolds and cattletracks,
So, cursed from morning until midnight,
A new curse on.

122–123, 125–126, 128–129 *within double quotes HE*

123 That] On the . . . lost, *HE*

124, 127, 130 *in italics HE*

126 fool, *HE*

128 raving] fool *HE*

129 must meet death] meet his death, *HE*

130/131 *insert entered ABY, but no comma after* it; *period after* leg; us all but great *for* them all but the Great; *and no period after* years. *Entry in ABY is over barely legible pencil which it follows except* Pretending *for* Pretends *and comma for period after* leg.

134/135 *no period HE*

136 cattle trucks, *HE*

137/138 There is not a quarter of an inch
To plaster a new curse on. *HE, then* on *rev to* upon *ABY, Texas (1)*

122–130 supplied (except for second half of refrain ll. 127, 130) in NLI 30, 485, but with "Thus" for "This" (l. 122), "legg" for "leg" (ll. 123, 124), "be changed" revised to "rave himself" (l. 126), "in the" revised to "to" (l. 128), and "fools" for "Fool's" (l. 129).

130/131 In l. 3 of the insert, "the Great Herne" becomes "Great Herne" in Texas (1); insert omitted HE

138 replaced in Texas (1) by two lines as in HE but "upon" for "on."

[Texas, p. 10]

- 10 -

CORNEY

Wriggling rascals !

CONGAL

139 **Say that he took a basketful**
140 **But paid with good advice, and then**
141 **Take to your bosom seven men.**

(Congal, Mike, Corney, Mattias, James, and Donkey go out. Enter timidly three girls, Kate, Agnes, Mary.)

MARY

142 **Have all those fierce men gone?**

ATTRACTA

143 **All those fierce men have gone.**

AGNES

144 **But they will come again ?**

ATTRACTA

145 **No, never again.**

KATE

146 **We bring three presents.**

(All except Attracta kneel)

MARY

147 **This is a jug of cream.**

AGNES

148 **This is a bowl of butter**

KATE

149 **This is a basket of eggs.**

(They lay jug, bowl and basket on the ground.)

138b Luck! *HE*
139 Adds that your luck begins when you
Recall that though we took those eggs *HE*
140 But] We *HE* advice; *HE*
148 butter. *HE*

141/142 Jane, present in NLI 8770, has disappeared.

[Texas, p. 11]

- 11 -

ATTRACTA

I knew what you would ask.
Sit round on these stones,
Children, why do you fear ?
A woman but little older
A child yesterday
All, when I am married
Shall have good husbands. Kate,
Shall marry a black-headed lad.

AGNES

She swore but yesterday
That she would marry black.

ATTRACTA

But Agnes there shall marry
A honey-coloured lad.

AGNES

O !

ATTRACTA

Mary shall be married
When I myself am married
To the lad that is in her mind.

MARY

Are you not married yet ?

ATTRACTA

No. But it is almost come
May come this very night.

MARY

And must he be all feathers ?

AGNES

Have a terrible beak ?

---

150 knew] know *HE*
151 on] upon *HE* stones. *HE*
152 fear *HE*
153 older, *HE*
154 yesterday? *HE*
155 married, *HE*
156 *no comma HE*
166 come, *HE*

[Texas, p. 12]

- 12 -

KATE

Great terrible claws ?

ATTRACTA

Whatever shape he choose
Though that be terrible
Will best express his love.

AGNES

When he comes — will he ? —

ATTRACTA

Child, ask what you please.

AGNES

Do all that a man does ?

ATTRACTA

Strong sinew and soft flesh
Are foliage round the shaft
Before the arrowsmith
Has stripped it, and I pray
That I, all foliage gone,
May shoot into my joy —

(sound of a flute, playing 'The Great Herne's Feathers').

MARY

Who plays upon that flute ?

AGNES

Her god is calling her.

KATE

Look, look, she takes
An egg out of the basket
My white hen laid it
My favourite white hen.

171–172 choose, . . . terrible, *HE*
182/183 Sound . . . Feather'.) *HE*
186 basket. *HE*
187 it, *HE*

In the stage direction, the last five words were added in NLI 30,485.

[Texas, p. 13]

- 13 -

MARY

Her eyes grow glassy, she moves
According to the notes of the flute.

AGNES

Her limbs grow rigid, she seems
A doll upon a wire.

MARY

Her human life is gone
And that is why she seems
A doll upon a wire.

AGNES

You mean that when she looks so
She is but a puppet ?

MARY

How do I know ? And yet
Twice have I seen her so,
She will move for certain minutes
As though her god were there
Thinking how best to move
A doll upon a wire.
Then she will move away
In long leaps as though
He had remembered his skill.
She has still my little egg.

AGNES

Who knows but your little egg
Comes into some mystery.

KATE

Some mystery to make
Love loneliness more sweet.

AGNES

She has moved. She has moved away.

---

209 mystery? *HE*
211 Love-loneliness *HE*

---

189 NLI 30,485 replaced “Look at – – – – glassy [? Etc]” with “Her eye grows glassy she moves.”

[Texas, p. 14]

- 14 -

KATE

Travelling fast asleep
In long loops like a dancer.

MARY

Like a dancer, like a hare.

AGNES

The last time she went away
The moon was full — she returned
Before its side had flattened.

KATE

This time she will not return.

AGNES

Because she is called to her marriage ?

KATE

Those leaps may carry her where
No woman has gone, and he
Extinguish sun, moon, star,
No bridal torch can burn
When his black midnight is there.

AGNES

I have heard her claim that they couple
In the blazing heart of the sun.

KATE

But you have heard it wrong;
In blue-black midnight they couple.

AGNES

No, in the sun.

---

223 star. *HE*
228 wrong! *HE*

KATE

Blue-black.

AGNES

231 **In the sun.**

KATE

Blue-black, blue-black !

MARY

232 **All I know is that she**
233 **Shall lie there in his bed,**
234 **Nor shall it end until**
235 **She lies there full of his might**
236 **His thunder-bolt in her hand.**

230b Blue-black! *HE*

231 sun! *HE*

236 thunderbolt *rev to* thunderbolts *Harvard* thunderbolts *HE*

[Texas, p. 16]

- 16 -

SCENE III

(Before the gates of Tara, Congal, Mike, Pat, Peter, James, Mattias, soldiers of Congal's, Corney, and the Donkey.)

CONGAL

This is Tara; in a moment
Men must come out of the gate
With a great basket between them
And we give up our arms,
No armed man can enter.

CORNEY

And here is that great bird
Over our heads again.

PAT

The great herne himself
And he in a red rage.

MIKE

Stones.

CONGAL

This man is right,
The great herne cursed us all
Beat him to death with stones.

(All go through the motion of picking up and throwing stones. There are no stones except in so far as their gestures can suggest them.)

PAT

All our stones fell wide.

CORNEY

He has come down so low
His legs are sweeping the grass.

---

scene: . . . Mathias, etc., soldiers of Congal, . . . *HE*

8 Great Herne *HE*

11 *omitted HE*

13 our *del to* those *Macmillan*

[Texas, p. 17]

- 17 -

MIKE

Swords.

CONGAL

This man is right.
Cut him up with swords.

PAT

I have him within my reach.

CONGAL

No, no, he is here at my side.

CORNEY

His wing has touched my shoulder.

CONGAL

We missed him again and he
Rises again and sinks
Behind the wall of Tara.

(<u>Two men come in carrying a large basket slung between two poles. One is whistling. All except Corney who is unarmed drop their swords and helmets into the basket. Each soldier when he takes off his helmet shows that he wears a skull cap of soft cloth.</u>)

CONGAL

Where have I heard that tune ?

MIKE

This morning.

CONGAL

I know it now
The tune of the great herne's feather.
It puts my teeth on edge.

23/24 . . . Corney, . . . unarmed, . . . skull-cap . . . *HE*
25 now, *HE*
26 'The Great Herne's Feather'. *HE*

[Texas, p. 18]

- 18 -

SCENE IV.

(Banqueting hall. A throne painted on the back cloth. Enter Congal, alone, drunk, and shouting.)

CONGAL

To arms, to arms ! Connacht to arms' !
Insulted and betrayed, betrayed and insulted.
Who has insulted me ? Tara has insulted.
To arms, to arms ! Connacht to arms !
To arms — but if you have not got any
Take a table leg or a candlestick
A boot or a stool or any odd thing.
Who has betrayed me ? Tara has betrayed !
To arms, to arms ! Connacht to arms !

(He goes out to one side. Music, perhaps drum and concertina, to suggest breaking of wood. Enter at the other side, the King of Tara.) drunk.)

AEDH

Where is that beastly drunken liar
That says I have insulted him ?

(Congal enters with two table legs.)

CONGAL

I say it !

AEDH

What insult ?

CONGAL

How dare you ask !
When I have had a common egg
A common hen's egg put before me.
Some coarse farmer's barndoor egg
And every other man at the table
A herne's egg.

(Throws a table leg on the floor.)

---

scene: . . . back-cloth. *HE*
1 arms' !] arms! *HE*
6 table-leg . . . candlestick, *HE*
9/10 . . . Tara, drunk. *HE*
11/12 . . . table-legs. *HE*
12c ask? *HE*
13 egg, *HE*
14 me, *HE*
15 An egg dropped in the dirty straw
And crowed for by a cross-bred gangrel cock,
An egg some common cockrel crew for, *then* gangrel *del to* gangling *and last line del Harvard; HE as revised*
17/18 . . . table-leg . . . *HE*

NLI 30,485 directed "take out 'me' at end of line", perhaps line 3.

[Texas, p. 19]

- 19 -

There is your weapon. Take it !
Take it up, defend yourself.
A turnip-headed farmer's egg.

AEDH

Some servant put the wrong egg there.

CONGAL

But at whose orders ?

AEDH

At your own.
A beastly drunken plot, a plot
To put a weapon that I do not know
Into my hands.

CONGAL

Take up that weapon.
If I am as drunken as you say,
And you as sober as you think,
A coward and a drunkard are well matched.

(Aedh takes up the table leg. Mike, Malichi, etc., come in, they fight, and the fight sways to and fro. The weapons, table legs, candlesticks, etc., do not touch. Drum taps to represent blows. All go out fighting. Enter Pat, drunk, with bottle.)

---

19 *del to* An egg some [*del to* a] turnip-headed wench *then to*
An egg that some half-witted slattern
Spat upon and wiped in her apron! *Harvard; HE as revised but* in] on
20 Some] Some *del to* A *Harvard* A *HE*
22 beastly] beastly *del to* murderous *Harvard* murderous *HE*
27/28 . . . table-leg. Connaught and Tara soldiers come in, . . . table-legs, . . . Drum-taps represent . . . *HE*

NLI 30,485 directed "instead of 'dont' read 'do not'", possibly for line 23; another direction, apparently 4 lines earlier, directed "leave out 'in the'".

PAT

Herne's egg, hen's egg, great difference,
There's insult in that difference,
What do hens eat ? Hens live on mash,
On kitchen odds and ends, slops, meal.
What do hernes eat ? Hernes live on eels,
On things that must always run about.
Man's a high animal and runs about.
But mash is low, O, very low.
Or to speak like a philosopher,
When a man expects the movable
But gets the immovable, he is inspired.

---

28 difference. *HE*
29 difference. *HE*
30 on] upon *HE*
31 Upon slop, upon kitchen odds and ends. *HE*
34 about, *HE*
36 Or, *HE*
38 inspired] insulted. *HE*

[Texas, p. 20]

- 20 -

(<u>Enter Congal, Peter, Malachi, Mattias, etc.</u>)

CONGAL

Tara had no chance, knew from the start
That he was overmatcher, at last
Fell with a broken head, died drunk,
Accused me with his dying breath
Of secretly practising with a table leg
Practising at midnight until I
Became a perfect master with the weapon.
But that is all lies.

PAT

Let all men know
He was a noble character
And I must weep at his funeral.

CONGAL

He insulted me with a hen's egg
Said I had practised with a table leg
But I have taken kingdom and throne
And that has made all level again
And I can weep at his funeral.
I would not have had him die that way
Or die at all, he should have been immortal.
Our fifty battles had made us friends
And there are fifty more to come.
New weapons, a new leader will be found
And everything begin again.

MIKE

Much bloodier.

CONGAL

They had, we had
Forgotten what we fought about
So fought like gentlemen, but now
Knowing the trust must fight like the beasts.
Maybe the great herne's curse has done it.
Why not ? Answer me that; why not ?

39–41 Tara knew that he was overmatched;
Knew from the start he had no chance;
Died of a broken head; died drunk; *HE*
43 table-leg, *HE*
49 egg, *HE*
50 table-leg, *HE*
56 friends. *HE*
61 about, *HE*
63 trust] truth *HE*
64 Great Herne's *HE*

---

58 NLI 30,485 revised "new leaders" to "a new leader".

[Texas, p. 21]

- 21 -

MIKE

66 **Horror henceforth.**

CONGAL

This wise man means

67 **We fought so long like gentlemen**

68 **That we grew blind.**

(Attracta enters walking in her sleep, a herne's egg in her hand. She stands near the throne and holds her egg towards it for a moment.)

MATTIAS

Look ! Look !

69 **She offers that egg. Who is to take it ?**

CONGAL

70 **She walks with open eyes but in her sleep.**

MATTIAS

71 **I can see it all in a flash.**

72 **She found that herne's egg on the table**

73 **And left the hen's egg there instead.**

74 **She brought James the hen's egg on purpose**

75 **Walking in her wicked sleep.**

CONGAL

76 **And if I take that egg, she wakes,**

77 **Completes her task, her circle;**

78 **We all complete a task or circle,**

79 **Want a woman then all goes — pff.**

(He goes to take the egg.)

MIKE

80 **Not now.**

68/69 . . . enters, *HE*

74–75 *spoken by* JAMES *HE*

74 brought James the] brought the *HE*

79 woman, *HE*

74–75 NLI 30,485 drafted as follows:

James

~~Wicked even in her sleep~~

She brought the hens on purpose

Walking in her wicked sleep

Then inserted the lines as drafted, but with "egg" after "hens".

79 NLI 30,485 inserted "goes".

CONGAL

This wise man says 'not now'.
There must be something to consider first.

JAMES

By changing one egg for another
She has brought bloodshed on us all.

PAT

He was a noble character, and I must weep at his funeral

JAMES

I say that she must die, I say
According to what my mother said,
All that have done what she did must die,
But, in a manner of speaking, pleasantly,
Because legally, certainly not
By beating with a table leg.

Insert here ——— As though she were a mere Tara man,
Nor yet by beating with a stone,
As Though she were the Great Herne himself.

MIKE

The great herne's bride.

---

84 And I must *begins new line HE* funeral. *HE*
85 die, I say, *HE*
90 table-leg. *HE*
90/91 *omitted HE. Entered in ABY, first as*

[?~~brawling~~]
~~As we kill~~ ^ Tara men, ~~nor yet~~
By beating with a stone
~~Nor yet by beating with~~ a stone
As if she were the Great Herne himself

Then as

As if she were knocked down in a fight
Like ~~[?]~~ Tara nor with stones & sword
As if she were the Great Herne himself

And finally as

mere
As though she were a ~~man~~ Tara man
Nor yet by beating with ^ a stone
As though she were the Great
Herne himself

91 Great Herne's *HE*

---

82 Inserted in NLI 30,485

90/91 The insert is in the editor's hand, not WBY's. It is copied from Texas (1), but with "stone" for "stone," and "though" for "Though".

[Texas, p. 22, cont.]

CONGAL

I had forgotten
That all she does he makes her do,
But he is god and out of reach;
Nor stone can bruise, nor a sword pierce him,
And yet through his betrothed, his bride,
I have the power to make him suffer;
His curse has given me the right,
I am to play the fool and die
At a fool's hands.

[Texas, p. 23]

- 23 -

MIKE

Seven men.

(He begins to count, seeming to strike the table with the table leg, but table and table leg must not meet, the blow is represented by the sound of the drum.)

One, two, three, four,
Five, six, seven men.

PAT

Seven that are present in this room,
Seven that must weep at his funeral.

CONGAL

This man who struck those seven blows
Means that we seven must in the name of the law
Handle, penetrate, and possess her,
And thereby do her good,
By melting out the virgin snow,
And that snow image the great herne,
For nothing less than seven men
Can melt that snow, but when it melts
She may, being free from all obsession,
Live as every woman should.
I am the Court; judgement has been given.
I name the seven: Congal of Tara,
Patrick, Malachi, Mike, John, James
And that coarse hulk of clay, Mattias.

MATTIAS

I dare not lay a hand upon that woman.
The people say she is holy
And carries a great devil in her gut.

PAT

What mischief can a Munster devil
Do to a man that was born in Connacht ?

99/100 . . . table-leg, . . . table-leg . . . *HE*

105 seven must in] seven in *HE*

106 Must handle, *HE*

107 And do her thereby great good, *del to* And do her great good by that action *then to* Do [*rev to* And do] her a great service by that action *then finally to* And do her a great good by that action *Harvard; HE as final revision, except* action,

108 By melting *del to* Melting *Harvard* Melting *HE*

109 image, the Great Herne; *HE*

116 James, *HE*

119 say] say that *HE*

[Texas, p. 24]

- 24 -

MALACHI
I made a promise to my mother
When we set out on this campaign
To keep from women.
JOHN
I have a wife that's jealous
If I look at the moon.
JAMES
And I am promised to a girl.
Her family are most particular
What would they say — O my God !
CONGAL
Whoever disobeys the Court
Is an unmannerly, disloyal upstart,
And no good citizen.
PAT
Here is my bottle.
Pass it along, a long, long pull;
The bottle's round like a woman carrying,
And yet the bottle is no traitor,
A most courageous, loyal bottle.

(<u>All drink.</u>)

MATTIAS
I first.
CONGAL
That's for the Court to say.
A Court of Law is a blessed thing,
Logic, Mathematics, ground in one,
And everything out of balance accursed.
When the Court decides on a decree
Men carry it out with dignity.

---

126 If I but look the moon in the face. *HE*

127 I am promised to an educated girl. *HE*

128 particular, *HE*

131 upstart,] lout, *HE*

134 The bottle's *del to* And although its *then to* Although its *Harvard* Although it's *HE*

135–136 No traitor bottle though like a woman,
A most courageous loyal bottle. *del to*
No unmannerly disloyal bottle
An affable and most loyal bottle. *Harvard; HE as revised but* unmannerly, *and* affable and] affable,

[Texas, p. 25]

- 25 -

Here where I have put my hand
I will put a mark, then all must stand
Over there in a level row.
And all take off their caps and throw.
The nearest cap shall take her first,
The next shall take her next, and so on
Till all is in good order done.
I need a mark and so must take
The herne's egg, and let her wake.

(He takes egg and lays it upon the ground. Attracta stands motionless, looking straight in front of her. The seven standing in a row throw their caps one after another. Attracta sings.)

ATTRACTA

Though beak and claw I must endure
When I take a beast to my joyful breast,
Sang the bride of the herne, and the great herne's bride.
No lesser life, man, bird or beast
Can make unblessed what a beast made blessed,
Can make impure what a beast made pure.

---

143 have put *del to* put down *Harvard* put down *HE*

148 next, and so on *rev to* next; so on *Harvard* next; so on *HE*

151/152 straight, *Harvard* straight *HE* She sings. *following* her *Harvard, omitted HE* Attracta sings. *omitted Harvard, HE*

152 endure, *HE*

152–153 *order of lines reversed HE*

154 Herne, . . . Great Herne's bride, *entire line in italic HE*

155 beast, *HE*

157/158 *stanza space HE*

152–169 NLI 30,485 prescribed revisions in "Song":
Insert stanza for last scene after present
last stanza, rearrange lines
begin 'though beak & claw' etc

Where is he gone, where is that other
He that shall take my maidenhead ?
Sang the bride of the herne, and the great herne's bride.
Out of the moon came my pale brother,
The blue-black midnight is my mother
Who will turn down the sheets of the bed.
When beak and claw their work began
What horror stirred in the roots of my hair ?
Sang the bride of the herne and the great herne's bride.
And who lay there in the cold dawn
When all that terror had come and gone
Was I the woman lying there ?

160, 166 Herne, . . . Great Herne's bride, *entire lines in italics HE*
162 mother. *HE*
163 bed? *HE*
163/164 *stanza space HE*
164 began] begin *HE*
165 Shall horror stir . . . *HE* hair? *Harvard* hair, *HE*
167 lay] lie *HE*
168 had] has *HE*
169 Was I] Shall I be *HE*

[Texas, p. 26]

- 26 -

SCENE V.

(Before the Gate of Tara. Corney enters with Donkey.)

CORNEY

You thought to go on sleeping though dawn was up,
Rapscallion of a beast, old highwayman.
That light in the eastern sky is dawn,
You cannot deny it; many a time
You looked upon it following your trade.
Cheer up, we shall be home before sunset.

(Attracta comes in.)

ATTRACTA

I have packed all the uneaten or unbroken eggs
Into the creels, help carry them
And hang them on the donkey's back.

CORNEY

We could boil them hard and keep them in the larder,
But Congal has had them all boiled soft.

ATTRACTA

Such eggs are holy. Many pure souls
Especially among the country-people
Would shudder if herne's eggs were left
For foul-tongued, bloody-minded men.

(Congal, Malachi, Mike, etc., enter.)

CONGAL

A sensible woman, you gather up what's left,
Your thoughts upon the cupboard and the larder.
No more a herne's bride, a crazy loon
Waiting to be trodden by a bird,
But all woman, all sensible woman.

MIKE

Manners.

---

18 crazy loon *del to* crazed loony *Harvard* crazed loony *HE*

- 27 -

CONGAL

This man who is always right
Desires that I should add these words,
The seven that held you in their arms last night
Wish you good luck.

ATTRACTA

I do not understand.
My husband came to me in the night.

CONGAL

Seven men lay with you in the night.
Go home desiring and desirable,
And look for a man.

ATTRACTA

The herne is my husband.
I lay with him, his pure bride.

CONGAL

Pure in the embrace of seven men ?

MIKE

She slept.

CONGAL

You say that though I thought,
Because I took the egg out of her hand
That she awoke, she did not wake
Until day broke up her sleep —
Her sleep and ours — did she wake pure ?
Seven men can answer that.

24b I do not understand. *del to* What do you say? *Harvard* What do you say? *HE*
28b Herne *HE*
29 with *del to* beside *Harvard* beside *HE*
32 hand, *HE*
34 up] upon *HE*

CORNEY

King though you are, I will not hear

/Bride of the Great Herne **The ~~Great Herne's Bride~~ defamed —**

/times a / ! **Seven-~~fold~~ liar!** A king, a king but a Mayo man!
A Mayo man's lying tongue can beat
A Clare highwayman's rapscallion eye.

38–39 The bride of the Great Herne defamed —
Seven times a liar. *HE; other insert omitted*

39 *Insert reads:*
A king, a king but a Mayo man.
A Mayo man's lying tongue can beat
A Clare highway man's rapscallions eye,
Seven times a liar. *ABY, over barely legible pencil, in which first line reads*
but
A Connaught [?] king^, . . .

37–39 The insertions and corrections are in the editor's hand, copied from Texas (1) with "king, but" and "man."

37–38 NLI 30,485 directed a revision to:
'but I hear
The great Herne s Bride defamed

NLI 13,593 seems to draft these lines as follows:
King m & men of Mayo
A Connaght, ~~a Mayo~~ man,
~~As I have always thought a Mayo boy~~
Everybody knows that a Mayo boy
Is worse than a rascalls eye
Out of Couny Clare

[Texas, p. 28]

- 28 -

MIKE

Seven men.

CONGAL

I, Congal, lay with her last night.

MATTIAS

And, I, Mattias.

MIKE

And I.

JAMES

And I.

PETER

And I.

JOHN

And I.

PAT

And I.

And no drop of drink since dawn.

CORNEY

One plain liar, six men bribed to lie.

ATTRACTA

Great herne, great herne, great herne,
Your darling cries to you,
Great herne, declare her pure,
Pure as that beak and claw,
Great herne, great herne, great herne,
Let the round heaven declare it.

(Silence. Then low thunder growing louder. All except Attracta and Congal kneel.)

42c And I; swear it; *HE*

43 no] not a *HE*

45, 47, 49 Great Herne *throughout, HE*

46 cries to you, *del to* is crying out. *Harvard* is crying out, *HE*

50/51 louder.] louder *Harvard* louder. *HE*

[Texas, p. 29]

- 29 -

JAMES

Great herne, I swear that she is pure;
I never laid a hand upon her.

MATTIAS

I was a fool to believe myself
When everybody knows that I am a liar.

PAT

Even when it seemed that I covered her
I swear that I knew it was the drink.

ATTRACTA

I lay in the bride-bed
His thunderbolts in my hand
But gave them back, for he,
My lover, the great herne,
Knows everything that is said
And every man's intent,
And every man's deed; and he
Shall give these seven that say
That they upon my lay
A fearful punishment.

(It thunders. All prostrate themselves except Attracta and Congal. Congal had half knelt, but he has stood up again.)

---

51 Herne, *HE*
58 hand. *Harvard* hand, *HE*
60 Great Herne, *HE*
65 my] me *HE*
66 fearful *del to* most memorable *Harvard* most memorable *HE*

57–66 NLI 30,485 instructed "instead of present speech insert"
I lay in the Bride-~~br~~ bed
His thunder bolts in my hand
But gave them back for he
My lover the Great Herne
Knows evry thing that is said
~~And~~ {E / evry thing man intends
~~And~~ Evry thing done & he
Shall give these seven their say
That they upon me lay
A fearful punishment.

ATTRACTA

Sharing his knowledge, I know
What punishment's decreed.
He will come when you are dead
Push you down a step or two
Into cat or rate or bat
Into dog or wolf or goose.
Everybody in his new shape can I see
But Congal there stands in a cloud
Because his fate is not yet settled.
Speak out, great herne, declare
That all I have said is true.

67–68 I share his knowledge, and I know
Every punishment decreed. *HE*

69 dead, *HE*

71 rat or bat, *HE*

73 can I see] I see, *Harvard* I can see, *HE*

76–77 . . . Great Herne, declare/ That all . . . *del to* . . . Great Herne, and make it known/ That everything . . . *Harvard; HE as revised*

67–68 NLI 30,485 revised to:

Sharing his knowledge I know
's
What punishment ~~is~~ decreed

73 Revised in NLI 30,485 to:
Everybody in his [?knew] shape I [?] see

[Texas, p. 30]

- 30 -

(<u>Thunder. All now, except Attracta, have prostrated themselves.</u>)

ATTRACTA

What has made you kneel ?

CONGAL

This man
That's prostrate at my side, would say
Could he say anything at all
That I am terrified by thunder.

ATTRACTA

Why did you stand up so long ?

CONGAL

I held you in my arms last night,
We seven held you in our arms.

ATTRACTA

You were under the curse, in all
You did, in all you seemed to do.

CONGAL

If I must die at a fool's hand
When must I die ?

ATTRACTA

When the moon is full.

CONGAL

And where ?

---

79 side would say, *HE*
80 all, *HE*

[Texas, p. 31]

- 31 -

ATTRACTA

Upon the holy mountain
Upon Slieve Fuadh, there we ~~shall~~ meet again
Just as the moon comes round the hill.
There all the gods must visit me
Acknowledging my marriage to a god;
/one man will I have **~~I would have one man~~ among these gods.**

CONGAL

I know the place and I will come
Although it be my death, I will come
Because I am terrified, I will come.

89b mountain, *HE*
90 we shall meet again *HE* there . . . again *del to* we meet *ABY*
92 me, HE
93–94 *rev first to*
Because I am married to a god
As I would have one man amongst them
Then to
Acknowledging
~~In witness of~~ my marriage to a god;
One man will I have among the gods *ABY*
94 I would have one man among those gods. *HE*
95 come, *HE*
96 come. *HE*

90, 94 The revisions are in the editor's hand, copied from Texas (1), where "One" is capitalized, comma follows "me", and "these gods" is "the gods".

[Texas, p. 32]

- 32 -

SCENE VI.

(A mountain top, the moon is about to rise; when it is the moon of tradition, a round smiling, . A cauldron lid, a cooking pot, and a spit lie together at one side of the stage. The Fool, a man in ragged clothes, enters carrying a large stone; he lays it down at one side and goes out. Congal enters carrying a wine-skin, and stands at one side of the stage. Fool re-enters with second large stone which he places beside the first.)

CONGAL

What is your name, boy ?

FOOL

Poor Tom Fool.
Everybody knows Tom Fool.

CONGAL

I saw something in the mist,
There lower down upon the slope,
I went up close to it and saw
A donkey, somebody's stray donkey.
A donkey and a Fool — I don't like it at all.

FOOL

I won't be Tom the Fool after to-night
I have made a level patch out there
Clearing away the stones, and there
I shall fight a man and kill that man
And get great glory.

CONGAL

Where did you get
The cauldron lid, the pot and the spit ?

Scene: A mountain-top, the moon is about to rise; the moon of comic tradition, a round smiling face. A cauldron lid, a cooking-pot , . . . stands at one side] stands at the other side Fool] The fool second] a second *HE* is about to rise *del to* has just risen *ABY*

8 to-night. *HE*

9 there, *HE*

11 that] a *HE*

NLI 30,485 inserted "grinning moon" in the stage direction.

1–2 Revised in NLI 30,485 to:

What is your name boy
Poor Tom ~~B~~ Fool
Everybody knows Tom Fool.

[Texas, p. 33]

- 33 -

FOOL

I sat in widow Rooney's kitchen
Somebody said, 'King Congal's on the mountain
Cursed to die at the hands of a fool'
Somebody else said 'kill Jim, Tom'
And everybody began to laugh
And I said I should kill him at the full moon
And that is to-night.

CONGAL

I too have heard
That Congal is to die to-night.
Take a drink.

FOOL

I took this lid
And all the women screamed at me.
I took the spit, and all screamed worse.
A shoulder of lamb stood ready for the roasting
I put the pot upon my head
They did not scream but stood and gaped.

(Fool has armed himself with spit, cauldron lid, and pot.)

CONGAL

But why must kill Congal, Fool ?
What harm has he done you ?

FOOL

None at all.
But there's a Fool called Johnny from Meath,
We are great rivals and we hate each other,
But I can get the pennies if I kill Congal,
And Johnny nothing.

CONGAL

I am King Congal,
And that is not a thing to laugh at, Fool, ?

---

14 Widow . . . kitchen, *HE*
16 fool'. *HE*
17 'Kill him, Tom'. *HE*
19 moon, *HE*
22 lid, *HE*
25 roasting — *HE*
26 head. *HE*

27/28 *stage direction* Fool arms himself with spit, cauldron lid and pot. *Harvard, then rev to* . . . pot, whistling, 'The Great herne's Feather.' *HE as revised but* Herne's.

27/28 for that is an unlucky tune *inserted below* CONGAL *then* for *del to* Hush, *Macmillan*

28 But *del to* And *ABY* must] must you *HE*

34 that is not] is not that *HE* Fool? *HE*

---

19 NLI 30,485 appeared to direct revision of "full moon" to "grinning moon".

[Texas, p. 34]

- 34 -

FOOL

Very nice, O very nice indeed,
For I can kill you now, and I
Am tired of walking.

CONGAL

Both need rest,
Another drink apiece — that is done —
Lead to the place you have cleared of stones.

FOOL

But where is your sword ? You have not got a sword.

CONGAL

I lost it, or I never had it,
Or threw it at the strange donkey below,
But that's no matter — I have hands.

(They go out at one side. Attracta, Corney and Donkey come in. Attracta sings.)

ATTRACTA

When beak and claw their work began
What horror stirred in the roots of my hair ?
Sang the bride of the herne, and the great herne's bride.
But who lay there in the cold dawn,
When all that terror had come and gone,
Was I the woman lying there ?

(They go out. Congal and Tom the Fool come. Congal is holding the cauldron lid, pot and spit, and lays them down.)

CONGAL

I was sent to die at the hands of a Foo.
There must be another Fool on the mountain.

---

37 rest. *HE*
46 Herne, . . . Great Herne's *entire line in italics HE*
48 gone? *HE*
49/50 holding] carrying *HE* . . . spit. He lays . . . *HE*
50 Fool. *HE*

[Texas, p. 35]

- 35 -

FOOL

That must be Johnny from Meath.
But that's a thing I could not endure,
For Johnny would get all the pennies.

CONGAL

Here, take a drink and have no fear;
All's plain at last, though I shall die
I shall not die at a Fool's hand.
I have thought out a better plan.
I and the herne have had three bouts,
He won the first, I won the second,
Six men and I possessed his wife.

FOOL

I ran after a woman once.
I had seen two donkeys in a field.

CONGAL

And did you get her, did you get her, Fool ?

FOOL

I almost had my hand upon her,
She screamed, and somebody came and beat me;
Were you beaten ?

CONGAL

No, no, Fool.
But she said that nobody had touched,
And after that the thunder said the same,
Yet I had won that bout, and now
I know that I shall win the third.

FOOL

If Johnny from Meath comes, kill him!

---

56 last; *HE*
59 Herne *HE* herne *Harvard*
66 me. *HE*
68 touched her, *HE*

[Texas, p. 36]

- 36 -

CONGAL

73 **Maybe I will, maybe I will not.**

FOOL

74 **You let me off, but don't let him off.**

CONGAL

75 **I could not do you any harm**
76 **For you and I are friends.**

FOOL

Kill Johnny !

CONGAL

77 **Because you have asked me to, I will do it,**
78 **For you and I are friends.**

FOOL

Kill JOHNNY !

79 **Kill with the spear, but give it to me**
80 **That I may see if it is sharp enough.**

(<u>Fool takes spit</u>).

CONGAL

81 **And is it, Fool ?**

FOOL

I spent an hour

82 **Sharpening it upon a stone.**
83 **Could I kill you now ?**

CONGAL

Maybe you could.

FOOL

84 **I will get all the pennies for myself.**

---

75 harm, *HE*
78b Johnny! *HE*

(He wounds Congal. The wounding is symbolised by a movement of the spit over and towards Congal's body.)

CONGAL

It passed out of your mind for a moment
That we are friends, but that is natural.

FOOL

(Dropping spit.)

I must see it, I never saw a wound.

CONGAL

The herne has got the first blow in;
A scratch, a scratch, a mere nothing.
But had it been a little deeper and higher
It would have gone through the heart, and maybe
That would have left me better off,
For the great herne may beat me in the end.
Here I must sit through the full moon,
And he will send up Fools against me,
Meandering, roaring, yelling,
Whispering Fools, then chattering Fools,
And after that morose, melancholy,
Sluggish, fat, silent Fools;
And I, moon-crazed, moon-blind,
Fighting and wounded, wounded and fighting,
I never thought of such an end.
Never be a soldier, Tom;
Though it begins well, is this a life,
Is this a man's life, is there any life
But a dog's life ?

FOOL

That's it, that's it;
Many a time they have put a dog at me.

84/85 over and towards] towards or over *HE*
86/87 (dropping spit) *HE*
88 Herne *HE*
93 Great Herne *HE*
101 fighting. *HE*
104 life? *HE*

- 38 -

CONGAL

If I should give myself a wound,
Let life run lout, I'd win the bout,
He said I must die at the hands of a Fool
And sent you hither. Give me that spit !
I put it in this crevice of the rock,
That I may fall upon the point.
These stones will keep it sticking upright.

(They arrange stones, he puts the spit in.)

CONGAL

(Almost screaming in his excitement.)

Fool ! Am I myself a Fool ?
For if I am a Fool, he wins the bout.

FOOL

You are King of Connacht. If you were a fool
They would have chased you with their dogs.

CONGAL

I am King Congal of Connacht and of Tara,
That wise, victorious, voluble, unlucky,
Famous, blasphemous man.
Fool, take this spit when red with blood,
Show it to the people and get all the pennies;
What does it matter what they think ?
The great herne knows that I have won.

(He falls upon the spit. Fool takes the spit and wine-skin and goes out.)

It seems that I am hard to kill,
But the wound is deep. Are you up there ?
Your chosen kitchen spit has killed me
But killed me at my own will, not yours.

(Attracta and Corney. The moon rises.)

---

109 lout] away, *HE*

114/115 (almost *HE* excitement) *HE* excitement.) *Harvard*

121 Blasphemous, famous, infamous man. *HE*

125 Great Herne *HE*

125/126 falls upon *rev to* falls simbolically upon *Harvard* falls symbolically upon *HE* It does not touch him. *following 1st sentence HE but not in Harvard*

128 me, *HE*

129/130 Corney.] Corney enter. *HE* The moon rises *del ABY*

[Texas, p. 39]

- 39 -

ATTRACTA

Will the knot hold ?

CORNEY

There was a look
About the old highwayman's eye of him
That warned me, so I made him fast
To that old stump among the rocks
With a great knot that he can neither
Break, nor pull apart with his teeth.

CONGAL

ATTRACTA!

ATTRACTA

I called you to this place,
You came, and now the story is finished.

CONGAL

You have great powers, even the thunder
Does whatever you bid it do.
Protect me, I have won my bout,
But I am afraid of what the herne
May do with me when I am dead.
I am afraid that he may put me
Into the shape of a brute beast.

Attracta

I will protect you if, as I think,
Your shape is not yet fixed upon.

CONGAL

I am slipping now, and you up there
With your long legs and your long beak
But I have beaten you, Great Herne,
In spite of your kitchen spit — seven men —

(<u>He dies</u>)

---

136 Attracta! *HE*
141 Herne *HE*
144/145 *all capitals HE*
148 legs] leg *HE* beak. *HE*
150/ dies.) *HE* dies) *Harvard*

ATTRACTA

Come lie with me upon the ground
Come quickly into my arms, come quickly, come
Before his body has had time to cool.

CORNEY

What ? Lie with you ?

CORNEY

The thunder has me terrified.

ATTRACTA

I lay with the great herne, and he,
Being all a spirit, but begot
His image in the mirror of my spirit,
Being all sufficient to himself
Begot himself, but there's a work
That should be done, and that needs work
The imperfection of a man. No bird's beak nor claw, but a man,

(<u>The sound of a donkey braying</u>.)

Corney ! The donkey braying.
He has some wickedness in his mind.

(<u>Attracta looks out at the side of the stage</u>)

Too late, too late, he broke that knot,
And there, down there among the rocks
He couples with another donkey.
That donkey has conceived. I thought that I
Could give a human form to Congal,
But now he must be born a donkey.

CORNEY

King Congal must be born a donkey.

ATTRACTA

Because we were not quick enough.

---

151 ground, *HE*
154/155 ATTRACTA
Lie and beget,
If you are afraid of the Great Herne,
Put that away, for if I do his will,
You are his instrument or himself. *HE*
156 Great Herne, *HE*
161 that work needs *HE*
161/162 *inserted line omitted HE; inserted as above but without punct ABY*
163 *spoken by* CORNEY The donkey is braying. *HE*
164/165 *omitted HE*
171 donkey! *HE*

161–162 The revisions are copied, in editor's hand, from Texas (1).

[Texas, p. 41]

- 41 -

CORNEY

I have heard that a donkey carries its young
Longer than any other beast,
Thirteen months it must carry it.

(he laughs)

All that trouble and nothing to show for it,
Nothing but just another donkey.

THE END .

175/176 he] He *HE* he *Harvard*
177/ *no period HE*